D1122010

Kinship with Strangers

362.734
M720

Kinship with Strangers,

Adoption and Interpretations
of Kinship in American Culture

Judith S. Modell

WITHDRAWN

LIBRARY ST. MARY'S COLLEGE

UNIVERSITY OF CALIFORNIA PRESS

Berkeley / Los Angeles / London

University of California Press
Berkeley and Los Angeles, California

University of California Press
London, England

Copyright © 1994 by The Regents of the University of California

Library of Congress Cataloging-in-Publication Data

Modell, Judith Schachter, 1941–
    Kinship with strangers: adoption and interpretations of kinship
in American culture / Judith S. Modell.
        p.   cm.
    Includes bibliographical references and index.
    ISBN 0–520–08118–8 (alk. paper)
    1. Adoption—United States.   2. Kinship—United States.
3. United States—Social life and customs.   I. Title.
HV875.55.M64   1994
362.7'34'0973—dc20   92–37617
                                                              CIP

Printed in the United States of America

1 2 3 4 5 6 7 8 9

The paper used in this publication meets the minimum requirements
of American National Standard for Information Sciences—Permanence of Paper for Printed Library Materials, ANSI Z39.48-1984 ∞

To my children, Jennifer and Matthew

Contents

Preface

This book originates in and is representative of the interpretations of the people I interviewed. With training in anthropology that included a particular focus on kinship, I also began the project with a general sense of the experience of adoption in the United States. As I began to collect interviews, however, I realized how little I had brought those two domains together and, by contrast, how effectively the people I met had used their experiences of adoption to analyze kinship. The people I interviewed are self-selected: if not members of a support group (some were, others were not), they were all willing to examine a complicated part of their lives with me. This did not mean they spoke out because they had taken a critical stance—they may or may not have. Rather, a critical stance and an analytic perspective emerged from personal, digressive, uncertain, joyous, confident, and angry anecdotes.

Virtually every interview with birthparent, adoptive parent, or adoptee took well over two hours. In a majority of cases, I saw the person several times, for further interviews, at group meetings, or at adoption conferences. Our lives were not intertwined—my work does not represent classic "participatory" fieldwork—but people's interpretations of kinship did emerge over time and in different settings. Although I do write, at times, as if "all" birthparents, or adoptive parents, or adoptees, experience adoptive kinship the same way, obviously that is not true: members of the triad did not always agree with one another, even when their experiences had been similar and their attendance at support group meetings equally faithful. Rather than present diverse points of view, I have tried to convey the gist of the birthparent, the adoptive parent, and the adoptee experience of this kind of kinship in late twentieth-century American society. And though my argument mutes the particularities of this experience, it *is* built out of the multiple perspectives and positions individuals conveyed.

While writing, I did not always find it easy to resist the temptation to let my interviews dominate the text. As it is, there are substantial sections in which my voice gives way to *their* voices, not simply because I succumbed to temptation but also (and primarily) because the birthparents, adoptive parents, and adoptees I interviewed are the "first order" analysts of the data. They were critical, and self-consciously so, about the terms of their relationships. They were also critical of the significance of "fictive" in being related. What is the content of a relationship that reflects or simulates a *real* relationship? The dichotomy of real and fictive (or "not real") pervades the everyday experiences of members of the triad. The dichotomy is not an abstraction or a theoretical point, but an aspect of daily interaction, manifested in the variety of ways in which people clarified what they meant by "real parent" in conversations with me.

Chapters 2 and 3 describe the context of this kinship. These chapters are somewhat different in approach from the subsequent chapters, primarily because they depend more thoroughly on secondary sources and on observer rather than participant analyses of adoptive kinship. The chapters do, however, indicate the extent to which a century and a half of developments in law and policy shape individual experiences of adoption in the 1980s and 1990s. The material in chapters 2 and 3 constitutes the backdrop for the experiences and interpretations foregrounded in chapters 4 through 9.

Embedded in discussions of adoption are cogent critiques of the assumptions of a fictive kinship, of the significance of biology in cultural interpretations of relationship, and of the importance of "blood" for a person's identity. These are powerful issues. In addition, almost everyone remarked on the lack of attention paid to adoption when so much attention is paid to the related issues of abortion, surrogacy, child abuse and neglect, and American family values. I hope my book will correct that. For adoption is not just about parent-child relationships, it is also about identity, "blood," culture, and nature. Furthermore, it is about the way in which individuals redesign fundamental assumptions about parent-child relationships—and thus begin to reinvent core cultural symbols.

The people I interviewed were pleased I was writing this book. I only hope I have done justice to their presentations of the complexities involved in a kinship with strangers.

Acknowledgments

The first people I have to thank are the people who let me into their lives. We did not just talk about adoption, but about parenthood and childhood, about family and marriage, sex, love, and commitment. And though a number of them had spoken about these subjects before, in relatively public domains, they let me ask questions, examine their answers, and occasionally push them in a direction suitable to my research. These people include: all the members of the Concerned United Birthparents (CUB) branch I attended, who welcomed me as an anthropologist and an adoptive parent—and who frankly expressed their opinions of adoptive families; the members of an adoptee and a birthparent search group in another city, who also welcomed me and sometimes wondered why it took so long to write a book. The people in these second two groups, like those in CUB, confronted me about my personal feelings; adoptees compared me with their own parents. All this was challenging and beneficial to my final interpretations. The adoptive parents I met, through various agencies, were wonderfully forthcoming and open. As a few of them said, talking about adoption was a familiar exercise. Knowing I had shared the experience, people discussed the difficulty of applying for a child, the first days of a child's arrival home, and their concerns about the impact of "telling." A few who had suffered through disrupted adoptions offered special insight into a contracted kinship. Though I cannot name any, I do thank them all.

I could not have done the study without the generous help of a number of social workers, who provided me with professional and personal viewpoints on the transaction in kinship in which they play a central role. In alphabetical order, they are: Kirsti Adkins, Allison Beynum, Ken Cole, Sue Collins, Brenda Dugan, Gloria Hein, Chris Leasure, Jean Logan, Betty Music, Azizi Powell, Martha Ross, Vera Smith, Marietta Spencer, and Susan Tabor. Jania Sommers played another part in the book, with her invitation to speak to social workers, lawyers, and others involved in adoption in Charleston, South Carolina. The following individuals gave me special help along the way: Pam Bolduc, Lee Campbell, Jon Ryan, Glenda Shay, Sandra Sperrazza, and Jean Vincent.

Another set of thanks are due to colleagues and friends who contributed to the project, uniquely and invaluably. Roxane Gudeman introduced me to the first adoption agency I worked with. Stephen Gudeman taught me kinship—and more—rigorously and well. Bill Davenport gave me lessons in theory and method that stood me in good stead in this, as in all my work. Rubie and Woody Watson cheered me along, and invited me to give a talk at the University of Pittsburgh that led to an article on birthparents, "In Search: The Purported Biological Basis of Kinship," published in the *American Ethnologist* (November 1986). Rubie Watson read part of the manuscript as well. I also presented an early version of my argument at Colby College, where an audience of eager listeners asked questions that significantly influenced the final form of the book. Thanks to Ron Grele, I wrote a paper on interviewing birthparents and adoptees (*International Journal of Oral History,* Winter 1987) and was invited to contribute "'How do you introduce yourself as a childless mother?'" to the volume, *Storied Lives* (ed. G. Rosenwald and R. Ochberg, Yale University Press, 1992). Richard Abel sent me articles and references on relevant legal issues, and read a draft of a paper on adoption as exchange, as did Steve Klepper. A lawyer and an economist, they each provided perspectives different from my own.

The research was funded by two NEH summer grants and by faculty support grants from Colby College and from Carnegie Mellon University. In addition, a number of people at Carnegie Mellon contributed to the book: Harold Scott and John Thomas were research assistants and listeners; Louise Morin, Louann Witherspoon, and Lori Cole transcribed tapes; Barbara Collins, Dot Marsh, and Cari Hoffman also helped with transcribing, printing, and generally seeing to the successful appearance of early drafts of the manuscript. Scarlett Townsend did final preparation of the manuscript and the bibliography; this involved some last-minute tasks, which she did efficiently and cheerfully.

Several people read the whole manuscript, each offering a particular perspective. Their critical comments helped and so, too, did the personal engagement with the work each showed. I thank Richard Scaglion, Laurel Cornell, and Judith Stacey for careful readings. I also thank Barbara Lazarus, Ellen Leventhal, and John Modell for readings that went beyond the ordinary. Stan Holwitz, of the University of California Press, stood by through the several phases of the project, always offering support, help, warmth, and friendship. He deserves special gratitude.

My own parents are part of the book. So are my children, to whom the book is dedicated with love and appreciation.

1

American Adoption

A Kinship with Strangers

"The fiction of adoption"

"And when I got off the plane we, neither of us had any problem recognizing each other. And we stood in the middle of the aisle, all the people are still trying to get, you know, the aisle just as you get out the gate. And people had to go around us. And we stood there and cried for a long time. With our arms around each other. And it was the most wonderful tears I ever shed in my life. The most wonderful, unashamed . . ." In the winter of 1990, Diana (a parent) told me about her reunion with the daughter she had relinquished to adoption over twenty years earlier. After an exhilarating phone call, the two had arranged to meet; the daughter came to the airport to greet the mother she had never known. Later in my interview with Diana, she revealed something of the difficulties that followed the ecstatic first sight. "I am perplexed about where we go now," she said. "There are no maps."

She was right: there were no maps. And there are more and more such reunions, reported in the newspapers, on television, and, increasingly, in published autobiographical accounts. Some end happily, others tragically. Sometimes, eager as two people may be to meet, they never actually do see each other. But whatever the outcome, reunions challenge the accepted views of adoption and, in the process, reveal the structures and the ideologies upon which adoptive kinship is based.

This book is about the particular kind of kinship American adoption *is*. Adoption is defined as "a procedure which establishes the relationship of parent and child between persons not so related by nature" (Leavy and Weinberg 1979, v). How do people in a culture in which parenthood is created by birth—a biological fact—understand a parenthood that is created by law—a contractual arrangement? The answer seems to be by making the constructed relationship as much like the biological as possible. It is a powerful fiction, but certainly not a new idea. A British jurist in the nineteenth century, asserting that adoption should not be a distinct kind of kinship, wrote: "We must try to regard the fiction of adoption as so closely simulating the reality of kinship that neither law nor opinion makes the slightest difference between a real and an adoptive connection" (Maine 1861, 239). No one doubted, then or now, that the "real connection" was the genealogical connection.[1]

A made relationship, American law claims, can be exactly like a natural relationship: the child is *as-if-begotten*, the parent *as-if-genealogical*. The adopted child is granted an entirely new birth certificate, with the names of his or her adoptive parents on the document and the name of the birthparent nowhere in sight. Adoption "terminates all such relationships between the child and its natural parents," continues the legal definition (Leavy and Weinberg 1979, v). Not the mother who bore the child, but the mother (and, probably, the father) who received the child are listed as the real parents.[2] After relinquishment, the birthparent does not exist: as birthparents said, "our parenthood vaporizes."

When Diana appeared at the airport to meet her daughter, she violated this assumption and more: the confidentiality of an adoption, the privacy of the adoptive family, the notion that a birthparent would forget the birth, and the assumption that an adoptee would forever have only one set of parents. Diana's reunion with her child destroys the presumption that an adoptive parent completely replaces the biological parent—the legal axiom of "substitutability" upon which adoption rests. The reunion also calls for a relationship between parents who, despite sharing a child, expect to remain strangers. "I have no earthly idea," Diana said, about what the new relationship might be like. "I'll have to make a new one." The challenge brought by reunions like Diana's, as well as the significance of the principles that are challenged, constitute the theme of this book.

In a conventional American adoption, the birth family and the adoptive family are not kin; they do not know one another.[3] Secrecy and sealed records see to that, and to the perpetuation of anonymity over the lifetime of the child. The policy has three accompanying prescriptions: that a birthparent forget the child and move on with her life; that an adoptive parent take on the characteristics of a natural parent; that an adoptee not "miss" a biological ancestry. The following pages show why these prescriptions work as well as they do and, too, their inherent paradoxes that led, in the late twentieth century, to demands for contact, reunions, and open records.

My theoretical framework also involves, in Maine's words, the "fiction" of adoption and, with that, the presumed "reality" of a genealogical connection. The theory derives from anthropological studies of kinship that start with the link between a parent and her child—the presumed core of kinship. The subject of adoption appears here and there in such studies, more often viewed as a mechanism for arranging social relationships, apportioning property, or caring for a child, than as a "story" of what it means to be related. But, as a fiction, that is also what adoption is: a delineation of what makes people "really" kin. In American adoption, as I have suggested, what makes people really kin is birth, symbolized by the notion of blood. That means that just as a book about adoption is paradoxically a book about biological relationship, so too a book about contracted kinship is a book about blood relatives. "I have no flesh and blood," adoptees said to me, explaining the "gap" in their lives.

That adoption mirrors biology is not a new insight. In Schneider's (1972, 35–36) terms, for instance, "adoption is not ruled outside the 'kinship' system but is understandable as a kind of 'kinship' relationship precisely in terms of the fact that it is modeled after the biological relationship. Without the biological relationship, in this view, adoption makes absolutely no sense." Yet my book does offer two new perspectives. First, I argue that adoption not only mirrors biology but also upholds a cultural interpretation of biological, or genealogical, kinship. Every time a child is given up and taken in, the script of "real" relationship is, as it were, written again. And so when adoption changes, interpretations of genealogical kinship will not remain unaltered.

Second, I show that "blood" makes adoption problematic for those who experience this kind of kinship. The significance of blood in American understandings of kinship means that adoption is always self-conscious; for a parent and child to be related by arrangement, and not by nature, compels an alertness to the terms of relationship that is unusual in an American context. Recently, too, the "unnaturalness" of adoptive kinship has produced a critique that demystifies the traditional symbols of kinship: blood, birth, and nature. When Diana appeared at the airport, she violated the axioms of adoptive kinship; she also exposed the principles of real kinship: blood is thicker than water, a birth bond cannot be severed, a parent's love is absolutely enduring. It is exactly the *sense* reunions make that prompts fascination with this meeting of long-lost relatives.

In meeting her daughter, Diana acted like a real mother. "I may not be her parent, but I am her mother," she told me, distinguishing the role of parent from the feelings of a mother. As Diana's comment suggests, a book on adoption would not be complete without a discussion of terminology. "And when I say my mother and my father, I mean my adoptive parents, ok? I want to have that terminology straight." Other adoptees were not as assertive as this woman was. She did not have any terms for her adoptive mother and father except the ones that connote a genealogical relationship, as she recognized in her statement to me. In fact, "mother" and "father" would have been more appropriate for those who gave birth to her, as she knew—which was why she was so insistent in her interview. The kin terms this adoptee used made the adoptive parent-child relationship seem real precisely because they evoked the "natural" link between parent and child.

The pervasive significance of "genealogy" in American kinship has been noted not only by anthropologists but also by philosophers and literary critics, as in the following: "We have a model that men and women couple to produce offspring who are similar to their parents and this model is grounded in genetics, and the semantics of kinship metaphor is grounded in this model" (Turner 1987, 7–8). One adoptive mother told me how she knew her son was really theirs. "I think now Lyle realizes that when you talk about parents, you talk about Mom and Dad." Calling them Mom and Dad, Lyle made his adoptive parents *as-if-genealogical*, corresponding with the *as-if-begotten* of his own birth certificate.

Adoptive parents, then, said in one way what scholars expressed in another way: "The meanings of kinship words are not free to commute away from these anchoring basic models and processes without some tension, fiction, and resistance" (Turner 1987, 7–8). In fact, in adoption kinship terms both do and do not "commute away" from the basic models; the *compromise* causes the tension I describe below. While kinship words transform those who participate in a contracted relationship by referring to a blood relationship, they also recall the "anchor" in biological processes. In American culture, moreover, "mother," not "father," is the crucial term for anchoring a transaction in parenthood to nature. "Whatever may be their ideas about physical parenthood, virtually all cultures attach symbolic values to both fatherhood and motherhood. I suggest that fatherhood is the freer symbol, able to take on a wider range of culturally assigned meanings, because it has a more exiguous link with the natural world" (Barnes 1973, 71). It is precisely because of the less exiguous link with the natural world that "motherhood" has primacy in the creation of artificial kinship.

"Mother" upholds the as-if premise, reminding an adoptive parent that she can be just like a biological parent. Mother also represents, as Diana reminded me, the unseverable bond between a birthparent and a birthchild. So powerful, in fact, is the symbol that it serves as the model of parenthood for adoptive fathers and birthfathers. The burden of the following chapters, then, is that "mother" is a condensed, contradictory, and crucial symbol in adoption. Moreover, this symbol constitutes a still point in the perceived fluidity of child exchange in the United States.[4] Shared understandings of "mother" render the whole transaction less haphazard, random, and commercialized—the presumed evils of adoption in the eyes of some and the source of the "frosty attitude" one nineteenth-century judge remarked, as well as of the "discomfort" twentieth-century analysts of the phenomenon comment on.[5] If adoption undoes, in order to re-do, kinship, the symbol of mother keeps the transaction from risk—keeps it, as the law says, in the best interests of the child.

The meanings of mother and the values attached to motherhood profoundly influence the behaviors of those who give away and those who take in children—as well as of the children who are thus transacted. An abstract symbol, "mother" determines an event that is life-course and life-crucial at once, and for all participants; in adoption, a child is moved from a birthmother to a social mother, who will become, and be recorded "as if begetter." The paradoxes entailed in thoroughly resting a contracted upon a blood bond, a legal upon a biological relationship, and "culture" upon "nature" are not academic for those whose actions the paradoxes frame—the person who raises as "one's own" a child who is a stranger, the parent who forgets the child who is "flesh and blood," and the individual who constructs an identity out of having been chosen instead of born. Members of the triad—adoptive parent, birthparent, and adoptee—face those cultural inconsistencies in their everyday lives. Those are also the inconsistencies that, as narrated, form the cornerstone of a sharp analysis of the "fiction of adoption."

How sharp and how critical the analysis is became clear to me the first time I attended a meeting of birthparents. The "social analysis" embedded in their stories had a jarring and formative impact both on myself and on the study of adoption I had undertaken.[6]

"The subjective experience of those conditions"

My project began to take shape when a social worker at an adoption agency sent me to a meeting of a birthparent support group. I had planned to do a book on adoption and visited the agency to talk about fieldwork for my study. Following the advice, I attended a meeting of the local branch of Concerned United Birthparents (CUB), a national organization for birthparents founded in 1976. The meeting surprised and disturbed me. Like most people and, until recently, most adoptive parents, I had not thought much about the parent who relinquished a child. The conversations, personal stories, and proposals for reforming American adoption I heard constituted a new version of fictive kinship and startled me into rethinking my own views as an adoptive parent and as an anthropologist. I had told the group of my research interest and also that I had an adopted son; I was welcomed at the meetings in both capacities. I attended meetings regularly, and also went to picnics, parties, and other events sponsored by the group.

Five years later I joined an adoptee support group, founded locally and not part of a national organization. This was in another part of the country, one that did not have a branch of CUB: birthparents as well as adoptees belonged to the adoptee group, and I was never the only adoptive parent there. After awhile, birthparents formed their own group, and I attended their Sunday afternoon meetings as well.

In addition, I participated in a seven-week training session for foster and adoptive parents, qualifying as a foster parent when I finished as well as learning how much had changed since I adopted over twenty years ago. In all these groups I met people who were willing and often eager to be interviewed. Besides wanting to tell and have their stories heard, they were interested in seeing more published about adoption as it seemed to be evolving in the late twentieth century. Generally, my full and active participation in the groups meant I was not just a scholarly observer, but one of them. Some people were interested in my family, others not at all.

In addition to my main informants—the triad of adoptees, birth-parents, and adoptive parents—I also talked with social workers, law-yers, and judges. Not all adoptees and birthparents I met belonged to a group or, in the case of adoptive parents, had been through a train-ing session. Social workers gave me names, I met people on my own, others were friends of people I had already interviewed. If not exactly a community, there was certainly a network of triad members in both places in which I did research.[7]

These are urban centers, with substantial suburbs and close-in rural areas. State laws differed in some respects, but not enough to make the experience of adoption widely divergent. The people I talked with were primarily white and middle-class, mainly Protestant in the first city and split between Protestant and Catholic in the second. Adoptive parents tended to be more homogeneously middle class, birthparents less so. Adoptees came from a variety of backgrounds. Probably the most important characteristic of the people I talked with, however, was that they were self-selected and, it could be argued, already criti-cal of adoption. And they *were* critical, in the sense of standing outside the relationship they had previously taken for granted. Every person I interviewed willingly explored the kinship in which they participated.[8]

Self-consciousness was in the air, even for those who had not joined a group. Support groups for all three members of the triad had been in existence for nearly three decades. They began in the 1960s, an out-growth of that politicized period and linked to other movements for "liberty" and individual rights. Adoptee groups were the first, soon followed by birthparent and adoptive parent groups. Most groups be-gan with the same general goal—consciousness-raising—and, in many cases, ended by being active advocates of change. This shift, however, did not reduce the significance of consciousness-raising, which persists as a central activity in virtually all adoption-related support groups. As

Kristin Luker argues in her book on the abortion debate (1984, 100), consciousness-raising implies "that people can be made to experience as problematic events or situations which they had previously accepted without complaint. It carries within it the belief that it is not necessarily the objective conditions of life that cause people to make social change but an individual's *subjective* experience of those conditions." At adoption meetings, too, as people discovered their subjective experiences were shared, they began to find adoptive kinship problematic and puzzling. Such sharing brought reassurance to those who came to the meetings; clearly, it was an important reason for attending.

In the setting of a support group, individuals exchanged personal stories and found their stories transformed into a commentary on adoptive kinship. The stories were not always critical or dissatisfied, but they were newly articulated and thereby revised old points of view. Piling up, in meeting after meeting, these stories formed a kind of rhetorical stockpile, offering, in technical parlance, "performative and narrative resources" for the "inchoate experiences" of participants.[9] Or, if not inchoate, these experiences had been forgotten or deliberately suppressed: "sewn up in a little box," as one birthparent put it. Meetings brought forth the "differences" that conventional adoption policy eroded; members learned to acknowledge that relinquishing, adopting, and being adopted were not just like the parent-child relationships everyone else had.[10]

My initial contact group, CUB, had started purely for reasons of support. As a pamphlet explained to new members, "Mutual help occurs when people help themselves and/or others who share a similar life experience." Adoptee groups, however, much more forthrightly argued for change, specifically for opening records and granting individuals the "facts" of their lives. The Adoptees' Liberty Movement Association (ALMA) told its new members, "The denial of an adult human being's right to *the truth of his origin* creates a scar which is imbedded in his soul forever." By the end of the 1980s, birthparent groups sounded as militant as adoptee groups. "Closed adoption records guaranteeing anonymity to all those in the adoption triad has succeeded with unprecedented effectiveness in demeaning and destroying the essence of family, kinship, genetic continuance and hereditary pride among people," said a newly formed birthparent group in 1990. Adoptive parent groups did not fall behind, arguing for recognizing the significance of the child's nature and for welcoming a birthparent into the family constellation. The idea of shared parenthood, of two sets of real parents, became a part of adoption discourse.

The rhetoric created at meetings gave people a sense of power and of leverage over decisions they felt others had made for them in the past. Whether or not a person became an adoption activist, proposed revisions of policy affected the experience of adoption. Moreover, support groups have clearly had an impact on this mode of transferring a child. Few agencies today avoid the issues of contact, reunions, and nonconfidential arrangements; few ignore the challenge to secrecy and sealed records brought by support groups. Many themselves argue for new ways of giving and of taking children—for a different kind of "child exchange" and a revised understanding of parenthood. Yet few people outside the adoption triad know about the adoption reform movement; proposals for change are lost on the American public. Except for a dramatic reunion, the occasional public television report or *New York Times* article, reforms in adoption mainly occupy the attention of those who are personally and professionally involved in this kind of kinship.*

Why is that? Adoption remakes a child's identity, creates parenthood without birth, and manipulates concepts of blood, law, nature, and culture—earthshaking notions that have not had much of an impact on general consciousness. Debate over adoption reform is silent compared with discussions of abortion, which, like adoption, is a life-cycle and familial event; abortion is rarely *out* of the news. The difference provides insight into the place of adoption in an American cultural and social context: "an apple pie institution," as one member of my adoption support group said.

The abortion debate, wrote Faye Ginsburg in her 1989 book, *Contested Lives*, depends on "antagonistic groupings" and polarized understandings. By contrast, adoption reform groups tend to blur differences and to emphasize the "family values" they have in common. Reform groups argue in the same terms as one another and, in fact, in the terms that have guided conventional adoption policy for over a century: the best interests of the child. They agree on the principle

*Since this chapter was written, there has been a great deal more attention paid to adoption in the media. The disputed adoption, known as the Baby Jessica case, in which a birthparent successfully regained rights to her child, has prompted a substantial amount of attention to American policies and practices of adoption. Whether adoption will ever be as significant as abortion as a national issue remains to be seen.

and on its implementation: placing a child with a loving family. Unlike the abortion debate, too, there seems to be little controversy about the meanings of parenthood, and of mother and father; core symbols are shared and beliefs do not profoundly differ. "Different beliefs about the roles of the sexes, about the meaning of parenthood, and about human nature are all called into play when the issue is abortion" (Luker 1984, 158); they are not called into play when the issue is adoption.

The American Adoption Congress (AAC), an umbrella organization for reform groups, does not diverge widely from the moderate Child Welfare League of America (CWLA) or even from the conservative National Committee for Adoption (NCFA). All embrace the family, the value of the child, and the importance of love, nurture, and enduring solidarity. The principle of the "rights of the child" has not (yet) warred with the rights of women—or of men; adoption groups are shy not only of feminism but also of references to "life and death" that are part of abortion discourse. Of course, there are differences among the groups: the AAC opposes closed records and anonymity, the CWLA modifies its proposals for change with an emphasis on professional supervision, and the NCFA argues forcefully for complete confidentiality. None opposes adoption, and all link adoption with the maintenance of the American family. To an outsider, the positions seem like variations on a theme, not a radical attack on family, marriage, or the "nature" of women and men.

Adoption reform groups have disadvantaged themselves by insisting on a common core of values and by avoiding issues that would split them apart and separate them from the central principles of child placement practice. State legislative amendments make small ripples, and federal guidelines go unheeded.[11] Consistent with the history of adoption in America, the proposed reforms uphold interpretations of kinship based on a biological model, inherently conservative.

On the other hand, as I suggest here, the behavioral changes that are occurring have the potential to disrupt interpretations of biology and revise American kinship far more radically than the reform rhetoric implies. The adoption movement rests on the particular decisions of individual actors, decisions that cumulatively may shatter the mirror of genealogy adoption has made. Birthparents who insist upon giving a child to a parent they can "relate to," adoptive parents who accept a birthparent into their lives, and adoptees who demand a certificate of birth and not a record of their parents' contract will create a "public problem," and the rhetoric to accompany it. The difference between adoption and abortion—as well as other public problems in child welfare—is a reminder of the significance of private actions for the content, and composition, of an effective rhetoric.[12]

Just as adoption reform advances behind the scenes, so too adoption occurs with little notice. An "apple pie" phenomenon, adoption has a surprisingly small archive, less well documented than virtually any other "life change" in American society.

"A matter of public record"

In gathering secondary sources to supplement my fieldwork, I discovered how limited, in some respects, the information on this form of kinship is. Participants complain about the "denial" of facts, and experts and scholars about the "scarcity" of data. Both can be attributed to the same cause: the prevalence of the as-if-begotten axiom. For if an adoptive family is *just like* any other, it gets counted, surveyed, and described just like any other. By the same token, "birthparent" is a null category since she (and he) disappears once the transaction has been completed. The adopted child becomes a full member of the new family and his or her characteristics part of its profile.

We do not even know with any certainty how many adopted people there are in the American population—something quite astounding in a rigorously record-keeping society.[13] There have been sporadic efforts to count: in 1944, the federal government, through the Children's Bureau and then the National Center for Social Statistics, began compiling statistics on adoption. Based on the voluntary submissions of states, each keeping records in a distinct fashion, for three decades these were the most reliable statistics available. In 1975, the effort ended partly because of budgetary and partly because of ideological constraints (Maza 1984). Some statistical data on adoption can also be elicited from a survey of women of childbearing age, conducted by the National Survey of Family Growth.[14] The NSFG, in contrast with the CB/NCSS data, tells about adoption in a woman's life, not about adoption in a child's life.

Faced with this chaos, in 1985 the National Committee for Adoption published an *Adoption Factbook*,[15] containing the most extensive statistical data on adoptions in the United States as a whole, including a compilation of annual adoptions in 1982.[16] In 1986, the NCFA did another survey published in its *Encyclopedia of Adoption*; in that year, there were approximately 105,000 adoptions, of which nearly 53,000 were "related" and 52,000 "unrelated" or "stranger" adoptions (Adamec and Pierce 1991, 316). Those figures do not, of course, tell how many adopted *people* there are in the United States.[17] One might do best by accepting H. David Kirk's (1984, 4) calculation: "Assuming a low figure of five million adoptees, that figure can be multiplied by eight, so that in a population of two hundred million, one fifth of the people are directly or intimately linked to the experience of adoption."

Not only do we not know exactly how many people are involved in adoptive kinship, we also know little about their sociodemographic characteristics, in effect, who they are (Jonassohn 1965; Bachrach 1983b; Moorman and Hernandez 1989).[18] This is most true of the birthparent, until recently the hidden member of the triad—and, from the birthparent perspective, another sign of the stigma attached to adoption altogether: "I would like adoption to be a matter of public record, like marriage, birth, and death," a reader wrote to a birthparent newsletter (CUB *Communicator,* 9/85: 6).

We do, however, know about expectations for this form of kinship and, often intertwined with those, about personal experiences—for, in another respect, there is a substantial literature on adoption, including novels, autobiographies, and a variety of case studies. In these, adoption is treated as a personal event, not unreasonably, but without attention to the social or cultural context. The few exceptions that do exist here can be found in social science and in history.[19] Manuals and guides form the other large body of literature: how to place a child; how to "beat the system"; how to search—though not, I think, how to relinquish a child. Embedded in these manuals are ideologies of the family, of gender, and of "true" kinship. Expressed in terms of instruction and guidance, such ideologies cannot help but influence the people who are themselves constructing a fictive relationship. To my knowledge, no one has argued, as I do, that the *experience* of adoptive kinship involves an *interpretation* of American kinship.

In the late 1970s, Betty Jean Lifton's books made an enormous impact on members of the triad and, as well, on those formulating adoption policy.[20] Her autobiography, *Twice Born*, a collection of lifestories called *Lost and Found*, and a novel for adolescents, *I'm Still Me*, all dovetailed with growing consciousness of the contradictions and constraints in American adoption practice. Lifton argues for the importance of contact between birthparent and birthchild, the necessity of knowing blood kin for forming a stable identity, and the denial of rights represented by an amended birth certificate and by the "tissue of lies" surrounding an adoptee's origins. Her books, more than any other autobiographically based comments on adoptive kinship, became a template for the experience of adoption.

"Their atypical reality"

Lifton urged adoptees especially, but by implication all members of the triad, to "awaken from the great sleep." My study reveals that very few members of the adoption triad are "asleep," unalert to their kind of parent-child relationship. Even those who are content with adoption examine the "fiction" of its kinship by reinterpreting kin terms, by developing behavioral strategies for making the fiction real, or by "forgetting" the ways they are different from everyone else. Whatever the method, it involves effort.

"All relationships need work," the coordinator of the adoptee search group told us. Yet, as she conveyed through her own story of growing up adopted and locating her birth family, adoptive relationships need special work. Her story also suggested that the "production" of kinship in adoption can come to have a positive value. At the various meetings I attended, I was struck by the emphasis on *work* in discussions of adoption. Ultimately, it seemed to me that work was a way of distinguishing adoptive relationships—according them a difference that was not a stigma. Work represented control over the terms of a relationship, important to individuals—like the birthparents, adoptive parents, and adoptees I met—who felt others had made decisions about parenthood *for* them. Working out and working on kinship suited a cultural context. In addition, such work was not considered antithetical to feeling, loving, and being passionate about an attachment.

Expanding on this theme, in his 1981 book, *Adoptive Kinship*, Kirk writes: "Given that the adoptive situation at the interpersonal level is objectively different from the situation of the family based on consanguinity, the solidarity of the adoptive family's membership is enhanced when their atypical reality is acknowledged in their daily relationship" (xv). The people I knew discovered that acknowledgment was a matter of constant and creative work: the production of a kind of kinship. *I* discovered how theories of kinship are articulated and revised by "natives"—natives, in my case, who constructed a critique that very much resembles those made by anthropologists, confronting (as these do) the "biologism" that dominates the construction of American kinship (e.g., Schneider 1984). The people in my study were not the fish-in-water Emily Martin mentions, but rather were fish out of water—people well aware of, and interested in probing, the contradictions in their lives.[21]

In doing so, and as I will show in the following chapters, they begin to dismantle the "simulation" of blood kinship that Sir Henry Maine proposed and American adoption law perpetuated. From the axiom of "as if" come the paradoxes in adoptive kinship: that a legal is exactly the same as a genealogical relationship, that a contract is unseverable while blood can be "broken." The solution to such paradoxes, apparently, is to recognize that adoptive is distinct from biological kinship: in this view, adoption could make sense without the biological relationship. Two questions follow: How far can adoption stray from the biological model and still be kinship? How much can kinship veer toward a "made" relationship and still be *real*?

Although complete answers to these questions lie in the future, the contours are nascent in the current experiences of members of the triad—experiences described in chapters 4 through 9.

In chapter 2, then, I begin by outlining the background of current adoption policy. I describe the development of laws and policies that were intent on designating "real" parenthood in the best interests of the child. Ironically, the growing legal recognition of adoption was accompanied by inconsistencies that continue to plague an effort to substitute "law" for "blood." Out of nineteenth-century custody and placement cases came an assignment of parenthood to that person who "cared for" but did not necessarily give birth to, or even have a blood tie with, the child. American adoption is unique in focusing on the child and in its willingness to place a child with a total stranger who will, presumably, love the child as his or her own. In chapter 3, I describe the entry of experts into this daunting transaction: the professionalization of child welfare services. With professionals came a move to systematize the criteria for a good (and a bad) parent and to find ways of predicting the outcome of a placement. This chapter, like the previous one, suggests the difficulties surrounding the making of kinship—in this instance, whether there can be a "scientific" measure of parenthood and, moreover, in advance of a person's having a child. Ought scientific techniques of inquiry and investigation be part of what is, in essence, a kinship event? These difficulties have not been resolved in over seventy-five years of professional child placement practice—and they profoundly influence the experience of those who give up and those who take in children.

Part II begins with the birthparent (chapter 4), in many ways the heart of an adoptive transaction. Without a parent to surrender a child, in a society that does not encourage the casual exchange of children adoption would not happen. For birthparents, as I show, surrender is a powerful, ambiguous, and central concept, organizing their experiences. The chapter indicates that birthparents, no longer passive victims, now refuse to surrender parenthood even though they have given their child to other parents. These other parents are the subject of chapter 5, and their experiences reveal a parallel effort to interpret parenthood in a context in which genealogy is the core of kinship. Unable to have a child "naturally," adoptive parents apply for a child and submit to testing, investigation, and the judgment of an expert on their fitness to be parents. In effect, they have to prepare a case for having a child while, as they put it, everyone else just has babies.

In chapter 6, I focus on the child, the individual who grows up adopted. Told she has been chosen, the adoptee works at living up to standards: "the duckling in a family of swans," an adoptee said to me. More than that, an adopted person in twentieth-century American society wonders about her heritage, why she does not look like anyone in the family and who she really does resemble. Some adoptees who wondered eventually asked out loud, doubting the chosen-child story they were told and "missing" a birth story. In turn, some would begin to search: for facts, for a parent, for a birth family. Their quests form the content of chapter 7, the beginning of Part III. Adoptees were the first of the triad to assert their rights to know and to claim the importance of biological ancestry. The founding of adoptee support groups initiated the reconsideration of adoptive kinship that unifies the three chapters in Part III.

Birthparents followed the lead of adoptees, claiming their equal rights to know. Chapter 8 tells that story: the impact a national birthparent organization has had on individual birthparent perceptions, bringing these parents (in their phrase) "out of the closet." Like adoptees, birthparents move from wanting information to wanting contact, a sight of blood kin, and an ongoing relationship. Encounters are no more easy for a birthparent to manage than they are for the child who meets an unknown parent. Each takes on the burden of reinventing kinship. Finally there are the adoptive parents, caught in changes seemingly beyond their control and, often, beyond their desire. Chapter 9 portrays the adoptive parent position, and the accommodations those members of the triad make to a prescriptive acknowledgment of the biological basis of kinship. In the 1990s, adoptive parents who are instructed in shared parenthood must decide what it means to be related to the other parents of their "own" child. It is baffling and confusing, as I discovered, and the process is only just beginning.

In chapter 10, the last of the book, I speculate on the impact recent changes in adoption practice and increasingly vociferous demands for reform of policy will have on fictive kinship. Open adoption plays a large part. The exchange of a child by people who know one another, expect to have an ongoing relationship and to share a child, transfigures the face of adoptive kinship: there is no *as-if* in an open adoption. Open adoption will alter the experience of the adoptive parent, who by convention is the exclusive and only real parent of the child; it will alter the experience of the adopted child whose "other" parents are by convention (in another paradox) fictive, and it will alter the experience of the birthparent, who by convention absolutely and forever relinquishes the child. Open adoption involves a radical modification of the policies and practices now in place.

But open adoption is also the culmination of a century and a half of tugging at what it means to construct a fictive parent-child relationship, and then make it real—the process of tugging that began with the first "modern" law of adoption, in Massachusetts in 1851.

PART ONE

The Setting:
American Adoption Policy

2

In the Best Interests

The Background of American
Adoption Policy

"The felt necessities of the time"

"Properly speaking a legal adoption is a procedure which establishes the relationship of parent and child between persons not so related by nature. At the same time the adoption terminates all such relationships between the child and its natural parents" (Leavy and Weinberg 1979, v). My book is about legal adoption and I describe the background of contemporary practice and policy through a focus on its guiding principle, "the best interests of the child." In the United States, adoption is presumed to be for the child's sake. Yet adoption is also a way of creating a family, and this other purpose complicates the application of "best interests."

In the middle of the nineteenth century, adoption laws came somewhat as a surprise and somewhat in response to the "felt necessities" of the time. The first law, in Massachusetts in 1851, apparently passed without much fanfare or debate, suggesting the time *had* come for such legislation. This was further suggested by the rapidity with which other states followed suit: Pennsylvania in 1855, then the rest of the nation. By 1929, all existing states had a law of adoption (Baran and

Pannor 1990, 320). These laws had elements in common: concern with the welfare of the child and with the "justness" of the transfer for the parents. The laws also uniformly took adoption out of state legislatures and placed the transaction in the probate courts, where it could happen quickly, efficiently, and democratically—not, however, without involving the court in interpretations of the parent-child relationship.

In the interests of the child, the concept of parent was deconstructed and its meanings analyzed. Yet this radical maneuver was combined with respect for the core symbols of kinship: birth, blood, and nature. Upon that combination, the transformation of kinship in an adoption rested. Furthermore, not only adoption—though adoption most severely—but also custody cases exposed the structures and symbols of kinship in the United States. Adoption *was* severe, as commentators, experts, and participants noted, inasmuch as the transaction severed the bond of blood. Unlike any other child placement, adoption permanently cut the ties of nature; yet decisions about adoption could not have been made without these other cases in which a child was removed from one parent and placed with another. A variety of judicial explorations of parenthood in the early and mid-nineteenth century contributed to the substance and the directives of adoption law.

These judicial explorations also gave adoption law the inconsistencies and paradoxes evident today. Like other domestic law, diverse from state to state, adoption law seems particularly chaotic, contradictory, and open to individual construction. Such lack of uniformity, I suggest, stems from a cultural resistance to the idea that blood can be severed and replaced by contract. The thrust of adoption law and policy is to pretend that blood is there; a fictive kinship is *just like* a biological relationship. But it is not: the "frosty attitude" toward adoption that one nineteenth-century judge remarked upon reveals an accompanying conviction that artificial kinship disrupts the true course of nature.

Why then were laws of adoption passed so rapidly and apparently inevitably in the late nineteenth century—laws that facilitated the creation of fictive kinship? Several explanations have been offered for why adoption laws came when they did in the United States. By and large, these explanations conclude by citing the intersection of social and demographic changes unique to the time with shifts in ideologies of family and of childhood.[1] Whatever the precipitating causes, adoption laws had the effect of at once protecting the parent-child relationship and subjecting that relationship to the oversight of the state. Deeming the family the right and natural place for a child, the state took the condition of the family as its responsibility. It carried out this responsibility first through the judges who supervised adoptions and then through the experts on child welfare who investigated the circumstances of a placement. But nothing was crystal clear and much depended on the individual case, the particular judge, and contemporaneous interpretations of mother, father, and child.

Adoption law asks who is the best parent for a child and implies a question about what a parent *is*. In the interests of a child, a parent must be evaluated, qualified, and approved. Reasons for wanting a child come under scrutiny, leading to a distinction between altruistically "rescuing" and selfishly "having" a child. The distinction between helping a child in need and taking a child in order to create a family is not easy to maintain: people who rescue children may also love them, just like their own. Yet efforts to preserve the distinction persist, a way of further refining the concept of "parent."

Sensitive to cultural assumptions about blood, nature, sex, and love, adoption law could not provide an unambiguous or unchanging interpretation of parenthood. Thus, the thesis of the present chapter is that neither "best interests" nor its accompanying emphasis on conduct in defining a parent eliminates the paradoxes attached to *making* a kinship that is *as-if-begotten*.

"The wholesale distribution of children"

The transfer of children was not a new phenomenon in the nineteenth century, nor was it new in the United States.[2] But the "felt necessities" had changed by the 1850s when laws were passed. Industrialization and urbanization, in the company of restrictions on child labor, did put more children on the streets; that a child ought not be at work but rather at school or at home seemed to have the effect of producing bands of wandering children (Howe 1983). At the same time, as commentators have noted, new views of childhood, of the family, of affection, and of individual rights took hold.[3] But these do not totally explain why laws of *adoption* were passed, laws that made the child a "real" member of the family that took him or her in. There are other ways of handling roving, hookey-playing children, and other ways of ensuring the continuity of relationship between an adult and a child.

One answer is that people were already engaged in transforming a "cared-for" child into a child as-if-begotten. Adoption had occurred in the United States, for over a century, despite the lack of precedent in English common law. Through a private legislative act, a child could become a full member of a family.

The number of such acts increased in the nineteenth century, demanding attention from state legislators.[4] Perhaps it was not the ideal use of legislative time to debate the petition of John Doe to make Sam his son or to assess Henry Smith's desire that Richard be adopted so he could inherit land and property.[5] Moving the transaction out of the legislature and into the probate courts *was* more efficient; adoption became a simple and, usually, automatic procedure. The more so, undoubtedly, since these adoptions tended to involve children who were blood related—nephews, nieces, cousins. Like their fellow citizens, legislators were reassured by the continuity of blood through the change of parenthood.[6] A typical petition of the times might read: "It shall be lawful for John Fonda to go before the County Court of Jefferson County, and to declare of record, that he does adopt John Edwin Blumenthal, his nephew, a minor, to be his son, and his lawful heir, as if said John Edwin had been his begotten son" (in Witmer 1963, 29).

The passing of adoption laws may also have been a response to the apparent flow of children in urban centers. As Howe (1983, 176) has pointed out, "By the mid-1800s many east coast cities were plagued by groups of street urchins. . . . Newspapers of the day carried advertisements for children wanted for adoption, and parents either sold or gave them away. No legal regulations existed to control the wholesale distribution of children to uninvestigated homes where they were used as cheap labor." From this perspective, adoption laws regulated a market in children and those who profited from such a market. But laws of adoption also regulated parents who, for good and practical reasons, "put out" a child. Laws about the "distribution" of children constrained the decisions individuals made about their families (Bellingham 1986). And, too, these laws regulated the charity societies that served as middlemen between the givers and takers of children. The 1851 Massachusetts law itself was viewed by a contemporaneous commentator as a "remedy for the distressing cases arising under the custom of adopting children, which was then increasing rapidly in that state, through the efforts of foundling societies" (Zainaldin 1979, 1044)—distressing, apparently, because irresponsible and self-interested. With adoption law, the state implemented an ideology of civic responsibility for children.

Although many factors led to the passage of adoption laws in the mid-nineteenth century, one effect was unmistakable: the official acknowledgment of a way of having children. A shift from the legislature to probate courts affirmed the ordinariness of the transaction: going to a local court did not have the exclusionary quality that petitioning a state legislature might. Adoption was democratized; not just governors, but average community members could take another person's child as their own.[7] By the end of the nineteenth century, farmers in Kansas and businessmen in Boston were adopting children, whatever the particular motivation was behind their assumption of a contracted kinship.

Adoption laws contained specific provisions for such kinship. These provisions evolved as more cases came to court, fewer involved blood kin, and some gave rise to controversy and dispute. Once embarked on the course of lawfully transferring parenthood and redefining kinship, courts had to delineate the meanings of parenthood and interpret the symbols of kinship. Judicial opinions examined concepts of blood and nature, as well as ideologies of sex and gender, in the context of protecting the rights of children. But the task was complicated. Parental rights were involved as well: one parent was permanently losing and the other permanently gaining a child.[8] Adoption law consequently required a test of parental worth, the more urgently the "thinner" the relationship between petitioner and child. By the end of the century, John Fonda and his nephew gave way to adoptions by strangers—and judges could not depend on "blood" to ensure the care of a child.

A test of comparative parental worth is evident in the 1851 Massachusetts law. Once satisfied the adopters were of "sufficient ability to bring up the child, and furnish suitable nurture and education, having reference to the degree and condition of its parents, and that it is fit and proper that such adoption should take effect," a judge might grant the decree of adoption (in Witmer 1963, 30–31). The child was placed with the "better" parents and gained full rights—just as if he or she had been born to these designated parents.[9] The test of parental worth focused on an individual's ability to furnish suitable nurture and education, appropriate to the child's nature; suitability was then measured by the "degree and condition" of the child's biological parents. Thus the Massachusetts law bequeathed to American adoption law the tricky matter of determining "suitable nurture" without bias, subjectivity, or prejudicial standards.

"Nurture" here also evoked a *kind* of care: loving and committed, affectionate and enduring. Nurture differed from the training provided in an apprenticeship or the moral discipline offered by a charitable person who took in a stubborn and unruly child (Chemerinsky 1979–1980). Adoption made a *real* parent, and that was different from the farmer who felt affection for the boy he trained or the child-saver who cared for the girl he disciplined into "good citizenship."[10] The latter were arrangements of convenience, not of kinship; only the adoptive parent was to be as-if-genealogical (Kawashima 1981–1982). For the purposes of legitimacy, custody, support, obedience, inheritance, "and all other legal consequences and incidents of the natural relation of parents and children," as in the Massachusetts Act, adoption made a real child, as if born "in lawful wedlock."

Under this provision, education was of a kind, too—not just passing on skills but also molding a child's temperament and forming her character. With its reference to genealogy ("blood"), adoption assumes the child will be like its parents, blending into the family. Such an assumption minimizes the threat of "bad blood" and the stigma attached to illegitimacy.[11] It also reveals a powerful faith in environmental influences: an adopted child can learn to resemble his or her parents, to grow up in their image, not just under their guidance.[12] The child becomes a *relative*, indistinguishable from anyone else in the family. Or maybe not quite indistinguishable. The recognition of difference when blood is missing is also part of the history of American adoption.

"The most troublesome question"

Inheritance, of course, is the most troublesome question. It "runs through the history of adoption and nonadoption so much more prominently than any other factor . . . that its importance can hardly be overestimated" (Witmer 1963, 23). Both Massachusetts and the next state to pass an adoption law, Pennsylvania, accorded the right of inheritance to an adopted child. The Pennsylvania law stated:

"That if such adopting parent shall have other children, the adopted shall share inheritance only as one of them in case of intestacy, and he, she, or they shall respectively inherit from and through each other, as if all had been the lawful children of the same parent" (State of Pennsylvania, Act 456, 1855). Though most states took these two laws as models, not all liked this way of dealing with property. The matter of inheritance reveals the persistent artificiality of adoptive kinship as well as the problematic links between "blood" and "money" in American interpretations of kinship. As two recent commentators claim, "the most troublesome question arising after adoption is that of inheritance" (Leavy and Weinberg 1979, 65).

Passed in 1873, the New York State adoption law prescribed that parent and child "shall sustain toward each other the legal relation of parent and child, and have all the rights of that relation, excepting the rights of inheritance" (Bremner 1971, II, 138).[13] Fourteen years later, in 1887, the state legislature had second thoughts and amended the law to include the rights of inheritance, possibly persuaded by an attorney's expressed fear that a child might be "trained up tenderly and in luxury, and then left in utter poverty, because the adopted parent had made no will" (in Grossberg 1985, 276). Other states persisted in the denial of inheritance rights to a nonbiological child. In 1898, in a disputed bequest case, the Ohio Supreme Court interpreted adoption law in its own fashion: "Adoption does not make the adopted child of the blood of its adopter nor of the blood of his [adopter's] ancestors" (in Grossberg 1985, 277).

A child might belong to the adopting parents but he or she did not necessarily therefore belong to the *whole* family. A stranger could be kept at a distance by not participating in the ownership of property; degree of relationship was delineated by the flow of material goods. And according to some state laws, in terms of inheritance only the parent and child were related. "The general rule seems to be that a statute making the adopted child the heir of the adopting parents does not entitle it to claim as heir of the adopter's relatives" (Leavy and Weinberg 1979, 65). By controlling the transmission of property, the law prevented a watering down of blood—a profound version of impartibility. In 1881, an Illinois judge wrote his opinion: "But another person [natural child], who has never been a party to any adoption proceeding, who has never desired or requested to have such artificial relations established as to himself, why should his property be subjected to such an unnatural course of descent? To have it turned away upon his death from blood relations, where it would be the natural desire to have property go, and pass into the hands of an alien in blood, to produce such effect, it seems to us, the language of the statute should be most clear and unmistakable, leaving no room for any question whatever" (in Presser 1971–1972, 503). There seemed to be no question in his mind about the primacy of blood.

The judge's words show a sharp suspicion of adoption, and a sense of its real and natural limits. Similar statements persist into the twentieth century, and laws still assume that property ought not be turned away from blood relations (Leavy and Weinberg 1979). The gist of such proscriptions is that those who have no part in the decision also have no responsibility for its continuity over time; neither forebears nor descendants are implicated in the kinship created by a member of the family. And so it is possible in some states for a child raised in luxury to experience poverty if a parent dies intestate. On the other hand, these exclusionary views of inheritance have another side—a reminder that adoption in America is for the child's sake and not in order to ensure the transmission of property. Somewhat paradoxically, failure to attend to the child's legacy affirms attention to the child: the child is to be nurtured in suitable surroundings, not designated to carry on the family estate.[14]

Cases of disputed inheritance challenge the assumption that birth can be "legislated" and the biological bond between parent and child replicated by a court. This brings up an even more troublesome question: under what conditions ought a child be permanently separated from a natural parent?

"The right of parental control"

The question of parental control involves not only the removal of a child from a natural parent but also the security of the child with a social parent. The two are connected. An adoptive parent is ensured of parenthood partly through the finality by which a birthparent surrenders or is denied rights to a child.

Pennsylvania law illustrates both the problems and the paradoxes of "freeing" a child for adoption. More than thirty years after passing an adoption law, Pennsylvania added an amendment, recognizing the necessity of "the consent of the parents or surviving parent" to an adoption. The amendment also considered the other possibility, that a parent might involuntarily lose all rights to the child (State of Pennsylvania, Act 66, 1887). Consent, presumably, is voluntary, while termination of parental rights is not. But amendments to Pennsylvania law well into the twentieth century suggest how hard it is to maintain the distinction, given that consent often comes in adverse circumstances or after the child has been removed from the household. Consent provisions do protect the rights of the natural parent, but they do not guard that parent against feeling coerced by circumstances, a child welfare worker, or a judge.[15] The main thrust of consent provisions has been to make sure a parent understands the reasons for and the consequences of relinquishing rights to a child.[16] In the late 1970s, the CWLA reiterated the point: "The relinquishment of a child should be accepted only when parents have had an opportunity to make a decision that they can feel is best for both themselves and the child, and that they recognize to be final" (1978, 21).

Termination is another matter entirely. In 1838, having removed a child from the father's household in order to place her in the Philadelphia House of Refuge, a Pennsylvania judge wrote: "The right of parental control is a natural but not an inalienable one. That parents are ordinarily entrusted with it [bringing up a child], is because it can seldom be put into better hands; but where they are incompetent or corrupt, what is there to prevent that public from withdrawing their faculties, held, as they obviously are, at its sufferance?" (in Grossberg 1985, 267). A crucial case, this decision recognized the state's right to sever biological ties in the face of a parent's opposition. Half a century later, according to Pennsylvania law a parent who acted incompetently or was "corrupt" could lose his or her child permanently: "If the father or mother from drunkenness, profligacy or other cause, shall have neglected or refused to provide for his or her child or children for the period of one year or upwards," he or she loses all rights to the child.[17]

The 1838 decision set a precedent and also created the most poignant aspect of adoption: the state's right to forcibly remove a child from his or her biological parent *forever*. The character and the conduct of a parent, in these cases, have ramifying consequences that lead almost any judge to struggle over the decision: "no judge wants termination cases," a lawyer told an adoption group I attended, "they are the worst to handle." Termination cases also occupy a good part of the literature on child placement, with discussions that range from examination of the behaviors that contribute to a child's well-being to condemnation of the "personal bias" these cases manifest—as judges decide about parenthood on the basis of their own experiences of having or being a parent.[18] In addition, termination cases introduce the knotty problem of prediction. If a parent is to lose a child forever, the flaws in parental conduct and character should be such that the child seems unquestionably subject to risk, regardless of the changes time might bring.[19]

Termination cases dramatize the conflict of interests that enters virtually every permanent transfer of parenthood: the child's right to protection and care; a biological parent's right to the child she or he has borne; a "petitioner's" right to the child who is to be cared for and raised. In an attempt to resolve the conflict, a court must weigh the consequences of alienating a child from her biological family against the advantages of placing her in a loving, if "strange" home. And it must do this without knowing much about the commitment of those who take in a child. Will a contract be as enduring as blood, an American court might well ask. And, in answer, the court would initially attempt to ensure that the contract held in law. New York State, for instance, passed an adoption law in order to guarantee adoptive parents their "security" as parents.[20] It was not enough to terminate one parent's rights or accept parental consent to a relinquishment; the petitioner for a child had to be granted an absolute right as well.

Emphasis in adoption law on terms of consent, on grounds for termination, and on the permanence of contract reveals a suspicion that the legal transfer does not erode the claims of nature. "I felt as if I had kidnapped a child," an adoptive mother told me—and not totally irrationally: courts still favor the natural parent in disputed cases, as they have for a century.[21] As Bellingham (1989, 27) describes the nineteenth-century situation, "Even if the child was being accepted into intimacy with the foster family, the ambiguity about who really had custody was resolved in favor of the natural parents without dispute or demand for explanation."[22]

Alienating a child from the biological parent, if necessary, also has profound emotional significance. Whatever the basis for removal or relinquishment, the course of "nature" has been disrupted: the person who gave birth is no longer the parent of the child. This seems so extreme an act precisely because in American culture the "physical realities of conception and birth" establish an enduring "emotional attachment" to the child (Blustein 1982, 142). Birth provides the model for parenthood, loving and enduring; the model, furthermore, leads to the centrality of "mother" in decisions about children. Adoption can be viewed as the movement of a child from one kind of mother

("unfit") to another ("fit"). In the words of the anthropologist Malinowski (1930, 136) adoption is "simply" the substitution of "one
maternity for another."

The focus on mother, and on maternal traits, did not happen instantly or consistently throughout all states. And it began with custody cases, in which maternal and paternal claims to a child conflicted.
Interpretations of parenthood that became part of adoption law had
their origins in these cases, in which women gained rights and "motherhood" ideological hegemony in decisions about the placement of a
child.

"Ties of blood weaken"

In custody cases, though not usually separated from
blood kin, the child did acquire a new parent. Under these circumstances, the links between biological reproduction and being a parent
were attenuated, and the way was opened for transferring parenthood
to a person who had no blood connection to the child at all. In designating a parent in custody cases, courts increasingly depended upon a
"demonstration" of care, concern, love, and affection—and this was
true whether the petitioner was related to the child or not.

In 1824, a Massachusetts judge denied a father the custody of his
biological daughter after the mother's death. "It is an entire mistake
to suppose the Court is at all events bound to deliver over the infant
to his father, or that the latter has an absolute vested right in the custody" (in Witmer 1963, 26). Custody was transferred to the maternal
grandparents, who had cared for the child and who had performed
parental duties. In this precedent-setting case, a father lost his common law rights to the child and those who demonstrated care acquired permanent custody. Nearly sixty years later, Mr. Chapsky, a father, lost his rights not simply because someone else took better care
of his child, but because he had failed to act lovingly. "[A]nd while
there is no testimony showing that the father is what might be called
an unfit person, that his life has not been a moral one," yet: "He
seems to us like a man still and cold, and a warm-hearted child would
shrink and wither under care of such a nature, rather than ripen and
develop," read the opinion of the Kansas Supreme Court in 1881
(*Chapsky v. Wood*, 26 Kansas 650). The father, though "upright" in
character, was not tender or warm—in a word, not motherly.

Mr. Chapsky's "unfitness" to be a parent indicated the very qualities that would render a substitute parent "fit." The judge in the case granted custody to the foster parent and drew a vivid picture of the good parent. "The affection which a mother may have and does have, springing from the fact that a child is her offspring, is an affection which perhaps no other one can really possess; but, so far as it is possible, springing from years of patient care of a little, helpless babe, from association, and as an outgrowth from those little cares and motherly attentions bestowed upon it, an affection for the child is seen in Mrs. Wood that can be found nowhere else. And it is apparent, that so far as a mother's love can be equaled, its foster-mother has that love, and will continue to have it" (*Chapsky v. Wood*, 26 Kansas 650). If years of patient care and attention constitute parenthood, the way is open for a stranger to become the "true" parent of a child. The judge in this well-cited *Chapsky v. Wood* case concluded: "It is an obvious fact, that ties of blood weaken, and ties of companionship strengthen by lapse of time; and the prosperity and welfare of the child depend on the ability to do which the prompting of these ties compel." In other words, a person grew into being a parent by demonstrating an attachment to the child.

Thus, by the end of the nineteenth century, the bond between a parent and child created by companionship was as "legitimate" as that created by blood.[23] Moreover, without a proper demonstration of such gentle companionship and motherly attentions, a mother was as likely to forfeit rights to the child as a father. As a child welfare worker at the beginning of the twentieth century claimed, "The mere begetting and *bearing* a child does *not* of itself constitute true human parenthood" (in Romanofsky 1969, 133). Yet acting as-if-begetter remained the test of parental conduct. And to gauge this, a judge needed evidence: signs of affection, manifestations of care, and patterns of behavior that could be observed. That had been true in the *Chapsky v. Wood* case. The child had lived with Mrs. Wood for five years and the little girl's "happy bearing" proved that she had been well loved. Decisions were not so easy when the petitioning parent had not had the child in the household and had no opportunity to demonstrate love and affection.

This would be especially, and increasingly, the case in conventional adoption cases. Without knowing much about a petitioner's parental qualities, adoption orders referred to an idealized concept of motherhood to support a decision. The qualities of warmth and tenderness the unfortunate Mr. Chapsky lacked defined a "suitable" parent.

Thirty-five years after *Chapsky v. Wood*, a Washington State judge transferred parenthood in an adoption, stating: "Mother love does not depend upon the pains and perils of childbirth. It is not every child that is welcome. On the other hand, there is an affection that grows from care and association and the tender ministrations which are prompted by a heartfelt sympathy for the weak and the helpless. These beget a love as real as the love of a mother, and more, for the one who voluntarily assumes such a privilege must have far deeper maternal instincts than one who is an unwilling mother." This 1915 order of adoption is a classic statement of the premises for transferring parenthood. It included a further significant standard: "a good home, good clothing and good food" (*in re* Potter, 85 Wash. 617).[24] Mother love evinced in tender care and gentle ministrations, and also the wherewithal to raise the child to adulthood, qualified a person to be parent. Lacking any evidence of conduct, then, a judge might consider good environment the basis for a placement.

Even the most sentimental judge knew that a child had to be fed, clothed, and housed. In the nineteenth as in the twentieth century, the (perceived) quality of the surroundings could influence a judge's decision. So in a case that occurred at the same time as *Chapsky v. Wood*, in a different Kansas courtroom, after a divorce a judge gave custody of the child to her maternal grandparents who "had an elegant home." Fortunately, the mother lived in the household as well, allowing the judge to conclude: "We may not ignore these universal laws of our nature, and they compel us to place these children where they will be within the reach of a mother's love and care" (Bremner 1971, II, 133). But obviously "universal laws" could be ignored under certain conditions: a mother's love might not be enough if resources were inadequate. And, in turn, a "plentiful" environment might be a persuasive reason *for* placing a child. The importance of material conditions to the child's welfare adds a further burden to the demands on judicial discretion.[25] That the environment was to be selected with the child's best interests in mind did not inform a judge of the elements in an environment that served this purpose. Yet when there is no evidence of parental conduct, as in infant placements, there may be no better guide than the "elegance" or "suitability" of the home.[26]

In fact, there is another guide. The continual effort to clarify "best interests" issued in a notion of the "psychological parent." In some ways a modern version of the "conduct and character" that had been a touchstone of nineteenth-century custody and adoption cases, in other ways "psychological parent" differed: the modern principle lo-

cated parental qualities more firmly in particular traits. Beginning with
the assertion that a "psychological parent is one who, on a continuing,
day-to-day basis, through interaction, companionship, interplay, and
mutuality, fulfills the child's psychological need for a parent, as well as
the child's physical needs," the originators of the concept—Joseph
Goldstein, Anna Freud, and Albert Solnit (1979b, 98)—go on to detail the psychological and physical needs a "parent" must fulfill. This
formulation of the concept was a culmination of decades of placement
decisions that released parenthood from "ties of blood," while anchoring it in "ties of companionship." The concept of a psychological
parent also epitomizes the trend toward freeing "parent" from biological reproduction, though not entirely from ideologies of gender. "In
this perspective," as Bellingham (1989) insists, "undelegated nurturance and socialization is the measure of love, and love is the criterion
of true, psychological parenthood."

In content and connotation, the notion of a psychological parent
reflects the persistence of a biological model and its gender bias. Parental *feelings* are tested against the kind of attachment that is presumed to come from the physical realities of conception and birth. A
child should be placed with those "who comfort him and brush away
his fears and tears and in whom he places his love and trust" wrote a
commentator in the *Rutgers University Law Review* ("Adoption . . . ,"
1972, 697). As this suggests, the notion of psychological parent evokes
cultural notions of motherhood; when moved from a "natural setting," the child should be placed with as "natural" a parent as possible. Here, once again, adoption substitutes one maternity for another.

The notion of psychological parent did not restore fathers to the
position they had lost over the course of a century.[27] Adoption laws,
and their amendments, had just about banished the father—except, in
a sense, as a completion of the mother's fitness. During the nineteenth
century, the father had lost his common law right to a child; in the
twentieth century, he had hardly any say in the placement of his child
if that child were removed from his care. The father was not consulted
about a relinquishment and he was not assumed to be the one who
wanted to adopt a child: in these instances, he was not a "parent" at
all. Adoption "required only the mother's consent, and the statutory
adoption scheme did not require notice to the father that the child
was being placed for adoption" (Mnookin 1978, 611). As birthfathers
discovered, the father of an illegitimate child had no "real" parenthood; it "vaporized," in the eyes of others. The law likewise presumed
a child had no claim upon a father's parental affections (Katz 1982).

In 1972, an unwed father brought a petition to the Supreme Court to be granted custody of his children. He won his case. *Stanley v. Illinois* "for the first time, accorded the unwed father Fourteenth Amendment due process and equal protection rights to notice and a hearing on his parental fitness before losing custody of his children" (Howe 1983, 186). But neither this nor subsequent decisions supporting paternal rights completely changed the picture. Although *Stanley v. Illinois* requires compliance by all states, not all states insist that social workers and lawyers comply with it.[28] Nor does the CWLA do much to support the rights of a male parent. "The natural father should be given the opportunity to help financially and to express his desires about the child, even though his legal rights are limited" (CWLA 1978, 30).[29] In the interests of the child and of a "timely" placement, the father must declare his parenthood quickly or lose his rights. The difficulty of effectively legislating in favor of fathers continues; in 1980, a congressional hearing on adoption reform attempted to "reinstate" the father, but the terms are vague and leave implementation in the hands of individual states (U.S. Congress, Oversight on Adoption Reform Act [P.L. 95-266], 1980).

The ideal in American culture, it seems, would be for nothing to disturb the biological model. As the CWLA (1978, 9) put it, "The biological family of father, mother, and their children constitutes the natural means of providing family life for children, and should for that reason be fostered and preserved whenever possible." When the biological family does fail—or, by this definition, does not exist—then parenthood enters the tangled arena of law. The "extreme act" of re-creating a parent-child relationship is exacerbated by the lack of uniformity in the laws that guide that act in American society. And though states passed laws one after the other, with Massachusetts and Pennsylvania as models, just enough room was left for adoption law to become filled with inconsistencies and ambiguities.

"Coercive meddling by the state"

"Each state has its own adoption statute and while many of such laws correspond in essentials, no two are identical" (Leavy and Weinberg 1979, v). To say that the "absence of uniformity betrays the uncertainty as to the appropriate policy underlying adoption" is an understatement, claimed an article in the *University of Iowa*

Law Review ("Natural Versus Adoptive Parents," 1971, 188). Absence of uniformity also betrays the extent to which adoption intertwines with other matters precious to state legislatures: marriage and sexual behavior, the distribution of property, the socialization of children. However persuasive congressional acts are in their rhetoric and their proposed regulations, they cannot establish rules for choosing a parent and re-creating the identity of a child that suit each state or, for that matter, each agency, social worker, lawyer, or judge who supervises a placement. At the same time, there is general agreement that the state has a right to intervene to protect the interests of children.

In 1922, in the course of approving an adoption, a Wisconsin judge stated: "[A]nd the state, entering also in its eminently proper and beneficent capacity as a guardian and conservator of the life, liberty, and happiness of its citizens, takes the children and supplies for the time that which the natural home cannot furnish them" (*Lacher v. Venus*, 177 Wisc. 558). The state carried out its responsibility for protecting its youngest citizens by ensuring that they had parents who would nurture, love, train, and discipline them. Over fifty years later, in 1987, a social worker described the child welfare system as a "parent surrogate system" (Kadushin 1987, 267). Echoing this *in loco parentis* idea, the CWLA (1978, 8) reminded its member agencies that "it is every child's right to receive love, protection and the kind of care that meets his needs, which he would ordinarily be expected to receive from his parents." The state guarded these rights in the interests of the child.

Agreeing upon the responsibility of the state does not eliminate doubts about its guiding principle, "best interests." As one commentator has noted, "From the perspective of rational discourse, the argument that anyone, including judges, can discover and articulate the best interests of children is tenuous at best" (Mnookin 1985, 11). An extensive legal system is of no great help. The law, according to more than a few child welfare experts, may be a clumsy instrument. "Child placement decisions must take into account the law's incapacity to supervise interpersonal relationships and the limits of knowledge to make long-range predictions" (Goldstein, Freud, and Solnit 1979b, 49).

What then is the answer? Critics of the principle advocate humility and a grain of salt about the application of "best interests." "More fundamentally, given the epistemological problems inherent in knowing what is best for a child, there is reason to doubt our capacity to know whether any given decision is a mistake" (Mnookin and Korn-hauser 1979, 958). Intervention should be cautious. "Familial bond-ing is too complex and too vulnerable a process to be managed in ad-vance or from a distance by so gross and impersonal an instrument as the law"; instead, "at best and at most, law can provide a new oppor-tunity for the relationship between a child and an adult to unfold free of coercive meddling by the state" (Goldstein, Freud, and Solnit 1979b, 114, 115). But as these same authors admit, crude as it is, sometimes the law must intervene. "The law also recognizes that there are situations when, on behalf of the child, the state is justified in breaching family privacy and supervening parental autonomy. Then the child placement process is invoked and the all-encompassing parental task is broken up and temporarily divided among specialists from law, medicine, child development, child care, social work, educa-tion, and other professions concerned with children and their fami-lies" (Goldstein, Freud, Solnit, and Goldstein 1986, 4). The state does well to arm itself with experts.

By the beginning of the twentieth century, parents and children could be permanently bound together by law as well as by blood. And, too, the family bound by blood, like that bound by law, could dissolve, or be dissolved. It did not take long before this transforma-tion became the province of professionals. In the words of the CWLA (1978, 1), "Adoption has evolved as a child welfare service, in the in-terests of the child and society, as it has been recognized to be not only a legal procedure, but a matter of social concern and responsibil-ity, discharged through legislation, the court, and the social agency to which responsibility for protecting and helping children and their par-ents is delegated."

The use of experts to decide when, how, and where to move a child is the subject of the next chapter. The ambiguities of the best interests principle led to, among other things, a dependence upon those who knew about children to testify about their welfare—though this, like everything else in adoption, is persistently called into question. In the end, one comes back to the deeply held conviction that removing a child from its biological parent forever poses a threat that can be lim-ited but not eliminated.

3

This Child Is Mine

*The Mechanisms for
Delegating Parenthood*

"A lifelong experience for all parties"

The permanent transfer of a child from one parent to
another has a profound and lasting impact on all three members of the
triad: birth and adoptive parents as much as the child her- or himself.
The child acquires a new identity, and the adults lose or gain parental
status. In this chapter, then, I will discuss the mechanisms: how the
transfer is made, how the right parent for a child is designated, and
how parents experience the kind of kinship adoption entails. I will also
demonstrate how complicated these issues are. Throughout the twentieth century, as both state involvement in child welfare and the professionalization of adoption grew, the ambiguities of a fictive kinship
remained.

In American adoption, social workers have the daunting task of delegating parenthood. The task involves disqualifying some and qualifying other people to have children. That the criteria for a "good parent" are variable, changing with time, place, and situation, does not
make the task easier. The task is further complicated by the awkwardness of the relationship between a person who wants a child and the

expert who intervenes in that decision. Consequently, next to social workers, the significant figures here are adoptive parents. During the twentieth century, adoption policy increasingly focused on the person petitioning for a child, as that person became not just a "caretaker" of the child but also an embodiment of notions of parenthood.

Yet techniques for selecting and approving an adoptive parent did not exclude the birthparent. The mother who had a child she could not keep represented traits that were considered undesirable in a parent; she was *unfit* to the adoptive parent's *fit*. At the same time, her "nature" was important; the genealogical parent presumably determined the child's personality and temperament. And that was important because, lacking any clear predictors of the outcome of a placement, social workers established a policy of "matching." The child should be like the people who adopt him, his "nature" in accord with theirs. If the child conforms to the adoptive parents, love and commitment will follow, or so the theory holds. Thus, social workers do attempt to "know" something of the character and material condition of the parents who will take a child and of the child they will take, in order to re-create a semblance of real kinship in the contrived family.[1]

Reactions to the investigative efforts of social workers are an important part of the story. Adoptive parents are not passive, or silent, about the process by which they "get" children or about the social workers who "play god" while giving children. Nor do prospective parents always turn to agencies in order to adopt: independent adoptions are both a viable alternative and a source of pressure on agencies. As a rule, adoptions without agencies provide a way of transferring children that allows participants to have more "say" and to feel less "bureaucratized." The appeal of this alternative, combined with the consciousness-raising affecting adoption in general, has pushed agencies into changing their policies. In a blending of foster care and adopting that is a striking development of late twentieth-century adoption practices, the "client" is now a partner of the expert, the child to be adopted is no longer a "perfect match," and prospective parents are presumed to be as interested in helping as in having a child.

My discussion concludes with the apparent transformation of expert involvement in adoption, as people turn toward nonagency adoptions and, more radically, toward the unmediated exchange of a child in a completely open adoption. If adoption "constitutes a lifelong experience for all parties" (Cole and Donley 1990, 280), it is also an experience that participants are constantly altering.

"Skillful investigation by
completely trained persons"

Michigan was one of the first states to require the investigation of potential adoptive parents. In 1891, an opinion held that any "judge of probate with whom such instrument [of adoption] is filed, shall thereupon make an investigation, and if he shall be satisfied as to the good moral character and the ability to support and educate such child, and of the suitableness of the home, of the person or persons adopting such child, he shall make an order, to be entered on the journal of the probate court. . . ." (Bremner 1971, II, 147). It is not clear who the investigators were; only marginally clearer was what they would look for: moral character and ability to educate, as well as a "suitable" home. But the course had been set. Trained workers were to assess the parents a child might acquire, and especially scrupulously when the change in parenthood was permanent.

A quarter century later, in 1917, Minnesota amended its adoption law to somewhat the same end. "Upon the filing of a petition for the adoption of a minor child the court shall notify the state board of control. It shall then be the duty of the board to verify the allegations of the petition; . . . and to make appropriate inquiry to determine whether the proposed foster home is a suitable home for the child" (Bremner 1971, II, 147). The institution of inquiry is cited, but the criteria—a suitable home—are not more specific. The amendment, however, also did something else; it included a reminder that there were two sets of parents involved in the transfer: the parents petitioning for and the parents losing a child. Investigation involved a judgment of comparative worth, not simply a test of capability to care for a child.

A Wisconsin statute of 1922 made the possibility of parents competing for a child more explicit. The statute recognized the difficulty of assessing parental capabilities, even if a suitable environment could be determined. According to the judicial opinion, adoption involves a "human triangle: the child at the apex, the living natural parents and the prospective adoptive parent completing the figure." Natural and prospective parents might not agree on the best interests of the child; a third person then had the responsibility of placing the child in a suitable home. This, the statute proclaimed, was a solemn responsibility, given the deprivation that accompanied a permanent reassignment of parenthood. As the statute described it: "Undoubtedly many children would be better cared for were the state to shift them to other homes than those nature gave them . . . ; but to transform a temporary separation of the family, incurred by reason of misfortune, into an absolute severance of those ties so interwoven with human hearts, should, and can, be done only under due process of law" (Bremner 1979, II, 151).

At the same time, the Wisconsin Children's Code Commission emphasized the primacy of the child's interests and, for that reason, insisted that experts supervise all child placement proceedings. "Adoption proceedings are, for the adoptable child, next to birth itself, the most important single transaction in his life. It is imperative, therefore, that the child at this time have the benefit of the most thorough and careful work in the procedure that is to determine his whole future. Essential to this is the need that the court shall have for its guidance full and complete facts about the child and the adopting parents. This can be secured only through skillful investigation by completely trained persons" (in Witmer 1963, 35). Thus, by the 1920s, social workers were thoroughly in charge of the movement of children; on their word, kinship was made or unmade.

The state had turned to families to protect its children and then called upon experts to judge the suitability of families for this responsibility (Tiffin 1982; Grossberg 1985). The emphasis on "completely trained persons" reflected a growing sense that parenthood ought to ˙ be supervised—especially in the dramatic circumstances of removing a child from his or her "natural," biological, parent. Social workers, even with training, moved warily into the arena of designating a "fit" and disqualifying an "unfit" parent. They did not always trust the claims individuals made about their own "capability" for being a parent; stated motives could be misleading. In response to the uncertainties surrounding the evaluation of a good and bad parent, social workers embarked on the task of developing concrete and consistent criteria—a task that has been never-ending.[2]

Tiffin (1982, 271) has described the state's growing involvement in the delegation of parenthood. "Whereas previously any family that was neither immoral nor in debt was considered suitable, in the later years [1920s] much greater care was taken in matching parent and child. Progressive agencies rejected the notion that a child should be placed 'without regard to temperament or suitability just because physical conditions in a home may be good' [Illinois Children's

Home and Aid Society 1909]. To guarantee that an individual child was suited to an applicant, it was necessary that the prospective parents be investigated as thoroughly as the child had been." A home that was "suitable," then, included the characteristic of being suited to the child's nature. To the criteria for a good environment, social workers added the idea that a child could be matched with her or his new parents. And though this did not mean birth and social parent were exactly alike—after all, one was losing and the other getting a child—it also did not leave the natural parent out; the traits of the genealogical parent predicted (it was thought) the child's temperament and promise.

"Superiority" was another factor in the transference from natural to adoptive parents. Matching, for example, followed upon the selection of a home that was "superior" and an adoptive parent who was more capable than the birthparent. Truly to achieve the well-being of the child, social workers were exhorted to choose "adoptive homes that are of average or better quality" (Witmer 1963, 255). Exactly how to implement that choice, however, was no clearer in the early part of the century than it is now: could there be "scientific measures" of quality? Or should a social worker depend upon individual intuitions and feelings in the matter of selecting a parent? Professional judgment in child welfare cases continues to oscillate between those two poles. And whatever the form of evaluation, there is still no guarantee that the arrangement will work, that the child will be loved and nurtured into a productive, contented citizen.

Of course, one might learn guidelines for placement from what *had* worked. In 1924, Sophie Van Senden Theis's pioneering study of 910 adults who had been adopted as children tried that approach. As head of the New York Charities Aid Association, she assumed there would be a link between adult "adjustment" and the environment in the adoptive home. What was the background like? "What are those children who are adopted in babyhood like, later in life? How do the children and foster-parents who have gone through periods of difficult adjustments feel when the children have grown up?" she asked. Unfortunately, her findings were neither definitive nor predictive. What she found did matter, however, were the "human relationships" in the family. In an optimistic conclusion to a nonconclusive study, Van Senden Theis wrote: "In many instances, particularly in the case of the child who was placed young, the relationship appeared to be a complete substitution for the natural parent-child relationship" (in Bremner 1971, II, 425). That has been the conclusion of most outcome studies since: a loving family will raise a well-adjusted child.

The implication of such studies is that good parents act like natural parents. Good parents, social workers said, "did not have to rely on intellectualized prescriptions; instead, they had a facility for understanding a child's feelings and needs and reacting in a positive, natural manner" (Witmer 1963, 157). The prescription for a suitable adoptive family has lasted—and been lastingly hard to apply, inasmuch as it relies thus on amorphous notions of "expressiveness" and "emotional attitude." Those who have tried to discover ways of predicting "adoption success" and "good adjustment" of the adopted child tend to conclude, like Van Senden Theis, that parental feelings make the difference. A crucial study by Alexina Mary McWhinnie (1967, 257), for instance, indicated that of the "many factors" that influence adoption outcome, "subtle emotional attitudes" were the most important. Yet how could subtle emotional attitudes, or parental love, be evaluated in people who had (usually) not had children? In the midst of such variables, the inadequacies of research become clearer. As Hoopes (1982) tells us, there are "difficulties in predicting functioning at a later time from early characteristics of adoptive parent and child. Knowledge of the qualities needed for good parenting is limited in the field of child development in general."

To compensate for the lack of predictability in parent-child relationships, social workers developed two major strategies: matching and assessing the "stability" of adults petitioning for a child. Referring back to Van Senden Theis's 1924 study, social workers found desirable qualities for parenthood in the "self-respecting, self-supporting, kindly families who make up the large part of every community" (in Bremner 1971, II, 423). In effect, not simply happy families but adults who were content with their roles in life provided the best setting for a child. Increased professionalization of child welfare practice generally led to more detailed descriptions of "happy families" and contented women and men. In 1943, for example, in a book that became known informally as the "Bible" for homefinders, Dorothy Hutchinson wrote: "These people have made reasonably satisfactory adjustments to the demands of everyday life. They can hold a job, make and keep friends, marry and enjoy love, and meet the common stresses of life" (in Hartman 1979, 20).

The 1940s and 1950s saw efforts to systematize the notion of "satisfactory adjustment" and to measure psychological stability in prospective parents. Recognizing the uniqueness of the situation, a social worker, Ruth Brenner, wrote in the 1950s: "In an adoption agency more than in most other case work agencies there is a heightened focus on the need to predict because of the irreversible nature of the adoption process and the fact that a child's whole life is at stake." In a self-reflective vein, she went on to bemoan the primitive state of adoption investigations. "To a large degree much of the work of the selection of homes has been left to the intuition of individual case workers because there has been no clear and definitive statement of the factors which might be prognostically reliable for the weighing and selection of homes growing out of observation, practice and research" (Brenner 1951, 18). Yet, in the end, this social worker, too, concluded that a good marriage was the best predictor of good parenthood. "A stable, satisfying marriage is basic to a child's growth; for family life is built upon a vital and meaningful marriage, the hub from which parent-child relationships radiate" (88). This is what the Child Welfare League told its member agencies in the 1950s and, without much change, for the next three decades.[3]

Emotional stability and contentment in marriage are still the main criteria for selecting suitable adoptive parents. According to a recent CWLA *Standards for Adoption Service* (1978, 60), "The study and evaluation of adoptive applicants should take into consideration the following characteristics that are presumed, on the basis of present knowledge, to indicate the capacity for adoptive parenthood: total personality functioning, emotional maturity, quality of marital relationship, feeling about children, feeling about childlessness and readiness to adopt, and motivation." Despite claims to the contrary, these imply that a good parent is the opposite of a bad parent and that "fit" can be drawn from "unfit."[4] Married, stable, thoughtful about childbearing: these individuals contrast with the (stereotypical) unmarried, emotionally volatile, and impulsive birthparent. Moreover, even when agencies accepted single adopting parents, they were distinguished from the single relinquishing parent. "The stability of the marriage of a couple or the stability of a single applicant" plus "handling of earlier life situation [*sic*]" qualified potential parents in one agency (personal communication). In the shadows stands the unwed mother, unstable and inept at handling crisis.

These standards of selection are also continually debated.[5] The difficulties of measuring contentment in marriage and emotional stability are real, and no social worker wants to determine a suitable parent solely on the basis of lack of "unsuitable" traits. Walking the fine line between scientific measures of parenthood and intuitions about a loving parent, social workers retreat to a policy of matching. The round peg in the round hole may be the best guarantee of a successful placement: the late nineteenth-century phrase can stand as well a century later. "It is of real value to fit the right peg in the right hole. A child that may be a torment in one family would be a blessing in another. And for children of promise, promising parents should be sought" (in Hartman 1979, 19).

A round peg–round hole prescription was easier to follow when an older child was being adopted, the usual case before the 1920s; an older child's temperament and promise showed and could be "suited" to the new home. Infant placement, which became popular after that period, posed a different challenge: what could be known about a newborn baby before placement?[6] How could the fit be ensured? One could know the biological family and, specifically, the birthmother and use her traits to judge the child's promise. As this premise increasingly dominated practice, relinquishing parents were asked to provide full "medical and background history,"[7] aspects of which were conveyed to the prospective parents. An alternative was to find out as much as possible about the infant her- or himself. The latter led to a program of testing babies, a parallel to the effort at developing "scientific measures" of a good parent; both peaked in the 1940s and 1950s. Infant testing, of course, delayed placement of the child.[8]

In the 1960s, influenced by the theories of the psychologist John Bowlby, social workers did away with prolonged infant testing. Bowlby had condemned such practice: "The third argument against early adoption—that there is less opportunity to assess the baby's potential development—is commonly used by psychologists but is the weakest of the three. It rests on the assumption that the various tests of development available in the first year of life have predictive value for the child's later development." Better place the child right away than wait six to twelve months, Bowlby instructed, "and adoptive parents like natural parents must be prepared to take a normal biological risk" (Bowlby 1963 [1951], 436–437). No time was to be lost between the child's birth and her placement into her new, and permanent, home. Adoptive parents understood they were taking a "normal" risk—or perhaps not quite normal.

The risk for adoptive parents was (presumably) minimized by careful evaluation of the birthparent. The adoptive family had a choice about genes. According to the director of the CWLA in the early 1960s, "Agencies were convinced and attempted to convince the public that they could guarantee them a perfect child; that by coming to an agency, adoptive parents could be sure that the child was without physical, emotional or mental defect, that his heredity was sound and adopting a child was a far less risky procedure than having one normally" (in Cole and Donley 1990, 277). The best children would be placed: the blond-haired, blue-eyed infant of adoption mythology represented all that was perfect in a child—health, intelligence, a good temperament. Yet so powerful was the belief in "matching" a child with his or her new family that the myth weakened in the face of the diverse looks and "temperaments" of adopting families. (It did not disappear: the image of the perfect baby—blond and blue-eyed—persisted, to be criticized in the 1960s and 1970s with growing concern about the exclusion of non-white parents and children from the adoption triad.) As long as matching controlled practice, the child could be as dark, as "promising," and as delicate in constitution as the adopting parents. The round-peg and round-hole philosophy continues to guide placement policy, with its expectation that a child would blend indistinguishably into the family.

The adopted child was the child the adoptive parents *could* have had. The child should resemble them in physical features, intelligence and habits, and, too, in race and religion (Huard 1956). Fitting a family, as a CWLA Task Force report proclaimed in the late 1980s, was a child's right. "Children who need adoption have a right to be placed into a family that reflects their own racial or cultural heritage and preserves their connectedness in history." "Of course," the report continued, children "should not have adoption denied or significantly delayed when adoptive parents of other races or cultures are available" (Watson and Strom 1987, 8). Likeness, the theory went, increased the chances that an adoptive parent would truly love and incorporate the stranger.[9]

For most of the twentieth century, infants were placed into families where they would fit, presumably to be given the love and care that went with belonging fully to a family. In the 1970s, however, adoption changed: the pool of adoptable infants diminished and adoptive parents could no longer be guaranteed a baby—let alone the kind of child that would grow up "as if begotten." Two consequences followed: prospective parents began to consider "special needs" children, and agencies developed mechanisms for placing special needs children in suitable homes.[10] Widening the definition of adoptable children had a counterpart in stretching the criteria for acceptable parents. The state still depended on families to fulfill its responsibility to the children, but by the end of the twentieth century these were not the same families they had been for the past fifty years.

They no longer so surely represented the average members of a community: some were single, some less than prosperous, and a few quite willing to care for a child temporarily. As the number of available infants decreased, adoption lost its family-building emphasis and once again incorporated the elements of charity and "civic responsibility" that had historically guided child exchange in the United States. By the 1970s, adopting and fostering were not absolutely distinct ways of having a child.

"The permanence and continuity of a caring relationship"

"Again, it's hard to come by clearly documented national data, but adoption professionals are seeing a tremendous increase in the number of foster parent adoptions. Roughly 60 percent of all special needs adoptions in this country appear to be such 'conversions.' In 14 of 17 states studied by the Office of the Inspector General in the U.S. Department of Health and Human Services in 1984, foster parent adoptions accounted for almost 50 percent of finalized adoptions" (J. Anderson 1990, 44).

Over the course of the twentieth century, adoption as a way of creating families had diverged from fostering as a way of caring for needy children. The divergence reflects the dual character of child exchange in the United States; a distinction between "child saving" and "child having" is less surprising, perhaps, than the earlier blurring of those motives for taking in children. Out of law and the professionalization of child welfare practice came two categories: in *foster care* a needy child finds a home, while in *adoption* loving parents receive a child. Both involve contracted parent-child relationships; neither family is the "natural setting" for a child. A foster family, however, is not supposed to be like a biological family, whereas an adoptive family is its facsimile. The differences tell a good deal about the notion of "parenthood" in American culture.

As an expert on foster care, Robert Holman (1973, 79), recognized: "On the one hand these private foster parents develop the attitudes and behavior appropriate to a natural parent. They give great affection, may be determined to keep the child whatever happens, integrate him into the family. On the other hand their actions and attitudes are not compatible with natural parenthood; they take payment for the child, and in many cases, as will be shown, accept—even encourage—visits from the natural parents." Those characteristics—accepting visits from the child's natural parents and, more especially, receiving payment for taking care of a child—make a foster family "different from" a real family in which, presumably, there are no "other" parents and conduct comes out of love, not for money. Confirming this strangeness, individuals in a foster relationship have been found to experience a "sense of falseness" (Triseliotis and Hill 1990).

A large part of the sense of falseness comes from the money involved. "There is evidence," for example, "that younger children do want from surrogate parents the love and commitment they think natural parents should provide, and that some of them are dismayed when they learn of the financial side of the [foster care] arrangement" (Bush 1988, 188–189). But the temporary character of the arrangement may be equally dismaying, to parents as well as to children. Foster children are never fully *there*; they can be re-placed—and both connotations are antithetical to notions of natural parenthood.[11] Foster children perceived an "unnaturalness" that legally adopted children did not, inasmuch as they *belonged* in the family. "While adoptees perceived themselves as growing up 'like any other child in a family,' many of those fostered were aware of differences in their situation in spite of most foster parents' efforts to make them feel secure and one with the rest of the family" (Triseliotis and Hill 1990, 112). Foster families also lack the conventional signs of "oneness" that establish security and compensate for the impermanence of the arrangement. The child keeps his or her birth name,[12] and probably does not look like the foster parents: matching is not a part of foster care policy. Foster parents are "resource" rather than "as-if-real" parents.[13]

But they are *parents*. They are expected to give the kind of nurture and education that is familial rather than institutional; their care is given with affection and commitment—if not for the child's lifetime. Foster parenting requires that one be a parent fully if not forever; performance does not presume enduring solidarity, but it does presume commitment. Like Diana, who distinguished "parent" from "mother," foster parents distinguish loving care from an exclusive bond of love. "It is hard to distance yourself and not be possessive of these children," a foster mother said to me. "Even the babies I have now, it's tough. You've had this baby for 3, 6 months and uh, oh. So it's real hard to get across to these people that I really, really love them but I can let them go." 277-1990

Foster parents expect to share parenthood with others. The child's birthparent is supposed to be a part of foster family life, her—or, more rarely, his—existence recognized in a way that would be unfamiliar (and probably discomforting) to those involved in conventional adoptive arrangements.[14] The idea of sharing evidently violates cultural ideas of parenthood even more radically than does the temporary quality of foster parenthood. At my training sessions we were given a short article by a social worker (Horejsi 1987, 77) reminding us that "not all foster parents are eager to have the bio-parents visit their child in care. Perhaps these resistant foster parents do not understand why it is so important. We need to remember that the parent-child bond is amazingly powerful. Its power cannot be denied or erased."[15] We also learned that each one of us, whether potential adoptive or potential foster parent, would have to recognize the importance of the "bio-parent" in our families. Fostering blurred with adopting, then, not only because adoption might not be an option while fostering was, but also because the conditions of a "contrived" parent-child relationship now link those ways of having children. With changes in the adoptable population in the past two or three decades, issues raised by foster care become appropriate to the (likely) adoptive situation: the child may not be an infant; he or she might have strong ties to a birthparent; the chances of the child blending perfectly into the new family are not great. Thus, even those able to adopt a child legally cannot count on replicating a natural family.

Members of my training group were aware of the changes that had begun in the 1970s and led to, among other things, the creation of a "fostadopt" category. The term referred specifically to parents who fostered in the hopes that the child would eventually be "freed" for adoption, but it also confirmed the lack of boundary between fostering and adopting. Now not only might prospective adopting parents choose to foster, but foster parents might choose to adopt. The latter marked a substantial alteration in policy: until the mid-1970s, in most states foster parents did not qualify as adoptive parents, even for the children in their care (Meezan and Shireman 1985, 13). The very terms of foster parenthood had disqualified them: they agreed to take a child temporarily; their (presumed) motive was charitable and not "reproductive"; their commitment was conditioned by the likely replacement of the child; and they were paid.[16]

This policy collapsed for both ideological and practical reasons. Concern about a floating population of foster children—drifting from family to family—contributed to the passage of the Adoption Assistance and Child Welfare Funding Act (U.S. Congress, Public Law 96–272) in 1980. The Act was designed to restructure the foster care, adoption, and child assistance program, and its main theme was the importance of permanency planning.[17] Under its provisions, foster parents could adopt or petition for permanent custody of the child (Derdeyn 1990). Simultaneously, "permanency" became the watchword for the CWLA: "The permanency philosophy seeks, first, to preserve and support the child in a biological family as the most natural environment and, when this is not possible, to secure an adoptive family. If neither of these alternatives is beneficial or possible for an individual child, then services should be directed to insure the greatest possible continuity of relationship with nurturing parents or caretakers" (Cole 1985, 69). The result was not only to encourage foster parent adoptions but also to ensure permanency to "all available" children. Under the 1980 Act, those who adopt "special" children can receive a subsidy.

But here a distinction emerges: "natural" families are not paid, and the provision of subsidies to adopting parents has caused a good deal of controversy. In my training group, we were told we would receive "reimbursement" for care of a child and "other kinds of 'paychecks' or rewards," like "the opportunity to develop new parenting skills." Real parents do not receive money for taking care of a child. Nor maybe, in the end, do real parents share a child or love a child "temporarily." Despite a congressional act and ideological shifts, foster parents are still not quite the "same" (Derdeyn 1990; Cole and Donley 1990). "And you know how foster parents are perceived. I mean, I can't tell you," a foster mother said to me in 1990. "One guy said to me, 'Oh, you have a farm?' A farm? He said a farm, with all these little babies crawling and working. But you know the stories. Even the agency, I'm not sure they understand why we do it."

My training group was probably a good example of the fading of such views of foster parenting. The participants were all prepared for what it might mean to have a child temporarily, to know the child's biological parent, and to begin parenthood with an 8- or 10-year-old child. As the social worker who conducted our meetings said to me, "There will always be 'the rescue people.'" But in her agency, the rescue people were likely to be the applicants for adoption as well. Faced with the merging of child-saving and child-having that potential parents had effected through their actions, agencies began to modify their policies. Although the guideline for placement is still "best interests," social workers are less likely to separate altruistic from narcissistic motives than to look for people who can make a lifetime commitment to a child.[18] With this in mind, too, agencies no longer examine applicants, following a list of desirable criteria; rather, they train people to be good parents.

"Nowadays we prepare families rather than study them"

An applicant for adoptive parenthood in the 1980s was not likely to be offered a blond and blue-eyed baby, ready to be taken home forever. That applicant was more likely to be asked to think about a "waiting" child, a child not yet freed for adoption, or a "special" child. Furthermore, that applicant was likely to find her- or himself being considered for parenthood along with people who came in planning to request special needs or foster children. Finally, given the policies embraced by many agencies, an applicant for adoptive parenthood would be "trained" along with those who meant to parent temporarily or in order to help a disadvantaged child. By the late 1970s, training became a mainstay of virtually every child placement agency, replacing the inquiries and screening techniques that had been popular in the 1940s, 1950s, and 1960s. The intake interview gave way to meetings at which feelings about becoming the parent of a "stranger" were elicited. As one social worker put it, agencies shifted from "interrogation" to "group education."

Petitioners for a child have always been confusing clients for a social worker. They do not have problems and failings; they simply, and "naturally," want a child.[19] Ruth Brenner, a social worker especially concerned with the selection process in agencies, in the 1950s voiced a distrust of this client that can still be heard today. The client in an adoption, she wrote (1951, 98), has "a stake in withholding whatever problems he may see within his situation. He is eager to get the child that he wants."[20] Such clients do not request treatment, but attention, respect, and generosity. Making it even more difficult, there are two other clients: the parent who is relinquishing a child and the child. But these two are easier to deal with; birthparent and baby fit the classic profile of the client in a social service agency: at risk, vulnerable, and in need of help. For some years, the very recalcitrance of the petitioner for parenthood as a client turned the professional spotlight on that member of the triad. And the focus fell on his or her, or most commonly their, relationship with a social worker.

This relationship tends to be awkward at best and hostile at worst. As one self-conscious social worker tells us, "The Them-Us Syndrome is quite simply the view from the client that the social worker is to be feared and the view from the social worker that those who are seeking to adopt are somehow different from the worker him/herself" (Hermann 1983, 22). Prospective parents cannot help but feel uneasy with and irritated at the person who can decide, or not, to give them a child. "After all, how many natural parents would take kindly to having their potential to be good parents assessed by someone who held the power to prevent them having a child?" asked one prospective parent, quite reasonably, given a culture in which natural parents are not evaluated (in Timms 1973, 7). "We had to meet all these criteria," an adoptive parent said to me, "when everybody else just has babies."

Social workers are aware of the difficulties that lie in requesting a child from a professional and, as well, of the combination of roles they are expected to play in the process of "transacting" kinship. A social worker described her job in the third person: "First, she is a professional. She has expertise in adoption, and can assess, teach, and counsel adoptive parents. . . . Second, she is a supportive friend. She is someone parents can safely bounce ideas off. . . . Finally, she is a mature human being who has a basic liking for and understanding of people. . . . In fact, parents are probably looking for the quality in her that she is looking for in them—the ability to be a good parent" (Ward 1979, 103).[21] In the exchange of a child, applicant and social worker each do best by acting parental—an equality disrupted by the fact that the social worker ultimately decides who is to have a child.

Social workers, say parents, "play god." And social workers admit to being humble before their "awesome" responsibility.[22] Applicants are petitioners, pleading for a child; social workers designate those "worthy" to be parents. In the 1970s, complaints by clients, as well as the disappearance of the infant that formerly constituted the adoptable population, led agencies to review their practices. The result was that, for a petitioner, adopting became less a matter of "meeting criteria" than of examining one's ability to "parent a stranger."

"The process begins with an adoption worker getting to know you," one agency brochure explained. "A series of group or individual meetings are held to help you to learn more about adoption and the children who wait. You and the adoption worker will come to know one another and can work to find the child who will call your family 'mine.'" To this, the director of another agency added, "Nowadays we prepare families rather than study them" (Bush 1988, 120). In practical terms, this meant that the social worker no longer sat behind a desk, trying out criteria on the clients before him or her. Now the social worker, like the prospective parents, was part of a group in which feelings were expressed, memories elicited, and opinions about a child's future exchanged. Group meetings, however, do not seem entirely to dispel a prospective parent's sense of being tested: "I've been to funerals that are livelier," a social worker said about such meetings. Exploring notions of parenthood at a meeting does not fit cultural understandings of becoming a parent any more happily than an interview does.

With all this attention to the adoptive applicant, the child seemed to disappear—as did the birthparent who could not decide whether to keep or relinquish a child (Inglis 1984; Else 1991). In the 1970s, one adoption agency distinguished itself from this apparent trend, asserting: Our approach "contrasts with that of many other adoption programs which may proclaim the child to be their major interest but continue to act in the best interests of parents who are seeking children" (in Unger 1977, xiii). The assertion reflected a growing sense that in half a century of professionalization, adoption had become a service for infertile couples. In response, child welfare workers called for reform and with significant results. As Hartman (1979, 13) recognized, "The most important shift in adoption practice in recent years has been the slow and halting change from viewing adoption as primarily a service for childless couples to redefining adoption as dedicated to finding families for children who need them."[23]

Agencies reinstated the child as primary client, but these children were different from what they had been before the 1970s. After *Roe v. Wade*, a woman with an unexpected pregnancy could have an abortion; welfare policies and a changed cultural climate meant she could also decide to keep the baby. Thus came the decade of the "baby shortage"[24] and the rise of adoptions taking place outside the arena of an agency. Those who wanted babies looked elsewhere; in non-agency placements, they found not only available babies but also leverage in the life-course decision they had had to make "public."[25] Birthparents, too, turned away from agencies to other ways of placing their babies; self-determination had become part of the climate of relinquishing as well as of "getting" a child. Non-agency adoptions are another part of the picture of adoption in the United States.

"A regular commercialized business of child-placing"

"It is through exerting control over who adopts children (as well as whom it permits to be adopted) that adoption law seeks to achieve its purpose of promoting children's welfare" (Witmer 1963, 130). But adoption laws have never exerted complete control. People make their own arrangements for giving away and taking in children, privately and without supervision. State regulations do not stop individuals from constructing (or deconstructing) a parent-child relationship as they wish.

Adoptions without agencies are called "independent." "An independent adoption may be defined as an adoption completed without the help or aegis of a licensed social service agency" (Meezan, Katz, and Russo 1978, 1).[26] Usually a third person is involved, a doctor, lawyer, or social worker who serves as the mediator, making contact between the potential adoptive parents and the relinquishing parents. Independent adoptions are legal in all but five states, and are finalized—as are agency adoptions—in court (Adamec and Pierce 1991, 153). In addition, a number of states require that an agency do a home study, evaluating the placement, before legalization. Yet these independent arrangements are still not the same as those made through an agency. Free of the restrictions agencies impose, they are also free of the control many think ought to be part of the exchange of children.

Independent adoptions have existed as long as the institution itself and have raised cries of alarm all along. Unsupervised exchanges, say opponents, pose a risk to the child, to the adopting parents, and to the surrendering parents. Worse, these unsupervised adoptions seem the next best thing to a market in babies—a first step on the way to buying and selling children (Meezan, Katz, and Russo 1978, 7). In this view, without appropriate supervision, greed and a profit motive inevitably enter the process of placing babies. Such alarm about non-agency adoption coincided, not surprisingly, with the growing involvement of social workers in adoption and foster care in the early twentieth century (Tiffin 1982). Deliberate or not, reference to a market effectively upheld professional involvement in the transaction of a child, inasmuch as social workers are considered "noninterested" parties, motivated by considerations other than personal profit (Zelizer 1985).[27]

Undoubtedly, there have been people in the "baby business" from the start. As Witmer (1963, 37) tell us: "The first field investigation of adoptions, so far as we could discover, was one made in Chicago in 1917 by the Juvenile Protective Association. This study was directed at the practices of 'baby farms,' unscrupulous organizations that, for a fee, assumed charge of unwanted babies and 'sold' them to would-be adopters. . . . 'It was found that there was a regular commercialized business of child-placing being carried on in the city of Chicago.'" An unscrupulous person could take advantage of the vulnerability of a person with a child she (or he) could not care for and of the desperation of an infertile couple who wanted a child of "our own." Sophie Van Senden Theis made the point in the 1920s, concluding that "it seems clear that no permanent transfer of a child should be made without the approval of some official body and that such a transfer should be properly recorded"—sounding rather like a good business person herself.[28]

Thirty years later, in 1955, a Congressional Commission led by Senator Estes Kefauver bemoaned the nefarious business of selling and buying babies, among other "evils" and delinquencies.[29] By then, "some babies sold for as much as $10,000" (Zelizer 1985, 199). The nefarious business continues to boom. Headlines in 1980s newspapers suggest this is a market worthy of attention: "Baby-marketing a big business"; "Lawyer profits from unwed mothers." And more soberly, as Malcolm Bush notes in his recent book on child welfare, "The work of finding adoptive placements for white babies has been taken over by consortiums of lawyers and doctors working for profit and the ethics of that development are disputed" (1988, 118).

Marketing babies *is* antithetical to cultural norms and to ideologies of the person in American society. But if not profit-making, there are principles of a market that may be appropriate to the exchange of a child, even in American culture. The point was made, in 1978, in a deliberately provocative article that argued: "Willingness to pay money for a baby would seem on the whole a reassuring factor from the standpoint of child welfare. Few people buy a car or television set in order to smash it" (Landes and Posner 1978, 343). People *do* value what they have invested in, and payments can be "legitimized as symbolic expressions of sentimental concern" by adoptive parents (Zelizer 1985, 207).[30] Those who are about to relinquish a baby may also appreciate the sense of value implied by a transfer of money. As the article I quoted suggests, willingness to pay indicates a commitment to care for that which is acquired at cost; such commitment is not, of course, antithetical to adoption principles. Simultaneously, and paradoxically, by referring to a market the article also reminds a reader that babies are not "products" but human beings, not to be bought and sold or distributed according to a cold calculation of worth.

Reference to a market offers another lesson for adoption, one that is relevant to the upsurge in independent adoptions. For, as the authors also note, a market evokes free choice and leverage: the control over a transaction that some birth and adoptive parents claim is missing from agency-arranged adoptions. People turn to independent adoptions not to sell and buy babies but to have a say in the "awesome" transaction of a child. In an independent adoption, birthparents have more say about the recipient of their baby and adoptive parents can "shop around" for the ideal parent of their child (Meezan, Katz, and Russo 1978). Birthparents and adoptive parents who chose independent adoption told me, "social workers never listen" and agencies "distribute babies as *they* see fit." From this point of view, agencies are the markets, providing "good" babies for those who can afford them—if not for profit, then without regard for feelings and love.

For those who chose it, independent adoption took child exchange out of the realm of commerce and into that of family. Without the red-tape and questions, the classes and training groups, adoption, people said, seemed "more natural." It was "more like childbirth," an adoptive father claimed. It also had the character of kinship: giving and taking a child can be seen as acts of generosity and of solidarity. But, opponents say, such sentiment is risky: for the child, the relinquishing parent, and the adoptive parent. The round peg may end up in the square hole. In this regard, "[I]t is clear that the possibility for the placement of a child in a home that cannot meet his/her needs is greater in independent adoptions than in agency adoptions" (Meezan, Katz, and Russo 1978, 223). On the other hand, there is little evidence that independent adoptions result in bad placements. The children grow up as "well adjusted" as might be expected, the same authors add (232).[31]

The number of independent adoptions is rising,[32] and this way of adopting evidently appeals to birth and adoptive parents. Agencies have responded by increasing their trust in clients and placing a greater part of the decision about child placement in parental hands. At the same time, too much choice is not comfortable: contingency and whim are not compatible with cultural notions of parenthood. However much relinquishing and adopting parents resent the "playing god" aspect of social work involvement, the resulting sense of the "rightness" of the placement suits interpretations of a parent-child relationship. Concepts of destiny and inevitability appear in descriptions of independent adoption and underline its resemblance to "natural" ways of having a child. Fate conveys the idea that a child "really" belongs. The same language appears in discussions of open adoption.

"Is it well with the child?"

Open adoption is an extension of the "free choice" that independent adoptions offer. It is also a response to the arguments against sealed records and secrecy made by adoption reform groups— and by adoptees, birthparents, and adoptive parents. In open adoption, "the birthparents and the adoptive parents meet and exchange identifying information" (Baran and Pannor 1990, 318). They may or may not continue the relationship (Lindsay 1987, 33). More thoroughly than independent adoption, open adoption allows individuals to make their own decisions, construct their own families, and work out their own understandings of kinship. Few have rushed into this form of adoption, but agencies and individuals are certainly moving toward it.

The first step toward openness, for an agency and for individuals, is usually an exchange of letters without identifying information. That may be followed by photographs, then names and addresses, and ultimately a meeting between the child's several parents (Silber and Speedlin 1982). In a genuine open adoption, a relinquishing parent selects the child's family; prospective parents receive a child from a person they know. Birthparents claim they feel less like they have given their child to a "complete stranger" (Lindsay 1987) or into the "great unknown," as one experimental agency put it.[33] Adoptive parents learn about their child through familiarity with the child's other parents. Open adoption does away with the distant and impersonal character of closed adoption, but it also collapses the conventions that have upheld a fictive kinship. If a biological and a social parent are present from the beginning, there is no "as if" or "juridical parthenogenesis." As Katz (1982) rightly explains: "Open adoption is controversial because it challenges the basic goal of adoption—to accomplish a complete transplant of a child from the birth family to the adoptive family." An adoptive parent shares with rather than substitutes for a birthparent; a birthparent is kin but not parent to the child. Because this is confusing, the arrangement demands creativity about the rules of being related and the meanings of "mother," "father," and "kin."

Why do people choose open adoptions, an uncharted and certainly challenging way of surrendering and taking on parenthood? The benefits for a birthparent are more immediately obvious than those for the adoptive parent. The birthparent knows where the child is and can follow his or her development; the birthparent does not have to suppress one whole chapter of her life. But the adoptive parent also benefits, knowing the adopted child better by knowing the child's other parent. Yet neither parent has a script for such sharing or a map for this kinship. *Are* birth and adoptive parents in fact relatives? "I don't know how our birthmother is related to me. She isn't my niece or my cousin, sister or daughter, but somehow, some way, we have a relationship. There just isn't a name for it" (in Lindsay 1987, 48).

Whatever its difficulties, open adoption is spreading—if not in its pure form, then through its impact on adoption practice in general. As individuals show themselves "open" to contact, agencies eliminate the strict application of confidentiality.[34] And, as with other changes in adoption, this one is assessed in the light of "best interests." "Through their growing years, children need a sense of their birth heritage, as well as an understanding of the transfer to their present family. Only then can they attain a congruous sense of identity," one agency wrote about an "openness in adoption pilot process." Staunch advocates of open adoption say the same thing as cautious social workers: it is an "inescapable conclusion that adopted persons not only have two families but that they need contact with both families" in order to achieve a sense of well-being (Baran and Pannor 1990, 330). Yet in the end, as one writer insists, "we must never cease to ask the basic question: 'Is it well with the child?'" (Katz 1982).

Open adoption accords the birthparent a lasting identity as parent, a status the birthparent loses in a closed adoption. With openness, too, a birthparent "makes a plan for" rather than surrenders her child: in such an arrangement, the birthparent can feel less the victim of circumstances—or coercion—and more the actor in a course of events. But whatever the specifics, it is the birthparent who initiates an adoption. Thus the birthparent, and the moment of surrender, begin my account of an experience of fictive kinship for its participants.

PART TWO

The Experience
of Adoptive Kinship

4

The White Flag
of Surrender

Birthparent Experiences of Adoption

"Let me share with you my story"

This is a chapter about birthparents, not about "pregnant teens" or "unwed mothers" or "children having children." The statement has several implications. The chapter is about a parent, someone with a particular status and role, and about interpretations of parenthood. Parenthood is complicated here by the fact that there is no child; the child has been given away and belongs to another family. The chapter is also about the process of becoming a birthparent and the significance of that term for interpretations of kinship in American culture. The term is not accidental but represents a choice by individuals who are consciously taking on an identity: parent by virtue of having given birth to a child. The term also, as I show in the following pages, contains a criticism of adoption policy and of the grounding of that policy in the best interests of a child.

Parents who relinquished a child have been the silent members of the adoption triad, until recently lacking a voice in popular or in professional literature.[1] They became invisible as parents when they gave up their children. Moreover, they were told to forget the episode so that life could resume its normal course. Within the past two decades, however, those who surrendered a child have begun to claim the parenthood they did not thereby relinquish. The claim rests on the importance of "birth" in cultural understandings of relatedness and on the presumption of permanence in the bond birth establishes. Birthparent narratives challenge the meaning of the fictive kinship upon which adoption is based.

"I have a book in me." "Let me share with you my story." The process of becoming a birthparent involved re-telling the story of adoption. Birthparents revised their life stories to include the missing scene, the "lost" child, and their own "never-forgotten" parenthood. My chapter, consequently, is partly about how birthparents used stories to establish the identity that had for years been denied, hidden, and suppressed. As one birthmother poignantly said, "I had kept my whole little past about being a birthmother all sewn up in a little box" (*Morning Sentinel* [Waterville, Maine], 3/9/83: 20). For her, the impulse to tell her story stemmed from awareness that others had "come out of the closet," in the phrase characteristic of CUB literature. A shared vocabulary provided reinforcement, reassurance, and context for an individual story, even for those birthparents who never went to a meeting or read a birthparent newsletter. The rhetoric of the birthparent movement made each experience, in Bruner's phrase (1986, 7), "storyable." The rhetoric also dramatized the story, and I have used such moments of drama to organize this chapter: a pregnancy that no one noticed and everyone condemned; a piece of paper that permanently severed a blood tie; a crucial scene in one's life that "did not happen"; a complete dismissal from one's own child's life.

It was not only a birthparent movement, however, that encouraged birthparents to claim their parenthood. Changes in adoption itself also helped set the stage. With special needs and older child adoption, more and more adoptees knew their birthparents, either actually or because they had a substantial amount of information about them. A birthparent was often part of their lives and almost always part of their memories. Adopted children had two sets of parents. In response, birthparents claimed their right to know, at least in the sense of "know about," the child they had given up. Moreover, adoptees who had been adopted as infants in an anonymous and confidential arrangement were demanding access to records that had been sealed and, often, contact with their birthparents. Influenced by adoptee outspokenness and emboldened to take their own position in the triad, birthparents moved to declare their parenthood in public.

For the birthparents I interviewed, one fact was immediately obvious: the extent to which they borrowed argument and imagery from the relinquished children who had been quicker to question adoption's anonymity and secrecy. Metaphors based on the concepts of birth, blood, and nature dominated birthparent narratives, just as they did the stories told by adoptees. But birthparents added metaphors that referred to a market in babies, to the greed and selfishness of those who took children, and to the "commerce" of child exchange in the United States. Their narratives went further than did those of even the most outspoken adoptees in criticizing the policies that had guided American adoption for most of the twentieth century. But then they had more reason to be critical.

I have placed this chapter on birthparents before the chapters on adoptive parents and adoptees by design. The birthparent can be considered the primary actor in an adoption. In a society where children are not freely exchanged or casually abandoned, without a relinquishing parent there would be no adoption. The significance of the relinquishing parent can be measured by changes in terminology; terms for the parent who gives away a child have changed far more frequently than those for the parent who takes a child or for the child (though now adoptees are asking to be called either "adoptee" or "adopted person," rather than the standard "adopted child"). From "pregnant teen" and "unwed mother" to "real" or "biological" parent, words for this member of the triad have slipped around the net of professional vocabulary. Changes in terminology also reveal the degree to which the birthparent incorporates cultural assumptions about sex, gender, adulthood, and family that are at the heart of adoption. Called a "pregnant girl" or a "natural parent," an "unprepared mother" or a "bio-parent," this figure links adoption to a wider cultural and social context.

The people I talked with rejected designations like "pregnant girl" or "children-having-children." They also rejected "real" and "natural" parent. Having given away a child, they did not want the child's other parent to be *unnatural*. But this scrupulousness did not always last through an interview, and a birthparent frequently referred to her- or himself as the natural parent of a relinquished child. The self-designation was equally a comment on the parent by contract. Nature stood for a permanent, unconditional bond with a child that for birth-parents transcended gender: fathers as well as mothers were "parents by birth" and therefore "natural." In coming out of the closet and asserting an identity they had long hidden, birthparents probed into the premises of American adoption—occasionally with sharp analytical insight and always with an urgency prompted by the sense of the risk they had taken in declaring themselves.

"Surrender" dominated every birthparent's story. Used metaphorically, the concept organized the experiences of becoming pregnant, giving birth, and giving away a child (Lakoff and Johnson 1980). Through the deliberate choice of this word, birthparents reinterpreted the meaning of the event: "surrender" conveyed the coercion, the force of social pressure that made it impossible to decide anything else. From the perspective this metaphor established for them, birthparents looked back to an event that had happened in some cases a quarter of a century earlier and in other cases just a few months before the interview. From this perspective, too, birthparents embraced the axiom that a natural parent had a bond with her or his child that might be modified by circumstances but could never be finally dissolved.

The past, then, provided the key scene, but always in the interests of establishing a present identity.[2] Reinterpreting the surrender, birthparents claimed an existing parenthood, and denied the possibility of ever forgetting the birth of a child. They saw through the advice they had once taken, to "turn back the clock and start again," and were now reinserting the chapter into their lives. In fact, the content of this chapter for them had never disappeared; they had surrendered a child, but not their memories. "And all that, you know, you don't forget."

I talked with twenty birthparents, including three birthfathers. I met most people at support group meetings, and some through word of mouth. Of the three members of the triad, birthparents were the hardest to contact but the most expansive when they did consent to be interviewed. More than adoptive parents or adoptees, birthparents wanted me to be a "porte parole" or messenger to the outside world, carrying their point of view (Crapanzano 1985, 27). Occasionally the message had already been given, to a social worker, a lawyer, a newspaper or television reporter; several of the people I interviewed had already told their stories in public. But whether I was another or a first audience, I was always treated both as an anthropologist and as an adoptive parent. In each capacity I served as a sounding board for the construction of birthparent identity that motivated the narrative. Nor would I be the only or the last audience. The stories I heard were part of a process, not begun or ended with the interview but forming a continuing interpretation of the meaning of parent-by-birth in the context of a parenthood delegated by law.

"Our parenthood vaporized"

Birthparents were "childless parents"—without a child, nevertheless parents according to the conventions of their culture. Their experiences exemplified the contradictions in adoption: a pregnancy that was invisible yet stigmatized, a birth without a baby, and a parental love that was demonstrated by giving away a child. How, birthparents asked, could it be in the child's best interests to be taken from the parent who acted out of love? In their accounts of giving up a baby, birthparents revealed the ambiguities in concepts of love and responsibility, nurture and competence, and well-being and wealth as these determined the designation of parenthood in American culture.

Like other parents, birthparents found that, at least initially, they relished the pregnancy, whether it was expected and planned for or not.[3] "So it was—everything as far as the pregnancy went was real normal. I mean just sort of a perfect pregnancy," said one birthparent. "I enjoyed going through those nine months, just fondling and feeling this little—you know, I remember never wanting her to be born. Just feeling her kicking," said another. The point here is that they did not feel unhappy or distressed until others told them they *ought* to. Then, in a milieu in which pregnancy was usually celebrated, they were stigmatized, denied their parenthood, and hidden away. In response, and in retrospect, birthparents made their experiences consistent with conventions about becoming and being a parent. Birthmothers said they had enjoyed the physiological and psychological changes; fathers and mothers remembered anticipating a new stage of life, even when they knew their parenthood would not last.[4]

But the "should's" prevailed; the pregnancy was supposed to disappear. Birthparents were hidden away or, under pressure, hid the pregnancy themselves. Mainly, they were ignored, the surrounding silence, in effect, eliminating the pregnancy. "Then again it was like it [pregnancy] wasn't real and my family came to visit me and they didn't say, 'gee, you're getting big, is the baby kicking? How do you feel?' It was like, 'so what's new,' you know." Pregnant at sixteen, this woman was sent away from her hometown to be "invisible" to others. She was not invisible to her family, who visited her, but her pregnancy was not, in their eyes, a real event. "There was never any talk, ever, about one, alternatives, or two, that I might perhaps go through something that would be emotionally difficult for me," another birthmother put it. People ignored the pregnancy and the change it represented. "Our parenthood," a birthfather said, "vaporized."

Most of the people I interviewed had surrendered a child over twenty years earlier, when "leaving home" was the conventional option. As one birthmother described it: "So anyway, the only option that was handed to me, oh yeah, mom said, 'well, we'll get you a home for unwed mothers far, far away.' And I said, 'I want to talk to a social worker in this state. I want to go downtown, there must be some kind of social worker that can help me keep my baby.' And mom said, 'I don't want anybody in this state to find out.' And she says, 'we'll find a nice home for unwed mothers down south somewhere.'" With positive feelings about having a baby vanishing, the birthparent came to feel "babyish" herself, utterly vulnerable and inept. "But I was just so alone and so scared and so homesick and so I came back to this city," another birthmother recalled. Such overwhelming emotions were common for most birthmothers unless, as some did, they fought to keep the pregnancy secret and for themselves alone.

"So I didn't tell anybody I was pregnant," explained one birthmother, "partly because I didn't want my aunt to be caught trying to decide whether to give me shelter or throw me out because if her husband's [second] wife found out, she could have made some trouble giving her a hard time. And because also I just didn't want to be hassled by people. In spite of the fact that I realized that I was probably going to give the baby up for adoption, I was really enjoying being pregnant and I just didn't want people bugging me. So I didn't tell anybody and nobody ever guessed."[5] By not telling, this birthmother kept her pregnancy and its pleasures for herself—along with the decision she knew she had to make. Her sturdy secretiveness was unusual, partly a matter of character and partly a matter of situation: at the time of her pregnancy she was out of college, working, and living with an aunt who was as much a friend as a parental figure.

Birthmothers faced a situation that birthfathers did not share. As their own bodies changed, they could not so easily hide their approaching parenthood. Fathers, by contrast, could remain "invisible," choosing to make their own parenthood disappear. A mother was "caught" in a way that the prospective, unprepared father was not. For the birthmother, then, the appearance of parenthood produced a vulnerability that, if she were living with her own parents, paradoxically turned her into a child—made her feel childish just as she was about to have a child. And so the women I interviewed hid the pregnancy as long as they could, and in retrospect complained about the social (and parental) pressures that forced them to distort this stage in their lives.

"I was petrified to approach my mother or my family at all. I told no one, and had been in ninth grade at the time and continued going to school. I was sent home probably several times a week. I would black out at school and would have problems. They didn't figure it out either. To this day it amazes me that I went through seven months pregnant before anyone knew that I was pregnant," said one birthmother. Another woman who was also pregnant in high school, but in the 1980s rather than the 1960s, described her experience: "Of course, I was scared to death. I hated throwing up. I was really scared of that. I didn't remember a lot of when I was pregnant because I blocked it out. I had these mental blocks so I wouldn't have to remember. This is the first time I'm really talking about it. This is really tough. This is really difficult to come up with the feelings that I forced out."

Yet the fact that "no one ever guessed" also constituted a kind of triumph and, in retrospect, a balance to the eventual surrender. The woman who lived with her aunt said, "She asked me once, after I got quite big, but you know, I didn't carry myself like a pregnant person. I didn't walk around sway-backed like people do. I don't know why they do that, there's no reason for it. I just looked like I was getting fat and I gained a little weight to cover it up. She asked me, 'are you sure you're not pregnant?' I said, 'no.' And she really believed me." When pregnancy could no longer be hidden, the birthparent became vulnerable and relinquishment seemed inevitable. One birthmother complained, in her interview: "Oh, well, my mother kept track of my menstrual periods. So *she* told *me*." And another: "And the only way that happened [her mother finding out] was one day I just could not hide it any longer. I couldn't fit in any of my tops. We were going some place and my mother said, 'are you ready? Are you ready yet?' I just couldn't find anything to wear. She said, 'boy, are you getting chubby or what? Boy, if I didn't know better, I would say you were pregnant.' And the next thing you know I burst out crying and she said, 'are you?' 'Yes.'"

When pregnancy was acknowledged, the person was not treated like a parent-to-be. Rather, this unexpected parent was treated like a "bad girl" or a "boy who didn't care." "At no time did any person at all treat me as if I was a young mother in need of help. I was a girl who had gone wrong" (in Inglis 1984, 28). Yet as birthparents recalled this period, their ambivalence grew and they talked about "needing" to be cared for, loved, and supported. One birthparent expressed it this way: "I felt really guilty about hurting them [own parents] . . . I wasn't sure of their love . . . I know I was glad to get their attention. I guess I was really grateful that they, their love was stronger than I ever thought it was. Because I was grateful I decided to see what they were saying and to believe that was best. And I felt that so much, that I didn't want to hurt them, I didn't want to cause them any trouble. And that's why I didn't fight for my babies as much as I should of."

The consequence of being childlike was giving up parenthood. As birthparents looked back upon their experiences, they realized they had been placed in a double-bind: they were treated like children and expected to make an adult decision. And though their own parents were not spared blame, the professionals who arranged adoptions came in for special vituperation. According to birthparent accounts, social workers manipulated concepts of responsibility, maturity, and love in order to "get babies." A birthfather complained, "I didn't have any parental rights that I was aware of and certainly no one was going to tell me if I had any" (CUB *Communicator*, 1/83: 4). "I remember detesting everything about it, those little talks we had to have every Tuesday afternoon," a birthmother recalled. "She [social worker] didn't listen to my feelings or anything."

Social workers had infantilized the birthparent while telling that person to act grown up about placement. One woman who had been pregnant in high school explained that the social worker had treated her as if she "didn't know anything and because she didn't know anything, [she didn't know] what was best for herself. How could she know what was best for a baby or she couldn't really know her own feelings either, she was just a kid." "And I just remember being patronized a lot, patted on the head," she continued. "I'd try to say something and she'd say, 'oh, that isn't how you feel. It's because of

this or that and it will go away' or 'that's natural.'"[6] Another birthmother tried to resolve the contradiction by saying, somewhat point-
edly, "Someone should adopt the pregnant mother."

Parents, in many cases, did offer to adopt their child's child. Yet, as
one woman said: "There was no way I could have my mother raise a
child the way she raised me . . . I just couldn't deal with that. So I
turned that alternative down and that only left adoption open." Or a
parent offered to take care of the baby. "And then my mother, I think
she was having a harder time with it [relinquishment] than I was,
being that she was older, and up to the last minute that we were leaving [the hospital], she said, 'you know, if you really want to keep this
baby, we'll manage, we'll think of something.' And I know she meant
it, but I kept thinking that she would have really been the mother."
Another woman whose mother offered to keep the baby realized,
"to have my own child call me sister would have been unbearable."
These comments suggest not only the difficulty of watching a mother
"mother" one's child but also the birthparent's further reduction to
childlike status in the family—being a child alongside one's own child.

The comments also suggest a resistance to the confusion of kinship
such in-family arrangements cause. A few birthparents told me a sister
had offered to take the child, and that was no better than leaving the
child with a parent. The baby would be there, but in the relationship
of niece or nephew. "And the other big thing was that my sister
wanted to keep my son. I would give her care [help with sister's chil-
dren] and she would raise my child. I said, 'how do you think I would
handle that? If I ever came to your house and this kid's calling you
Mom when he should be calling me [that]? If that was the case I
would never come and see you or anything, because I would have just
said, 'here, let me have it [her child].'" Having the child in the family
would just make it tempting to take the child back, and birthparents
meant to stick with the relinquishment. If they had initially given up,
they would not subsequently "give in" to wanting the child back.

"How can you give a baby up for adoption, you didn't want to,
but then here your family is raising her, you got to be around with it.
I wouldn't think that was a good idea, you know," said a birthmother
who thought the temptation to take her child back would be "too
great" if her mother raised it. Birthparents claimed that if they had
surrendered under pressure, they had not lost their willpower. "Surrender" itself suggested a fight to them, a battle against the odds
which, in terms of their own sense of self-worth, was something they

needed. A woman who had begun to describe her submissiveness, "So it was in fact like a little two-year-old," suddenly corrected herself: "I was so grateful . . . because I thought I gave in really easy and I felt so guilty about giving in. If I had really given them a fight I may not have felt so bad and I never thought I did. But here years later when my mother and I could finally talk about some things she says, 'Oh no, you gave us a real fight.' So I was stronger than I thought I was."

A few birthmothers had an ally in the fight: the father of the baby. In my study, and probably to an unusual extent, birthmothers considered the other parent as being in league with them and equally pressured to "give up." "And his family," a birthmother said, "his parents told him that he would lose his scholarship and it would be a ruination of his life and they forbid the whole relationship at that point." Birthfathers corroborated the story birthmothers told. They were too young to marry, not "ready" to be fathers, irresponsible. One birthfather, for instance, recalled: "I wanted to marry Jessica and keep our daughter. We were a family and should have been together" (CUB *Communicator*, 1/83: 4). Gender stereotypes came into play here as well; women were told they could not "nurture" the child they had unexpectedly had, men that they could not support the mistimed family. A man's sexual behavior had proved he acted carelessly, a woman's that her feelings were out of control.

As birthmothers put it, they were condemned for being "too loving." "Some people have closed doors because I have 'sinned,' but I really loved" (in Rillera 1982, 41).[7] The punishment exceeded, and misjudged, the crime. "A lifetime of suffering is too much to demand for any woman's expression of her sexuality" (Anderson, Campbell, and Cohen 1982, 6). To take a child away was not only extreme but also inconsistent with cultural assumptions; being "caught" at sex distorted the meaning of love and its connection with being a mother. In response, birthmothers insisted on the positive aspects of being in love: not a sin, but a valued emotion. The one exception was a woman who grew up in a strict religious family. In her milieu, sex *was* wrong—and she was practically the only woman who did not talk about falling in love with the baby's father or being "passionately" attached to him.

"But then when I found out I was pregnant, it was a disaster," she said. "And I'll tell you something funny—I don't have a real good memory of details of that. Because it was the worst thing that could have happened to me. It was like a self-fulfilling prophecy. Everything

I had been told not to do. And I also knew that it would bring out of the closet with my mother the fact that I was not living this straight and narrow life that she assumed that I was living." She was also the only person I met who thought it right to atone: "Whatever I went through was very, very small payment in my, the environment that I lived in. Very, very small payment against what I had done to the family." But for most birthmothers, losing a child was too big a price to pay for having made a mistake through "love." It was also too big a price for getting caught at what everyone else was getting away with.

"How dare you say to me, 'well, you're pregnant.' You fooled around just as much as I did. I got caught, you didn't. You didn't get caught, don't treat me that way," a young birthmother reported what she had (or wished she had) said to her friends. Being caught, in fact, could be interpreted differently: "And I think it was my mother who explained to me that that's what happens to nice girls. The bad girls know better and don't get caught." Another, older woman had also learned that lesson. "It does not happen to somebody who is good. You know, I thought I was good, I was a good old prudish schoolteacher."

This same woman explained how she had been pressured into sex. "If they want to, if they take you out for dinner and a movie, and you want to see them again you've got to thank them the way they want to be thanked. And all of a sudden, after three months of that, I was pregnant." She did not say she had fallen in love, but she conveyed the same impression that those who *did* had conveyed: they had been naive, trusting, and implicitly *female* in their behaviors. "I was dating a seventeen-year-old guy who I thought I was in love with. And he convinced me that he loved me and what we did was right." There was a good deal of romanticism in this, and appropriation of cultural clichés, along with a justification of their actions—and a condemnation of those who punished them. "I met him when he moved from Illinois to this state when we were in the sixth grade and it was love at first sight," said a woman who became pregnant in her senior year of high school. "From the time we were in sixth grade, I'll never forget the day he walked into that sixth-grade classroom, I just thought my heart had stopped."

Birthmothers were angry at other people, and ultimately at a hypocritical society. "And all my friends turned against me and were ashamed to be around me and just saying things about me." Their friends were sometimes the worst. "A lot of the people who I thought were close friends told me that their parents wouldn't let them—forbid them to see me. I guess they thought that it would rub off." Having a baby seemed like having a disease. "It really bothered me that I was shunned by a lot of my friends," said an 18-year-old. "I had a whole bunch of friends when I was in high school and then when I got pregnant, Tom [baby's father] and I both had a lot of friends, and when I got pregnant and we were going through all those problems, we had two, two good friends. And that killed me. That really hurt. It's like, 'wait, I don't have a disease. I'm carrying a child, not, I have gonorrhea or AIDS.'"

Once "out of the closet," birthfathers and birthmothers equally condemned the society that had punished them for getting caught at what everyone else did and the "bad one's" got away with. "You weren't allowed to mingle with the normal people who were allowed to have children." You weren't allowed to *have* children.

"And it's all lies"

"I remember my sister calling me once and I told her I was in labor and she said, 'how long have you been getting pains?' And I told her all day and she said, 'it must be false labor' and, you know, it was like you didn't even know if you should call anybody when you delivered," one birthmother reported with a sad anger. False labor was a powerful symbol in birthparent accounts, representing a birth that, like the pregnancy preceding it, was "not real" in the eyes of others. "It had been two weeks prior to when I went into labor, which it turned out that I went into the hospital and it was false labor," another woman remembered. "So about two weeks later, about ten o'clock at night I was watching TV and I started labor, and being so naive I thought I was having false labor again. I was in labor all night. I never slept the entire night, it was horrible." Then the next morning: "And my mother got up and was getting ready for work and I didn't say a word to her, and she was getting ready to leave and she went past my room and she came out and said, 'are you awake?' I said, 'yes.'" The birthparent decided her labor was real and, after her mother left, went to the hospital.

Falseness extended from labor to a birth in which there was "no child." This disappearance was supported by documents that lied about the event. "And it's lies. The whole thing is lies," this woman

recalled of the event of twenty years earlier. "It says it was a spontaneous birth, it wasn't. I was in hard labor for a good twelve hours and
in total labor twenty-eight hours. And they put down that my labor
was like six hours or something. I can't remember what it was. But
they lied about that and they said it was spontaneous and it wasn't.
For four hours I was on the delivery table and they finally had to take
forceps and pull her [baby] out." Giving birth represented the birthparent's truth, a physiological experience engraved in memory and a
social experience incorporated in the actuality of a parent-child relationship. The truth of having a child was conveyed through descriptions of the baby, of the feelings that came with holding an infant, and
of the significance of naming the child.

Birthfathers and birthmothers described their babies as beautiful,
wonderful, perfect. "She was very, very attractive for a baby. And I am
not one of these people that think all babies are cute. A lot of babies
are really ugly when they're little. Even when they get older, they're
still pretty ugly a lot of times. So even as a really little, tiny, fresh baby,
she was really pretty," said this woman, who then trailed off into a
memory of the birth. "They [nurses] didn't tell other people that their
babies were gorgeous," another woman told me. "But she was gorgeous, though, and they would say, 'your baby is so beautiful.' And
she was. She was a really beautiful baby.... They were all raving about
her."

Like these examples, descriptions did not individualize the baby
but imposed its existence on those who had not "seen" the pregnancy. The beauty of the baby also redeemed the birthparent in her
own eyes. "And once you see the baby you realize if there was any
mistake, it certainly wasn't that—that beautiful baby was not the mistake. And because your baby is so beautiful it makes you feel better
about yourself because you can see something so beautiful that you
have produced. It shows that you are not a rotten person. Otherwise
this baby would look rotten." In some sense, birthparents were rewarded and justified by the beauty of their child. "And I wanted her
[own mother] to come down and see. Cause it was the most beautiful
baby—there were thirty-five babies in the nursery, in the big nursery,
and there were about five newborns in the smaller nursery. And of all
the babies, mine was the prettiest. And that's just not my opinion."

The baby's beauty also made the relinquishment tolerable: a beautiful baby would be adopted, as would a smart baby. One birthmother
overheard a social worker describe her son as their "number one

baby" and add, pointing to her, "because she's so smart." (The birthmother laughed then and said to me, "I wanted to say, 'if I'm so
smart, why am I pregnant?'") Just as surrender was not so bad if there
had been a struggle, it could also be redeemed by the "good" of the
child. "Because I also thought, 'what if she had never been adopted?'
But I didn't think that would be the case because she was a beautiful
baby. Anybody would have wanted her," said another parent. This
kind of remark insists that a birthmother is a *mother*; her concern for
the child's well-being does not vanish because she cannot "keep" the
baby. Nor does her attachment. A young birthmother experienced this
strongly: "I was allowed to look at my son for three short minutes,
very short, very short, and I was extremely attached to him."

Birthparent comments also insisted that being a mother was more
than a biological event. They were not the "bio-parents" some agencies called them. "They call me: biological mother. I hate those
words. They make me sound like a baby machine, a conduit without
emotions" (Dusky 1979, 75). The physiological link with the child
was only one strand of "real" parenthood; the other was a social link,
expressed in interactions: seeing, touching, feeding, and naming the
child. "Seeing and holding your baby will help to connect you with
the reality of your experience," CUB told its members in a pamphlet
(Concerned United Birthparents, n.d.).[8] "But I made my mother
come. I also told them [nurses] that my mother had to see this baby.
There was something, you know—a very strong need I had to live
through the reality. I know a lot of girls didn't do that; for me it was
terribly important. I was really happy that I didn't terminate the pregnancy and that I lived through the delivery, that I felt all of the stirrings of her, and that I saw her and held her and did as much as I possibly could. I felt like it was facing a reality . . . not to terminate the
experience before it had gotten finished."

One young woman, who was fourteen when she gave birth, described her somewhat different experience:

So when I wanted to see her, they [nurses] wouldn't let me see her through
that night or the next day. I kept asking and they wouldn't let me see her, and
I believe it was the second or third day after, and it was the day before I was
going home and they had not allowed me to see her. I kept telling them that I
had to see her and I really felt that I could see her, that I couldn't go through
with it without seeing her. It's strange but that's how I felt. So they just kept
trying to talk me out of it. I guess it was the next morning when Dr. King
came in and we talked, and he felt the same way as they did. He acted more

like a father with me. He said, "I know what's best for you and I know it's hard, but it will be easier if you don't see her." I insisted and he finally agreed with it and it was hours later when they finally brought her in to me. The nurse brought her in and I held her, and the nurse was standing over me, wanting to take her back instantly. So I can't say I had her more than three minutes when they whisked her back away from me. And I thought they were doing me a big favor.

Some birthparents, on the other hand, had relinquished at a time or in a setting in which seeing the baby was official policy. "If you're a good girl and if you sign the papers, you could hold her," was a birthparent's version. This did not mean that the doctors, nurses, and social workers really liked or acted on the policy.[9] A birthparent who relinquished in the mid-1980s reported a nurse's objection to her unwrapping the baby from his blanket. "I said, 'so what? What are you going to do, not bring him to me? I'll complain. He's my baby.' I hated it when they used to—. I had a wrist band and he had a wrist band, and they would say, 'is this your son? Let me check your wrist band.' I mean, they would bring him to me four or five times a day, 'let me check your wrist band.' Well, wait a minute, of course he's mine, you just brought him in here three hours ago."

With the same sense of a battle, one birthmother told me she had been "forced" to see her baby.[10] In her view, not having contact with the baby would have better helped her through the relinquishment. But hers was a minority position. For most birthparents, seeing and holding the baby was important; it normalized the birth and legitimated their parenthood. "He had these little, teeny weeny, skinny things [legs], about this big [circling thumb and forefinger]. And the bottle was an ounce, maybe two, and he couldn't even drink half of that bottle. Maybe half." A woman who had twins recalled: "And after the first baby came I remember the doctors—and I heard the cry and I remember, my mother always said, 'just so it's healthy, it has all its toes and all its fingers.' And so that's what I said, that's the right thing to say. Because I was laughing to myself, I said, 'that's your little baby' when I could hear its cry."

Birthfathers who "came out" described their parenthood as more than biological, but their contact was even more circumscribed and controlled than a mother's—especially if the Supreme Court decision *Stanley v. Illinois* was ignored. "I never had the chance to hold her, to bathe her, to tell her that I love her" (Birthfather, *Today Show*, 4/86). On the whole, nurses and doctors were less sympathetic to male than to female parents. "I just barely got a glimpse of her tiny face when the nurses came pouring out of everywhere to chase me away from the forbidden window," one birthfather wrote with bitterness (CUB *Communicator*, 1/83: 4). In this situation, the surest way a man could be a father was if the mother let him. Of the group of birthmothers I met, one or two went even further in involving fathers in parenthood. "Actually he was the one that chose the name [Danielle Marie]. There was some movie, some French movie, I can't even remember what it was. He loves that name, Danielle. And Marie was his sister's name," said the woman who had fallen in love "at first sight" in sixth grade.

Naming was a sign of attachment a birthmother did not often relinquish—even to the father of the child. Birthparents gave names knowing the name would disappear with adoption. A name placed the baby in a social world, located him or her in the birth family, established a connection with the birthparent, and accorded the child a unique identity—the things names do in American culture. The name could be fanciful, recalling how young most birthmothers were. "I had always wanted to call her Kim," said the birthmother who had given birth at fourteen. "There was a little girl right next door to us with dark hair and big brown eyes. And she was always what I pictured my baby would look like. And her name was Kim. And that's what I wanted to call her [own baby]." Often the name had resonance in the birthparent's life, though not usually as precisely as in the case of a woman who had recently relinquished: "I named him Jayson William. With a 'y' [in Jayson] because he was a special baby." There was even more to that baby's name. "William was Tom's [baby's father] middle name. And Jayson, it might have been because of my mother when my stepfather—he was dying—that this baby be named after him. So I gave him the name Jayson to make her happy, but I changed the spelling because I couldn't stand her husband. So, yes, he's special and he has the name Jayson but it's not like my stepfather. And his name has a lot to do with every guy I ever went out with [using similar letters and so on]. . . . I put everything together in one cute little package."

A name served as a token of the child's identity, a sign of who the child really was, in an echo of ancient terms of relinquishment (Boswell 1988). Several birthparents were quite self-conscious about this, telling me they had planned the name as a legacy, a bequest that would tie the child to his or her natural family. A few said they expected the name to provide a clue for a child who might want to find his birth family in the future. One woman, for instance, told me she gave her son his birthfather's name in addition to her own last name, "so he can find me when he is ready."

But if the name were to be a legacy, the child had to learn it or, ideally, be given it by the adoptive family. "Now I don't know how true it is," said another birthparent who had just surrendered, "but Joan McDevitt, the caseworker for the adoptive family, told me they're keeping her first name. Now this is what she tells me, I don't know."[11] For a birthparent, keeping the name meant the adoptive parents respected the child's nature, her ancestry, and her birthparent. "Yes, I named her Liza and her family kept her name which I thought was really nice. I named her Liza Louise and they kept her first name. I don't know whether the mother did it as sort of a gesture or just because she liked the name," said a birthmother who did trust the social worker. Names awakened a kind of mysticism; birthparents had a sense that an aspect of the birth name would persist in an initial or an echo of the "real" name. Like the symbolism of blood, a name indicated the persistence of a birth tie despite contracts and the "contrivance" of a family. Signed and sealed papers did not sever the bond between parent and child.

"Once that paper was signed, they wouldn't give us the time of day"

"Like the white-flag surrender of a losing nation in war, most birthparents surrendered not because they wanted to but because their situations gave them no other choice" (Concerned United Birthparents, n.d.). Signing a child away was the dramatic climax in all birthparent stories, and the drama was important. The birthparents I spoke with constructed a world peopled by villains and victims, and one in which values were scrambled in the interests of "marketing" a child. "We were all fed the same line! We were all such vulnerable prey for the baby market!" (CUB *Communicator*, 12/82: 12).

Birthparents felt tricked into a transaction that was at once unnatural and uncultural. Vulnerable and uneasy, they fell prey to people who "distributed" babies. Parenthood became a matter of negotiation, and birthparents were not given the resources with which to bargain. "We were given no information," they remembered. The decision was my own, said a mother, "but it was misinformed." She added, "I didn't even know about welfare." In this view, the greed of social workers for babies made them stingy with information.[12] "But I didn't have any money, nobody told me I could go on welfare till I could get a job again. Nobody told me about foster care," said another mother. "I guess I'd heard the word 'foster care' but didn't really know that it was for that situation, thought it was for brain-damaged kids or kids that can't get along in their home. Never knew it was for babies, until the mother maybe could get her act back together and take the kid back."

Not provided with any resources, even information, a birthparent had no choice but to surrender; there was nothing "voluntary" in giving up a baby. " 'Surrender' fits the experience. Because the child is 'given up' without options, often under pressure tactics, and because there is no emotional compensation for the loss, there is a real 'surrender' " (Concerned United Birthparents, n.d.). "Signing away" a baby further emphasized the powerlessness of the birthparent, and underlined the unfeeling, bureaucratic quality of the arrangement. So brutal and unnatural did the action seem that some birthparents blocked it out entirely. "I cannot remember being in the hospital. I cannot remember signing anything," said a birthmother, who then did not say much more about the "surrender" of her child. And some birthparents claimed they would not have signed had they realized what they were doing. "No, I wasn't aware of anything, what the decisions were. Years after that I didn't know if it was legal or not, I didn't know. We just went through the whole thing."[13] "I was at a lot of stress and I didn't read the forms as closely as I should have," said a woman who was in her 20s when she relinquished. "When I got to the agency, I signed the adoption form. I didn't know that at the time. I just thought it was just the paper work."

One woman blamed her numbness and lack of attention on those who wanted her baby.

You know, I was crying so hard. They had me doped up because I was in horrible pain. It was only two days after I almost died from childbirth. And so they had me doped up. I had double the dose of sleeping pills that I was supposed to have because I couldn't get to sleep. And I had tons of pain pills in me plus all kinds of other things. And they got me up at midnight because this person from the County that moonlighted, and would come and take care of the stuff at midnight, came for the surrender—for me to sign the surrender papers. And that was only two days after I had given birth. And so I had no idea what I was doing and they said the only—and I didn't want to sign it, I was crying and crying. And I have no idea what I signed. I did not get a copy of the surrender papers.[14]

She was not alone in feeling she had been literally or figuratively "doped up." "But after I got back home, into the maternity home, I got to—oh, a big mistake they made was—I went into the infirmary then and I had just been back a couple of hours and the social worker came in with the adoption papers for me to sign. And I was not feeling well and out of it with medication and all sorts of things and I said, 'well, that's it,' you know. 'I'm not signing any paper, I have to see this baby and so you can't do this to me right now,'" said this birthmother, who next apparently exerted her will. "She [social worker] got real angry and everybody got angry and they all, the preacher came in and everybody came in and tried to talk me out of it. I said, no, that I was gonna see her [baby] and take care of her until she left. Or they wouldn't have a baby to sell."

It was not only that they were bewildered and brainwashed. Their maternal feelings were also exploited, turned to the project of getting their babies. An outspoken birthparent summed up her old feelings of anger:

And these are all the things I think the social worker, the message she gave and like, "how can you possibly take care of this baby? You're not even through high school, you're going to hate the baby when you want to go out on a date and you're going to be stuck with this kid. And how are you going to pay the baby's doctor's bills? What are you going to be able to give that baby for her birthday? What can you possibly give that baby? We're going to give her to a home where they are, where they have money. She'll have everything, what can you possibly give her? So sign the paper. This is the biggest and hardest thing you've ever done in your life and she'll be happy and you'll just go on with your life and forget about it." And I'm hysterical. I don't want to give away my baby, and I signed the papers and I'm bawling and I could hardly see the paper to sign it and big drops are dripping all over the paper.

What emerged from these and other accounts of relinquishment was a strong sense of the *business* of adoption, as social workers bargained for the babies they would distribute. "Greed" prompted the actions of those in charge, while birthparents were motivated by feelings of love, tenderness, and concern for the child. "And the babies were all crying in the nursery, ready to be fed, and the nurse was going to be the witness and had to get back to the babies. . . . And I have no idea what I signed." This birthmother's emotion made her vulnerable to the social worker's argument, which seemed completely cold and calculating. "And we know that once that paper was signed, they wouldn't give us the time of day and we were nobody," a different birthmother concluded. *They* wanted the babies and did what they could to get them. "This woman in authority," a birthmother wrote in a newsletter, "didn't care about me or my child, what I was feeling or what my child would feel later. . . . Her main concern was not my hurt at that point, only my name on that contract" (CUB *Communicator*, 2/83: 5).[15]

As for the birthfather, he was rarely even given the opportunity to sign a contract. When the mother was on the scene, birthfathers said, a man lost both the status and rights of a parent. "The loss of a child is difficult enough to bear but, coupled with the loss, men are forced to cope with social stigma that the child is the personal property of the mother. . . . The birthfather is expected to leave the scene of the accident" (CUB *Communicator*, 12/82: 4). In addition, the birthfathers I met complained of being betrayed by the mother, along with everyone else who ignored their feelings. As one birthfather told me: "She [the mother] never again talked about the baby, or having other children. But I thought about the baby constantly."

Gender stereotypes underlay the terms of surrender. Relinquishment drew on emotions the mother who had carried and given birth was supposed to have: putting "her" baby before everything else and wanting the best for a child. That was how both mothers and fathers remembered the situation—mothers with mixed feelings, proud of their love but not their vulnerability, and fathers with anger. "We [birthparents] were told, 'if you love your baby, you'll give it away'" (*St. Paul Pioneer Press*, 10/13/85: 1G). These comments did reflect social work policy as conveyed, for instance, in books about adoption. Birthparents "can often be helped to see that agreeing to adoption is the one generous gesture they can make for the child," said one such book (Smith 1980, 204). Convinced then of their generosity, birthparents gave away a child, only later to consider the manipulation inherent to the act. As one birthmother put it: "And then, you know, I realized just last year that here I had the most important thing that my daughter ever needed and they say, 'what could you have given her?' And now I answer 'me.' My god, what else does she need, you know, it was like it was so obvious. It just, you know, well I hit myself over the head, you know, what more could she want? And so what if she didn't have the party dress, my god, she has her cousins, her grandparents, her family. What the hell is more important than that? And they made me buy that, the fact that I couldn't provide a party dress or a nice toy made me unworthy as a mother."

Of course, birthparents also wanted their children to be well-placed. One birthmother was told, for example, that a married couple could provide "everything" she couldn't for her child and concluded, "like any mother, I wanted the best for her [baby]" (CUB *Communicator,* 8/84: 10). A married couple was one thing; that made sense. But the provision of "everything" was another matter, suggesting judgments based on comparative worth rather than love for a child. Yet the two were hard to separate, for birthparents as well as for social workers: a married couple did have more resources than the unprepared, usually young, birthmother. A birthmother who relinquished in the 1960s remembered being persuaded by a social worker: "You have to give her two parents. If you love her, you'll give her up. You want to do what's best for the child. It's selfish for you to keep her, for even thinking about keeping her, because what can you provide for her?"[16] Another birthparent was reassured that her adoptive family was both well-off and loving. "They love money or something," the social worker said, and added: "'as for a good home,' she said, 'perfect. Rosa, oh, they love her,' she says."

Birthparents did want the best for their children, but they did not want to be misled into an understanding of what that was. "I wanted him to have a family. I did not want him to grow up just with a single mother," said one birthparent. Nor were they naive about the importance of security, support, and stability. Evidently accepting cultural assumptions about family, a birthmother explained her relinquishment: "Because that person [child] is not able to live with the natural parent and they should have the best. Which would be a mother and a dad who are able to provide things, who really are deserving of a child, who really want to have a child. And I think that that's all that's necessary." By and large, birthparents really wanted the stereotypical American family, exactly what the social workers hoped to find. The same woman continued her analysis: "Although I can see single women and men with children, I think, I guess I feel like it was going to be a—I guess I feel that a child first of all should try to go to a couple. If that's not possible, then single parent is certainly second best. Homosexuals and gays, I don't know, I just don't think—. I wouldn't want my child raised in that kind of environment."

Despite the coming-out metaphor, no birthparent I met (and no one at meetings) had sympathy for adoption by gays, even gay couples. The desirable family was not just heterosexual, it was also an old-fashioned family, in which the father worked and the mother stayed home with the children. Otherwise why have relinquished?

"You know, at least that's what every birthmother, I think, expects—to be giving their child to a better situation than they can give them. And I definitely feel that she got, was in a better situation. And I, you know, the parents are at least staying married and everything seems very stable," said a birthparent who had heard a good deal about her daughter's family. "I do feel very fortunate," she added. "That was the main concern, the main goal was to get her somewhere decent, a nice environment, you know, financial too. And also people that love her. That's important too."

But some birthparents became suspicious about the placement, fearing that social workers chose parents who were rich but not loving. They distrusted what they had been told. "Naturally they're covering the tracks and they don't tell you anything. They just make something fictitious up"—in order to get the baby, this birthmother implied. Another birthmother was more explicit about her experiences. The social worker said, "'don't you want to give her [baby] to people that are economically sound and can provide everything for her and give her this joyous, wonderful home?' That's a joke." Others were equally sarcastic. "Of course, the baby gets a family, a mother and a father guaranteed for life, supposedly." "I was given the 'Hollywood version' of adoption, that they always work out." And an especially angry birthparent shouted at me: "They really sold me a sack of shit and I bought it and I can't believe that I bought it."

It was not that birthparents had necessarily learned more about the adoptive families. Rather, the public declaration of their own parenthood brought with it a greater awareness of the placement process and of the people who petitioned for babies. By the mid-1980s as well, adoptive parents were no longer considered perfect or perfectly stable, and this had special meaning for birthparents who had been "disqualified" from parenthood. In some cases, too, a changed official interpretation of adoptive parents led a birthparent to find out as much as possible about the family with whom her child lived. "I was told that the mother looked so much like me that she could be my sister. That couldn't be further from the truth than the sun and the moon. This woman has light hair, fair features, and we are just not at all even built the same or anything. I mean, obviously I was told so many lies, and I was told the father had blond hair and that he was very, very similar in feature to her father," said a birthparent who learned about the family twenty-five years after she relinquished. "So I was just told all these lies," she concluded.

A woman who had relinquished a few months before I met her felt equally deceived. "I didn't like the fact that her reason to adopt [to have another girl in the family], when they told me that, and I didn't like the fact that she did have kids and here, you know, Rosa [child] is going to be the youngest. . . . They told me, 'oh, her reason's this,' and I didn't like her reason, you know, for adopting and . . . when I went down there . . . the agency was asking, 'oh, what kind of family would you like?' . . . and I told them but yet when I made a comment Nancy [social worker] says, 'well you have the choice of going private adoption—'" and, presumably, picking out the family she wanted. The social worker's suggestion did not make her feel any less betrayed by the agency.

Even when a birthmother did not feel betrayed or lied to, it was hard not to wonder about the parents who were selected as "better" than she. As another, also recent, birthmother explained: "And I know these people have enough money, too, so he [baby] doesn't have to want for anything. I'm sure that they don't just give him everything so that he is a spoiled, rotten brat, but that he doesn't have to want. That was my biggest thing, that he would have to want for things if I kept him." Then, referring to the familiar dichotomy: "The only thing I could give more, . . . was to be more loved. If people could live on love in this world, he would be the richest, happiest baby." Regretting the necessity of relinquishing, this young woman also found intolerable the assumption that, once surrendered, the child would totally disappear from her life. "So I am standing there, calling him Jayson and he lifted up his little head and he turned it over and looked and smiled and then he turned the other way."

"And all that, you know, you don't forget"

"'You'll forget it. It will go away.' And we bought it because they were the professionals. We were the scared." For the birthparents I interviewed, this perhaps was the hardest part of giving up a child, being told they would forget and "start all over again." That such "advice" contradicted both cultural assumptions about having a baby and their own experience in the days and years following the surrender speaks to the difficulties it both caused and perpetuated. Like descriptions of signing a child away, birthparent accounts of being advised to "put it all from your mind" served a quite opposite function, reanimating past memories and feelings in the interests of a present identity.

"We cannot forget the most profound experience of our lives nor does the pain of losing our children diminish," states a CUB pamphlet (n.d.). Having grown up in a culture where childbirth is often considered a profound event and always the beginning of a new stage in one's life, birthparents viewed the prescription to forget as another deception to which they had succumbed. In the same CUB pamphlet, the social worker's questions are viewed as an attempt to "persuade the frightened young parent to believe that adoption can turn back the clock to before the conception" as if parenthood had never happened.

Nonetheless, birthparents do remember that at the time they found the advice they received from social workers appealing. "And I think, now I admit to it, at that time [of relinquishing] I was thinking that if I gave up this baby, I would still have a chance with Mike [baby's father]. I don't think I ever admitted that to anybody before but now I admit it." Indeed, they *might* be able to start all over again. Another woman told me, "My parents said I could come back home if I never mentioned the baby again." A young birthmother who had recently relinquished was still tempted by the possibility of returning to the time "before conception," yet she also did not want to give up the experience she had just had. "I am more of a kid than I am anything else. Now I have to be this grown-up person in this grown-up world that I am not ready for. I still want to be sixteen and seventeen years old and just start all over again. The part that I missed when I was pregnant. Of course I'd have to grow up again and that was tough."

When they came to talk about it further, though, birthparents considered the prescription to erase a chapter of their lives the most unforgiving aspect of adoption. It had been hard enough to lose a child, but to be told that memories of the child should also disappear did not ease the situation. Their own parents never mentioned the subject again. "You know, it was just they never spoke about it. They never said, 'gee, do you have stitches? Do you hurt?' I mean, you know, my mother had five children and she couldn't ask how her 16-year-old daughter was feeling. Do you hurt? How was your delivery? Nothing.

Not a word was ever mentioned. We never discussed it again." And another woman commented on the lack of sympathy shown by her own mother. "Now, looking back on it, I say to myself how really strange it was that my own mother would not ask me if I had a bad delivery, would not ask me if I was having pain after I got back home or any question. Nothing! Can you imagine that a mother wouldn't think, 'gee, you're rotten but I wonder if you're getting—maybe you need, a doctor should give you a check-up or something.'"

That no one paid attention did not, however, make the baby go away or the memories disappear. Not mincing words, a birthmother summarized her view of the situation: "But it was all a bunch of lies. 'You'll forget. You'll close this chapter in your life. You'll do all these wonderful things. This is not the end, it is the beginning.' And all that, you know, you don't forget." Birthparents, then, never forgot the birth, no matter who else ignored it and how often they were told they would forget.[17] This claim constituted a severe criticism of adoption and of the people who arranged adoptions—people who not only took a child but also attempted to take a parent's memories away. "They [maternity home] assured me that the way I remembered things was not the way it had happened," a woman wrote to the CUB newsletter (CUB *Communicator*, 6/83: 36). And social workers did see it differently. "I don't get to have a lot of contact with my clients," a social worker said to me. "They pretty much want to forget it and put it behind them."

The absurdity of the idea that forgetting was not only possible but advisable came out repeatedly, not necessarily with the passion of the following remark but with much the same interpretation of birth. "I mean, that's a part of my flesh that they took from me and it's gone. And it's like they cut off my arm or my leg, it's just that conceivable of a scar. Because I don't believe adoption as it is right now, you know, saying I'm going to take your leg and you're going to forget that it ever existed and you're gonna go on through life—. It's impossible. They can't take my child and say that I will [forget], you know." Fathers made the same point, dismissing the fact that they had not experienced pregnancy and recognizing that a flesh-and-blood tie nevertheless existed for them as much as for a female parent. "I never forgot about my daughter, and her birthdays were very difficult" (Birthfather, *Today Show*, 4/86). And like mothers, fathers claimed the tie lasted forever and the pain of relinquishment did not vanish. "It's a pain I've lived with every day for nineteen and a half years," one man told me, knowing this kind of statement did not perfectly fit conventions of fatherhood in contemporary American culture. It was easier for women to admit to the grief, pain, and overwhelming emotion—to me and in general. "I cry every single day, I mean, I cry every single day, every, every single day," a young mother said. "I mean, this is something I'll never get over."

But even mothers who cried were violating the cultural dictates surrounding adoption. Parents who relinquished children were not supposed to mourn.[18] "If she [baby] had died I would have been allowed to mourn her loss" (CUB *Communicator*, 2/86: 11). On this issue, birthparents themselves became prescriptive. "You need to grieve for the baby that was lost to you. You need to mourn the life that you might have shared." Nor was there any possible replacement for the loss. "And then I had the second child and the third child," a birthmother told me. "And all this time I would not allow myself to grieve. I never allowed myself to grieve the loss of Lorna. I never allowed myself to get angry over any of the circumstances. And I, as a matter of fact, I shut it down so bad that I wouldn't read any articles on adoption."

"And it gets worse as the years go on, too," another parent said. "It's not something that heals itself. Other things, you know, after a death, how time heals? Or some tragedy like your house burning down, or things like that. Those things time heals. This is something that gets worse. Isn't that crazy?" And a birthfather: "and that's a pain I'll carry until I die" (Birthfather, *Today Show*, 4/86). References to death accentuated the extent of a loss that was not supposed to have happened. "So now I have come to the conclusion that I'm going to take it to my grave. You know, that the sorrow that I have and the loss that I have I will suffer forever, nothing will change that." And the grief was both more persistent and more poignant because the child was, in all likelihood, alive.[19] "It can be difficult to put 'the past' behind you when your child exists in the present—but without you" (Concerned United Birthparents 1981, 43).

The phrase *a childless mother* perfectly captured the paradox of being a parent whose child was nonexistent. The child was real, but not *there*; nor was its absence noted. "How do you introduce yourself as a childless mother?" (CUB *Communicator*, 12/82: 13). This also marked a central contradiction in adoption: a parent by birth who was then not a parent at all. She or he presumably forgot the experience; parenthood was invisible and the child a full member of another family. The birthparents who did not forget exposed the contradiction. That a childless parent fit the logic of adoption did little for birthparents who resisted that logic by remembering the experience. They had not surrendered their parenthood when they gave away a child.

"If they think we're such trash, why do they take our babies?"

Just as adoptive parents would deal with the presence of another set of parents in the child's life, so too did birthparents think about the parents with whom *their* children lived. And like adoptive parents, birthparents delineated their own parenthood in juxtaposition to that of the "other" parent.

Not knowing much about the parents who adopted their children, birthparents drew on the descriptions in adoption literature, in popular journalism, and in support group newsletters. There they learned that adoptive parents were average members of a community—normal people with normal problems. Yet, prompted by memories of the surrender, some birthparents converted the adoptive parents' fall from the pedestal on which they had been placed into a sheer drop. Adoptive parents were portrayed as greedy, possessive, and selfish. They had taken children as "consumer durables," to add to a household and to compete with everyone else. As one CUB newsletter noted, the birthparent "feels selfish for wanting her child, [and] too naive to realize how much more selfish it is to try to get someone else's" (CUB *Communicator,* 11/86: 3).

In this interpretation, if the adoptive parents were selfish, the birthparent was generous: giving up a child became "giving" to the adoptive parent's "taking." As one birthparent said to me: "So the biological mother is important, you know, she's making this step. And I feel [if] she wasn't selfish in giving her daughter or son away, I don't think *they* should be selfish about having the child." Clearly considering the adopting parents unsympathetic and mean-spirited, she continued: "But you know, they're being so selfish with her. It's like I was told, I wasn't selfish when I gave her up and they don't want to have no parts of her, you know, natural background." At the heart of her comments was a simple feeling: the adopting parents could not share, they could only possess a child. They would not give out any information, or equally selfishly, receive any information about the child's "real" parent. Birthparents were not asking for the exchange of identifying information, just a sense of the child in her new family.

"I wouldn't have bothered her [adoptive mother], just so that I can have pictures to see what she [daughter] looks like, I mean that's all I'm asking. So I wouldn't have bothered her, just, you know, drop a letter or two now and then, a picture. You don't have to be in them. Just snap them on a clear wall, you know, or something"—thus birthparents interpreted the "entitlement" adoptive parents learned. "It's that need to have that other individual all to yourself which some people feel, people feel about how husbands—you know, if he, I mean this has got to be mine and only mine and nobody else's," another birthparent explained adoptive parent stinginess. "You know that they have, that's a need so much to cling to this thing that belongs to them, you know, that this paper makes that belong, and that it makes that person who brought you into this world not exist."

"This paper," as she put it, referred to the adoption papers, and also to the "contracted" nature of adoptive kinship. "Paper" also evoked the flimsiness of such a bond. "Why is she [adoptive mother] so scared?" a birthmother asked her social worker, who responded: "you had her [the baby],' and I said, 'what?' Nancy said, 'Jackie, listen to me, you had her.'" Another birthparent recognized the implied threat here, especially to a woman who could not have a child of her own. "Like this girl next door [an adoptive mother], now, she has never had her own children and she can't and she never will and so maybe a birthmother would be very threatening to her because I was able to have this child and she could not." And there was a further implication of infertility. "Yeah, well, if you feel inadequate because you have inadequate ovaries and here this person is able to have it and give it away and, you know, rather than feeling gratitude they feel envy and envy, what grows from that but hatred?"[20]

By the same token, an adoptive mother who had had a child of her own should have been sympathetic with a birthmother. "She's [adoptive mother] had a kid for sixteen years and she can't understand how a mother would feel to give, they're not thinking on that level, you know, and they said the mother was fishing for bad things about me." Regardless of having had the experience of biological parenthood, an adoptive parent still shut out the parent of the adopted child. In the eyes of birthparents, this further confirmed the tenuousness of a contracted parenthood. "Adoptive parents are possessive; they want complete ownership of a child," a birthmother told me without hesitation.

The contrast was for her a fact of nature: a biological mother, secure in her bond, could share, while an adoptive mother could not.[21]

But what finally condemned adoptive parents in the birthparent's eyes was the rejection of their "own" child's natural parent. As one said, "I was good enough [for them] to take my baby but not good enough to acknowledge." Adoptive parents refused to accept the "whole child." "Adoptive parents are encouraged to deny birthparents' humanity and continuing concern and to forget our existence even though they see us reflected in our children's faces, bodies and personalities every day" (CUB pamphlet, 1980). And for birthparents, this represented a profound contradiction: a parent who valued the child yet denigrated the child's mother. "[B]ut to them, what am I? Some tramp that got pregnant at fifteen years old? It's quite possible, let's face it. Once they have the baby, they have each other, and pray, I'm sure, that I never do contact her [baby]." And with unimpeachable logic: "if they think we're such trash, why do they take our babies?"

From this it was a short step to assuming the adoptive parent would "spoil" the child's nature. The well-off parents who "provided everything" would turn the child into something like themselves: materialistic and competitive, *spoiled*. "She's in private school," a birthparent told me about her relinquished daughter.[22] "She might be a snotty little thing," this mother worried. Raised by others, her daughter would take on their characteristics. It was no longer just a matter of the difference between an unprepared birthparent and adoptive parents with resources, but also a question of whether environment did overwhelm nature.

Usually, birthparents knew almost nothing about how their child was being raised. With little beyond a sketch of the family, they imagined the child through the ordinary stages of growing up.[23] As declared childless parents, they participated in the child's life vicariously: the child's first steps, first day of school, sicknesses, and birthday parties. "I wish he was here to say, 'let's go take a walk,' and go to day care, and all that happy stuff that I missed," a young birthmother admitted. Vicarious participation also proved to them the reality of their parenthood. "I said [to the social worker], 'look, you can sit on the other side of that desk and say this and that . . . but you don't go to bed every night feeling guilty. You don't go to bed every night with your heart actually hurting, you don't—I dream about her [baby]. Oh, you don't picture what she's looking like. What does she say, "momma or da-da.'" She should be talking now and pretty soon, another month, she should be walking, a month or two."

Not forgetting, then, had its painful side. "Almost two years later I thought it would be better and it seems to be getting worse, because the older he gets and the more ready I am to handle him, the harder it gets. So I missed out on the baby stuff, the crying. You can have the crying baby, I'll get the one who . . . now he's set. He knows what he wants, well, he doesn't know but he's ready now, he's two. He's ready to go for walks and play on swings. That's a big thing for me to go to a shoe store and I look at those little teeny tennis shoes." Given the nature of the bond, it was impossible to forget. One birthmother repeated her conversation with her social worker: "'Honey, I know she'll be theirs,' I said, 'but she is still my daughter biologically, she still has my blood running through her.' I even said *this*. I said, 'I don't care how much by law she's theirs,' I said, 'but I'm blood back to my daughter.'" The social worker was uneasy. "Nancy just looked at me and she turned red as a beet. I mean, I said, 'you know, of course they're her legal guardian over her, but she still is mine as far as I'm concerned.' I could never say she's not mine. She'll always be mine, that's how I feel. And you know they look, I say I have two kids and she's one. I say, 'well, one is just not here with me, that's all.'"

"She'll always be mine." Birthparents did not oppose adoption. Rather, they insisted that a birth bond could not be severed no matter what happened to a birth certificate. In making this argument, they drew upon cultural interpretations of kinship, family, and parenthood. From their point of view, adoption "reinterpreted" these notions to justify moving a child forever. But they did not think it had to be that way: both birth and law could be part of the child's experience growing up adopted. Birthparents did not want a child back; they wanted *birth* to be acknowledged in fictive as it was in "real" kinship. The problem, of course, was that adoptive parents learned that the birthparent would disappear. They learned, as I show in the next chapter, that a legal attachment could replace the bond of nature.

5

Everyone Else
Just Has Babies

Becoming an Adoptive Parent

"We had to meet all these criteria"

Adoptive parents are "chosen" parents—they have to
pass a test and meet established standards to become parents. As they
put it, "everyone else just has babies," while they must be approved
by experts to "receive" a child. "It seemed funny," said one, "that we
had to meet all these criteria and anybody else that was just going to
have a kid could just go out and have a kid." In fact, the entire process seemed "funny"—unconventional and unnatural. Moreover, the
process kept the birthparent very much in the mind of those who
were applying for parenthood. A contrast with the "natural parent"
shapes the experience of becoming an adoptive parent; biological kinship determines interpretations of fictive kinship. And so the present
chapter, about adoptive parents, is also about birthparents.

Genealogy was the model for parenthood, no less for parents who
adopted than for parents who surrendered a child. Adoptive parents
did not ignore the significance of a blood tie. "Even though I love
those children as if I had given birth to them, there's still that thing
that you won't ever get to experience that part of it. It will always be
different the way we get our children, the way they arrive," one adoptive mother confessed. The effort to establish a bond equivalent to

that of birth began with the first inquiry to an agency and did not end when the adoption had been legalized in court. Adoptive parents, as I show in this chapter, worked on establishing a bond as enduring and solid as, presumably, the genealogical connection. With genealogy their model, adoptive parents constructed a parenthood against the image of a parent by birth—the person who just had a baby, naturally.

Furthermore, adoptive parents, like birthparents, found the meanings of "good parent" and "bad parent" to be ambiguous, inconsistent, and perplexing. The ambiguities exposed the paradox at the core of adoption. To be good, not just "worthy" or "capable," the adoptive parent had to demonstrate traits associated with a natural mother: unconditional love and attachment—feelings presumed to come from the "physical realities" of conception and birth. Yet these traits were also associated with the woman who, as designated "unfit" to be a parent, had lost her child. In working out this inconsistency, adoptive parents made their own parenthood. They also, like birthparents, contrasted themselves with the professionals who, in another sense, made their parenthood. As a result of their encounter with professionals, in which calculation took precedence over emotion, and "distributing" a child took precedence over caring for a child, a number of prospective parents turned away from agencies altogether to find another way of "having a baby."

In this chapter, then, I provide an account of a "social" parenthood made natural, of the difficulties of applying for a child, and of the accommodations to a *contracted* parent-child relationship. Like the previous chapter, too, this one indicates the extent to which American adoption is changing; the parents I met did not assume adoptive parenthood without awareness of the other parent, of an ideology of shared parenthood, and of the possibility that their "own" child would know his or her "real" mother. Change affects even those parents, like those I interviewed, whose adoptions were conventional: closed and confidential. Whether adoptive parenthood can be "as if genealogical" is the question adoptive parents confront.

"The average members of a community"

"There is no typical adoptive parent; the one common characteristic is the ability to accept as a member of your family a child who was not born to you" (Phillips 1980, 3). The adoptive parents I interviewed also shared other characteristics: they lived in the same area and had had interactions with the same adoption agencies. Their views of family and of being parents were somewhat influenced by the general conservatism of the region. They were not all equally sure about their ability to accept a child who was not born to them, but they all knew they wanted a child and that adoption was the way they would "get" one. A few had biological children and were adopting in a second marriage or to bring a sibling into the family. Most could not become pregnant: adoption was their *only* option. In the end, the people I interviewed—average members of the community—adopted for the range of reasons described in the literature: to help a child, to have a child, to express love, to provide a home for someone who needed one.[1]

Their sociodemographic profile was also generally characteristic of adoptive parents: white, largely middle class, and dominantly Protestant and Catholic, with a sprinkling of Jewish couples (Bachrach 1983b; Bonham 1977).[2] Eleven of the twenty-seven families had adopted biracial children. Almost everyone already had an adopted or a fostered child in the house when I did the interview. Two couples were waiting for infants, and two couples had experienced a disrupted adoption so the child was no longer living with them. Fifteen families had adopted infants (under six months); the rest had adopted older children or sibling groups. I interviewed two single fathers (never married) and one single mother (divorced). Nor was the educational background of the adoptive families I met substantially different from what has been reported.[3]

All but two of the families had adopted in the 1980s. This bias toward recent adoptions is not unusual in adoption research, given that families whose adoptions are completed tend to disappear from record, their initial applications confidential and protected by an agency or lawyer. Applying for a child in the 1980s, these individuals faced a so-called baby shortage, an emphasis on special needs adoptions in agencies, and the growing acceptance of independent adoption in most parts of the country. In the state in which I did my research all legal adoptions must be preceded by a home study; consequently everyone I interviewed had had contact with social workers.

Several people remarked that my being in the house and asking questions reminded them of the home study. Undoubtedly, a few used the occasion to correct or reinforce statements they had made in earlier interviews. They were used to talking about "becoming parents."

They also said there was a difference when "getting a child" was not at stake in the encounter; they *had* their children and could talk "freely" with me. For them, I tended not to be the messenger that I had been for birthparents; rather, I was someone who shared their experiences.[4] And primary among those experiences was that of being selected, judged, and approved in order to have a "child of one's own." The steps of applying, the seemingly endless investigation of character, and the discomforts of feeling out of control of this life-stage transition dominated our conversations.

"They just were calling all the shots"

People adopted a child because they could not have one or because they wanted to help a child in need.[5] The motives were not always separable; love did not differ entirely from charity nor did "building a family" mean a person was not concerned with the plight of an unwanted child. Whatever the dominating motive, people felt they were "taking action" when they began to apply for adoption— only to discover how little they really *could* do. They took action only to come across rules, regulations, and obstacles—in response, they learned how to play the game. "And that, that was another ball game, all this required," a father recalled. "We just couldn't believe what all you had to go through."

Contrasting their situation with that of the natural parent, who not only did not have to play the game but who had not followed rules, one adoptive mother said: "This is very extraordinary. You get two horrible people who can produce a child naturally and there's no restrictions whatever on them. Then you get two people that probably are going to be great parents and they've got to subject themselves to all this, all this stuff, and it just doesn't seem right sometimes. But you've got to play the game and it's somebody else's rules." At the same time, adoptive parents valued the sense of responsibility that distinguished them from those "other" parents. They also valued the purposefulness and determination that carried them through seemingly arbitrary rules and regulations. Like birthparents, adoptive parents were proud of not being passive about their parenthood.

"In adopting, you're not sitting back and doing nothing," said an adoptive mother, "like you are when you're going through infertility treatments." The inability to give birth, to reproduce a child biologically, was particularly devastating; not only was one's body not working right, it was impossible to make a change. "And my impression is that infertility is kind of like alcoholism," said another woman. "You don't, you don't quit until you hit your bottom. You know? You really, everybody gets frustrated and fed up at a different point." A man offered his version of the same sentiment: "Frustrating, frustrating. It [infertility] kept, it was like something that you didn't have any control over, that you couldn't affect. Really and it was—frustration was the biggest thing." He continued: "Then when we started adopting, it was like, 'well, we can do something about it.' It was great, it was [interruption], yeah once we got started doing it, it was like 'well, now we can actually do something about it' and we were pursuing a positive line of thing here."

But their sense of moving forward and taking control disappeared almost instantly with the first phone call to an agency. A professional and quite sophisticated woman in her early 30s told me: "We had loads and loads of forms to fill out and they ask everything and they asked us to fill things out separately and they wanted to know everything. They even wanted to know about your sex life. And you know, I even put, 'this is personal.' You know, come on." Neither gender, age, background, nor social class made much of a difference; the questions were probing, intrusive, and humiliating for everyone. "It wasn't as depressing as the medical part," a young man said, "but it was, I always called it 'jumping through hoops' for somebody. You jump through the hoop and you could be rewarded by jumping through the next one." The process, he concluded, "was really a wreck."

One woman who agreed to put up with "all of this" grew afraid her "stubborn" husband would "mess things up." "Robert scared me a few times during this adoption in that he refused to give out certain information that they requested. . . . He knew that it was just routine, out of habit, they've gotten used to asking these questions, and a couple of times I thought that adoption was going to go right out the window because he would refuse to give out this or that piece of information." That questions about one's sex life, contentment in marriage, and feelings for one's parents were routine did not make them less of an ordeal.[6] And though such questions often did not seem relevant to becoming a parent, going through the process of being questioned and probed served another purpose: testing one's endurance, it transformed one's "identity."[7] That is, the experience of applying for a child altered an individual's sense of being a parent. Applying for a child, then, provided a transition into parenthood that was different from, but could be as powerful as, becoming pregnant and giving birth. Several adoptive parents, annoyed at the tests and ordeals, also conveyed the impression that these established their commitment to adoptive parenthood.

"It amazed us," one woman said. "It seemed like what they [agencies] wanted was they wanted you to be married twenty years, to have tried to get pregnant ten years at least, to make $70,000, but they only wanted you to be twenty-five years old. And I'm not sure how people, I mean I don't know how they do it, and maybe they find people but it seemed like almost impossible qualifications." Yet even as she complained about tricks and impossible qualifications, she struggled to pass the test: adoption was the only way she could become a parent. An adoptive father had much the same thing to say about the process: "Yeah, a lot of them [application processes] were like a catch-22 thing. By the time you were old enough, or by the time you waited ten years for the child, then you'd be too old to qualify and meet the criteria and so forth." He, too, put up with the confusions and learned to play the game that would grant parenthood. The penalty for not playing was too great. A woman who recalled being excessively cooperative said, "Here I am waiting to get this baby and I didn't want them to be angry with me. You know, they just were calling all the shots."

"They" were the social workers, who came in for a fair amount of blame and anger. They set rules, they examined the applicants, and they made a prospective parent—a worthy member of the community—feel like a criminal. "We complained about that, you know we'd try to tell everybody else, they'd say, 'oh, I thought it was easy to adopt.' You'd start explaining to them what you had to go through and there's criminal investigations and child abuse records and just, it's terrible." No one thought there should not be *any* regulations, only that these should be reasonable, in the best interests of the child, and without the assumption that an applicant was "unfit" until proven fit. "I do agree that families have to be checked out who are adopting. I feel that it is true that the government or state or whatever agency has to make sure that they are making a good placement. Or [an] attorney via the court system. But I think that some of the restrictions are not necessarily in the best interest of the child."[8]

Reflecting the dualism in American adoption, adoptive parents remarked that though they "wanted" a family, they were also *helping* a child. Under these circumstances, they ought not to have required such thorough investigation. The sense of being distrusted by the state that considered them resources was a personal experience, not just a comment on policy. One man remarked: "So we have all these kids. Like in this state, we have these ten thousand waiting children and yet there doesn't seem to be anybody, whether it be the courts or the Department of Social Service or anybody that really wants to move these children out of their foster or institutional lives and into parents. And the legal system and the bureaucracy and the red tape actually turns people off to do it." He had himself adopted a special needs child, but only after several months of close examination.

He continued his account.[9] "And yet I was put through a State Police check, what do you call it—the other check they put you through with the bureau for child molesting? There's two checks they put you through, police check and that other one. I had financial statements. I had to have credit references. I had to have personal references." He then made the comparison that underlay his resistance to being investigated. "I mean if they put every parent, if they put every mother and father through that before they had their first child, there would be a lot less loose children in the world. But they actually put, they put adoptive parents—I can understand now why a lot of people say the heck with it and don't do it." His point was unmistakable. "Of course after waiting almost two years for Raoul, like I tell them [social workers], I could have made a few kids faster than I've waited for Raoul."

Whereas "making kids" could be ruleless and random, applying to care for a child resulted in a close scrutiny of one's life: the policy did not make sense. Rules were applied to those who had the characteristics that conventionally defined a "capable" parent. "At first I thought, gee, why do you have to do this?" said a woman, remembering her application process. "People don't—young kids you see in the mall holding hands that are pregnant don't have to go through this. Why should somebody that is financially and emotionally ready to do this not be able to do this?" An adoptive father was blunt: We "have to go through all this crap and yet other people can have babies."

There was another side to being tested that contributed to the transformation of identity for adopting parents. In jumping the hoops and playing the game, they demonstrated their seriousness about the endeavor; adopting was not impulsive. As one social worker told me, with sympathy: "No one goes through this [adopting] for fun."

Another said, with rather less sympathy: "It's incredible what people do to themselves to get a baby." And a third: "The one thing that they want they can't have and somebody else made the judgment." She meant that having a child was not under an adopting parent's control—that being a parent depended upon the judgment of others. This same social worker also conveyed her perception of the urgency and insistence in a prospective parent's behavior. But adoptive parents denied that they felt urgent or desperate; they were merely persistent. In talking with me, they distinguished firmly between wanting a child and having a "consuming desire" for a baby.[10] A few did this by assuring me they had "always" wanted to adopt, well before they knew adoption was the only way they could have a child. "Ever since I was a kid I always thought it would be so neat, that once I got older whether I had my own kids or not, to adopt." In other words, they had not been pressured into adoption, coerced by an inability to give birth. Another parent conveyed a similar self-image: "I always had the feeling that I wanted to have children not on my own, I wanted to have a family."

A few parents counteracted the characterization of being desperate by suggesting they could have extricated themselves along the way. "We decided if he gets [his degree] and gets a better paying job, then we would try to adopt. If not, then we wouldn't bother because of the financial aspect of it. But," this wife added about her husband, "since he did graduate and he finally got his degree, we decided to give it a whirl." Or they claimed a casual, almost indifferent, attitude. "No, it was more I-go-with-the-flow sort of thing. If I decide to do this, well, I'm going to do this. I'll stick with it, good or bad, and we decided to do that so I was willing to run the—run it out to see how it worked." Mostly they contrasted themselves with other parents who *were* desperate. "And, but it's like that desperation to have a child which my sister, I think, at some level had," a woman said. "And I've never felt that." Another parent remembered rejecting international adoptions: "My understanding was that the folks who were there were rather desperate, like there was this desperate look on their faces, and everything about them was desperate."

Some adoptive parents presented themselves as pragmatic about having a child. There were reasons for wanting a child, apart from desire or instinct or social pressure. "And it wasn't until after my father died that I even thought about it, and I was just sort of driving home

one day and I don't even know what it was but just something triggered and I said, you know, this idea of my memory of him, sort of
keeping him alive. And then I thought, well, who will be there to
keep my memory alive when I am gone? And that's what really started
me thinking about the kid, about having a kid," said an adoptive
mother. Another mother sounded even more practical: "I think we
were just—part of the decision was we didn't want to grow old and
not have anybody else there. You know? I think you really, you miss
something if you don't have someone there to grow old with you and
to call you Mom and Dad and to see how you're doing."

In a sense, then, adoptive parents reclaimed the process of having a
child by defining their participation in adoption differently from what
they perceived (often accurately) the view of social workers to be.
"And to be truthful, too, I feel that we were preoccupied with so
many other things that adoption was not a centermost in our mind.
To complete our family we wanted to adopt, but it wasn't the—our
lives would not have been empty had we—" and her husband interrupted: "it wasn't a consuming priority."

Another adoptive father conveyed his lack of urgency by emphasizing his interest in the child's well-being: "Right there, and my objective was if I could ever save a kid from going through that experience
[of an institutional setting], you know, that I would. Because that's
very, very wrong for a kid to have to go through that type of situation." His emphasis on altruistic motives was unusual among the people I met, and may have reflected his position as a single adoptive father. To have a family was not as prominent a part of his discussion of
adoption as it was in other interviews: "Like I say, I wasn't intending
to find a son," he told me more than once. His explanation of his motives recalls the history of American adoption, in which "charity" and
"child-having" oscillate as poles of policy. For him, or so he said, the
important element was his ability to give a child a better home than an
institution could provide; he did not *need* to be a parent. His sentiments were echoed by another adoptive parent, a woman who had
five biological children and described adopting as a way of "doing
good." "It wasn't that we wanted a child in the house; we had had a
lot of children," she said. Rather, "My husband and I are acutely
aware of the severity of what I see happening in our society in terms
of problems. We're not involved in any kind of social movements or
anything like that, we simply had to find a way to help that we

thought fit into our life-style and about the only thing we thought we could do is raise kids well. We had a good home." They adopted two girls.

Whether desperate or not, wanting to have a baby or to help a child, in choosing adoption, people chose to become *parents*. They had embarked on a process whose goal was establishing an enduring kinship with a child who was a "stranger." And for some the child remained "different," not quite like a biological child. One adoptive father regretted he did not have a "real son" to carry on the family name, and another remarked: "There are a lot of losses in adoption; you give up a lot, starting with the genetics." Later this man added, "you give up control. There's a sense of defeat." And a woman who claimed she was perfectly happy about adoption said: "And it's my fault that Rob is fatherless [i.e., not a real father] except for the adoption."

She, like other adoptive mothers I interviewed, managed the transition into adoptive parenthood by putting family above pregnancy and birth. "Along the way I was starting to talk about adoption because what I wanted more than anything else was a family. I mean, I didn't—I, you think about it, you think real hard—what is it I want? Do I want to be pregnant? Do I want an infant in my arms or do I want the long term? Do I want to have PTA and football and grown-up children with grandchildren? And you realize that you don't have to be pregnant to have a family that you want." Accepting the traditional gender stereotype helped: she would have not only the "long term" but also the day-to-day involvement with a child that, in American culture, constitutes parenthood. (She told me later in the interview that she wished she could be a "stay-at-home mom.") Conduct, she expected, would bind her to the child as effectively as the pains and perils of childbirth. But the expectation came after the process of self-exploration required by adoption agencies when she began adoption proceedings.

"A self-education experience"

In the late 1970s, responding to complaints of clients and some loss of clientele to other ways of having babies (including "high tech" births), agencies began to change their policies. Questionnaires and interviews gave way to group meetings and parent-

training classes. "Our Agency places a very strong emphasis on education and 'becoming acquainted' rather than on making a judgement,"
noted one agency, in a typical introductory brochure. The agency, also
typically, still required an autobiographical statement from applicants,
but presented this as a benefit to the applicant rather than as a screening device for the agency. The idea was that autobiographies gave people an opportunity to explore their feelings about parenthood and to
remember their experiences as a child in a family. Agencies regarded
autobiographical statements as a kind of expanded introduction: people explaining what they were "like." This was true of the agency I
worked with; the County Youth Agency (CYA) instructed its applicants: "This worksheet is a way in which you can help us to begin to
know you as an individual and as a member of your family."

Thus, becoming an adoptive parent was a matter of self-searching.
Retrospection and introspection were encouraged at group meetings
and in training classes. Another agency—a private Catholic agency—
put it this way: "Adoption classes are a self-education experience that
assists couples to look at themselves and to determine their readiness
to adopt." The social workers who facilitated group meetings urged
people to focus on the meaning of making a stranger a full member
of the family. "However, when people broaden their ideas about
how families come together and what constitutes a family," one social
worker told me, "they will find there are a variety of ways to bring
children into their home." In the 1980s and 1990s, social workers
were further convinced that this was a matter of education and not
just intuition or self-knowledge on the part of applicants.

Adoptive parenting, CYA proclaimed, required "more training than
evaluation." I participated in the seven-week training course, along
with ten prospective adoptive and foster parents. "Alternative parenthood," we were told at the start, was not different from other parenting or any job.[11] "Like any other job, parenting requires that you have
special skills and knowledge in order to perform that job well. . . .
However, in most cases, no one trains us in these skills and that kind
of knowledge. We just become parents because there is a child living
with us," a short handout informed us. Over the seven weeks we did
learn parenting skills; we also developed interpretations of being a
parent by role-playing, reminiscing about childhood, and describing
our principles of child rearing. Partially at least, the goal here was to
transform the application from a cognitive and verbal exercise into an

emotional experience; becoming an adoptive parent ought to be *felt* as well as considered.

Training sessions focused on the adopting parents. Yet the birth-parent hovered in the background of almost every session, presented either as a figure in the triad or as part of the child's nature. One evening we watched a skit: one of the social workers came in dragging a heavy suitcase. Silently, puzzled, we all waited for an explanation. The adopted child, we were soon told, brings her own baggage with her, and that included "pieces" of her biological ancestry. The social worker unpacked the suitcase, bringing out a photograph, a toy, and a worn blanket. The message was clear. We had to learn to accept a child's past. As the CYA handout for that evening explained: "Perhaps by educating adoptive parents to the importance of these past connections, they may feel less threatened by a child's past relationships. Consider your own reaction and feelings if you were told, 'starting today your past ties do not exist.'" On another evening we acted out a relinquishment scene, trying to put ourselves in the place of a parent who had to give up her child. But our empathy here was by no means complete. "I just cannot understand a person who would give away her child," one person remarked. "I just kept thinking I would try to get the help I needed."

We were also asked to put ourselves in the place of a parent with a child who was not related by blood, who had traits, features, and memories that might be completely unfamiliar.[12] We did this in various ways, by anticipating our reactions to "bad" behavior—we learned a number of disciplinary techniques—or our reactions to a nosey neighbor who wondered why the child "looked so different," or our reactions to a visit by the biological parent. Then we set these reactions within the framework of experiences with our own parents. Comparison with one's own parents "naturalized" alternative parent-hood; we could continue their practices, but with more "skill."[13] And we were encouraged to make the comparison. "Please tell us about the people who parented you, your relationship with them, and how they parented you."

People especially liked this aspect of the classes.[14] "Well, it made us see right away the different parenting techniques that we had been raised and reared with," one woman told me. There was something comfortable about assessing one's own parents; people tended to be forthcoming, and we learned from each other rather than from a skit or presentation. "Something I thought was so edifying, too, was, you know you usually only get to see how people close to you behave as parents. And I thought it was real neat to see how people you don't know would behave as parents too." At those sessions, alternative parenthood appeared to be just like any "loving" parenthood.

But we also learned about the children we might be asked to parent through case histories and a one-time videotape of an autistic child. We were reminded forcefully then, by vivid descriptions and a view of "special needs" children, that our parenthood would be different from that of our parents. "Well, one other thing, too, that I thought was good in the classes, and I wished they had done more of it—I enjoyed hearing about the case histories of the kids who were possibly up for adoption. Or foster care. And I also enjoyed hearing how the present foster parents dealt with the situation. To me, that's really practical information. I think they didn't give us enough of that," a woman who was still waiting for a child said, several months later. There was a consensus about the importance of case histories. "The thing that we may not have seen and I think that may be important is to go through a case history. And to say, ok, here's a child and take an actual—. Here's a child, here's some of the situations that the child has gone through." The classes, an adoptive father told me later, "really crystallized what we could and couldn't accept."

Once involved in a "chosen" parenthood, people thought they ought to be able to assess the consequences of a choice. "And I really think that you should have some parents with special needs [children] come in and say what it's like, if people haven't been exposed to that. Say, gee, I think that people are a lot more capable of parenting certain types of children that they automatically don't think they could parent," an adoptive mother commented. The classes helped people determine the kind of child they could accept—and they reminded everyone that this was an *alternative* parenthood. If not artificial, it was not real either. But it could be a relationship that endured, upheld by love and commitment.

Our group fell back on the strength of attachments that were developed over time. Love, people said, came from the performance of parental duties. An adoptive father phrased this in terms of another couple's behavior: "I thought, they're so generous and so kind to open their homes up and their hearts up and they were such loving parents. . . . I was just so struck by how much they had to offer." And his wife added: "The love and concern that those people all had I thought was just wonderful. It was really uplifting, you know, at the end of the session to realize that all these wonderful people want to become parents."

While classes were a welcome relief from the questionnaires and "checks," they also felt like an examination. "So I wondered sometimes, should I say something or should I not? And then I just better bite my tongue and keep quiet," said a man who was waiting to become an adoptive father. Clearly, people who went to an agency engaged in a particularly self-conscious transition to parenthood, constantly reminded that the way they had children would always be different. Agencies, however, are not the only route to adoption.

"Out of the clear blue sky"

People turned to non-agency adoptions in order to avoid red-tape, gain leverage, and, in the 1980s, get babies. "Well, the standard stuff that any agency asks—income, assets, how long you've been employed, what your education is, what your house looks like, relatives, race, and then all the questions about 'if this happened, what would you do?' . . . Oh, my goodness, we must have written ten pages of various questions," said an adoptive mother, to explain why she then adopted independently.

Some felt not only that they were scrutinized but also that in an agency they were on the "market," asked to describe their ideal product. As Lynne put it: "But it was, it simply started with, 'yes, we'll adopt but the baby will be an infant. It will be, well, it will be white, it will—.' I mean, all of these things we were going to have." And, as Walter added, "[with] blue eyes and blond hair." Lynne: "Or green eyes and red hair." Walter laughed: "Or green eyes and red hair." Another parent expressed a similar discomfort with the agency "laundry list." "I thought that question ['what kind of child do you want?'] was kind of unfair though, because what they were forcing you to do was come up with an idea of an ideal child. For an ideal situation. Of course we all know that doesn't exist. And I don't even think it's healthy to be thinking about stuff like that because then that's boxing you in. It's either getting your hopes up or it's causing you to think in specific terms when you were happy thinking in general terms." Contrary to popular and professional opinion, independent adoption seemed to its participants less like a commerce in babies and more like a kinship arrangement.

Mrs. Granger was a well-known figure where I did my study. A woman in her late 60s, she had been placing babies independently for nearly forty years. She worked with a home for unwed mothers, helping the "girls" with their babies. And by the late 1980s, she had no trouble finding adoptive parents—news about "Granger babies" spread through the community. Everything she did was legal; she simply mediated between a birthmother and a prospective adoptive parent.

"So we set up our appointment time and invited her to dinner and it was just so unorthodox, just so different from any agency that we had ever dealt with. She was a sweet little, old plump lady that looks like anybody's grandmother with the little hose tied up at the knee and a little knot there and a little bun on her head and those sweet little rosy cheeks and she just was so different." Then, reflecting her prior experience with an agency, this woman added: "You know, of course I had the house spotless and had everything all made. She's just this neat little down-home lady and came in and sat down and Tracy [child] kept lifting up her dress to see the knot on her hose. I mean, she's just a really nice lady. She absolutely asked nothing about financial status. . . . She kind of wanted to get our philosophy of parenting and how we felt. And she was here, I don't know, maybe four hours but a lot of that was just chitty-chatty."

Another adoptive parent described their visit with Mrs. Granger. "And we've been told that rhubarb was her favorite dish and I had made rhubarb, and I made this nice dinner and it was really nice to have her here. We, and I can remember when she left. She's a short, plump woman and she left and she gave us both a hug and she said, 'I love you.' And I can remember very clearly going, 'I don't know. Does she?' " This couple had apparently passed Mrs. Granger's test, whatever it was.[15] "And I remember the next time Mrs. Granger hugged me was after she left, after putting Jill [baby] in my arms and she said she loved me and I knew she did."

Decisions were fast, intuitive, and not excessively discussed, and people liked it. "I guess Walter's and my feeling was, 'isn't it nice that somebody makes the decision?' When you talk to agencies nobody makes decisions. They just go, oh you don't fit the rules. You know? And so for us it was refreshing, I think, even if Mrs. Granger had said, 'no, you don't fit.' At least somebody had taken into consideration that we are different people and that we're not going to fit the mold but that doesn't mean we can't love." With Mrs. Granger, getting a child happened without rigamarole, right away—or not at all.

The speed with which she made the decision, and the suddenness with which she brought a baby, made a Granger adoption seem more natural—more like "real" childbirth. "Yeah, it seemed awfully funny that you had to meet all these requirements for these agencies and Mrs. G gave you the once over and said, 'Fine, the kids are yours. You get them tomorrow.'" This father added, "it seemed a lot more natural the way Mrs. G did it. It seemed like childbirth. You're pregnant, here comes the kid, you know, like it or not, here he is. You know, you may not have any money, but you got a baby." The way people described the day a Granger baby arrived underlined its likeness to the day of birth—with a rush of preparation and a gathering of appreciative friends and family. "And two hours later Mrs. G arrived and they put the kids in my arms. Ken was out buying Similac because she was early. I turned around and there were six neighbors with cameras going click, click, click."

This quality of suddenness was attributed appreciatively to all independent adoptions. The lack of time to prepare, and the spontaneity and impulsiveness on everyone's part, brought these adoptions as close to a biological birth as possible. It "came out of the clear blue sky," said a husband, and his wife added: "It was wild. And we just got off the phone and we were like, we were laughing, it was like funny. It was like hard to believe or something. It was a thrill." The surprise in an independent adoption also gave parents a sense of inevitability; no one had carefully calculated the "match" of this baby to that family. "And we're sitting around having coffee and talking about something totally foreign to adoption and babies. The phone rings and it's Mary and she says, 'This baby boy has been born this morning at five o'clock and he needs to be adopted, do you want him?' I mean, I was just, I was like, 'Say that to your brother,' and I handed the phone over to Rob. . . . And he's thinking all along, this is God's will and that we were meant to be and why did this baby come to us?"

Exactly what parents relished, social workers distrusted: the failure to pay attention to qualifications, to shared traits, and to the comparative capacities of relinquishing and adopting parents. What to participants seemed like a loving, generous, and kinlike transaction in parenthood seemed to professionals to raise the specter of exploitation, baby-selling, and violation of the child's best interests. The compromise reached in many places, including where I worked, was to require that independent adoptions be approved by an agency before they went to court for finalization. Thus anyone who adopted independently experienced a "home study," an evaluative visit by a social worker.

This was not easy. "Adoptive families have reported time and time again how defensive they felt and how agonizing the home study process was" (Hartman 1984, 3). Aware of the tension surrounding these visits, agencies tried to minimize the investigatory aspect. "A home-study is a comprehensive document which describes you and your family, your thoughts about adoption, your ideas and expectations about being a parent, and those things which are important to you in life," explained one typical agency. But parents experienced the home study in much the way they had experienced contact with an agency, and they expressed a similar ambivalence about the bases of judgment. They were split between demanding professionalism, as long as an expert was involved, and considering intuition and fondness appropriate to the designation of parenthood. "We had a good feeling about Bridget. She had an intuitive feeling about how we were going to be as parents."

Given all that hinged on this encounter, fondness should be combined with doing the job right. One couple compared the two social workers they had seen. Karen said: "So it was very different that way. I mean, she asked us questions and she looked at the house but that was half hour to an hour. And with Jennifer [adopted child] it was paperwork and paperwork, business, which was fine." Henry added: "She started asking us a couple [of] questions and we said, 'we have a home study done already, would that be helpful?' And she said, 'oh, you do? Ok, I'll take a copy of that.' She never asked us anything else." Under the circumstances, parents were not sure how to draw the line between having a conversation and being evaluated. This couple concluded, in Karen's words: "you never know what it's going to be like. Someone coming into your home and evaluating you. But it was a very nice meeting with the lady, the couple of times we met."

Nor were parents any more sure during the home study than when they first applied what the social workers wanted to find out. "You never know what's going on at the other end and we had, we were personable with the people at Chapel Social Services when they came down and did a home study. So we got to know them, they got to know us. But from that point on . . . it was, you know, off in the wind. It was just, we didn't know why decisions were being made, really," said a woman, disliking the feeling that she was subjected to someone else's whims.

In the end, the most satisfactory home studies seemed to be those that incorporated an element of friendship or kinship. If not professional, at least these encounters had something to do with being a parent. "I thought it was going to be a real strenuous type of interview and it wasn't at all," an adoptive father said. "Actually it got to be a lot of fun because you start talking about yourself and you hope that who you know most about is yourself—or it better be. We had a lot of fun doing it." And, if not grandmotherly like Mrs. Granger, a social worker could still become involved with the child—an interested rather than an investigative visitor. One mother remarked that her home study "was very helpful because she has a son who is essentially Joey's age, so for me especially, she really helped to say, 'Well, this is, Adam does the same kind of thing.' All the input, I mean I just needed so much input on what . . . is normal kid behavior, . . . to normalize the stuff."

So, whether they had gone the agency route or the seemingly "more natural" route of independent adoption, parents had to be approved by an expert before the baby was *theirs*. The expert could be stern or friendly, act like a professional or like a kind of parent, but either way it was the expert who made the final decision about one's "own" parenthood. In addition, whether they had adopted through an agency or independently, adoptive parents recognized that the social worker knew more about the child's "real" parents than they did. Approved as parents, they had to decide how much of the other parent would be part of family life.

"Their many sets of parents"

The first night of our training classes, we read in a CYA handout that foster and adoptive parents "must share parenting with the birth parents—if not through direct contact—then through the child's feelings about his or her family of origin." Sharing was in the child's best interests; a child had a right to his or her past "in order to be a whole person." As a CYA brochure stated, "foster parents and adoptive parents must demonstrate an ability and comfort level in helping children feel comfortable with their many sets of parents." But it was one thing to contemplate, in the abstract, a child's "nature" as part of the baggage brought into an adoptive family, and quite another to think of a birthparent.

Those who did constructed a picture out of "facts" combined with conventional interpretations of the woman who gives away a baby. They were women pressured by circumstances, sent away to a "home," and never given "any counseling, which I think is so sad," one adoptive mother commented. A few adoptive parents also recognized, with sympathy, that a birthmother might not forget. "With his [son] birthday being July 3, I can't help but feel that every July Fourth holiday that she has got to remember and must wonder where he is. I know if the positions were reversed that's the way I would feel." Most adoptive parents leaned on stereotypes, and not always ungenerously. "Cause I think about what it must have been like for her, with all these little kids at such a young age. That sort of thing. And I'm curious about her."

Some, however, were less than sympathetic, especially if the relinquishment had been delayed. "I went and saw the dad before I left the country, trying to convince him to change his mind and sign the [papers] giving up the rights to the boy. And he refused. The guy is, mentally he's not all there. He's got some problems. The case against him is extremely strong," said an adoptive father about the biological father of his son. It was almost as if adoptive parents had to feel the birthparent was *wrong* in order for adopting to be *right*. A woman who had met the birthmother told me: "So I had to justify it [adopting] to myself. . . . And I thought, which road will do the least hurt [to the child]? Nobody ever told me about her until I saw her at the termination of rights hearing and she needed a momma herself. I mean, she's just a pathetic little—as far as I know she had seven children out of wedlock, five of whom she has lost [terminations] and the last two—she may have had more, I don't know. And she just really needs a lot of support to function at all."

In the eyes of adoptive parents, too, a birthparent might not only be emotionally immature but also manipulative and cunning. "I'm tired of hearing about the 'poor birthmothers,' etc.," said a man, whose experience had been particularly painful; the birthmother kept changing her mind. "It was a long four weeks and sure enough, when it came—when the girl had to go into the courthouse to sign the interlocutory agreement, she didn't show. And she backed off for two more weeks. . . . And they [social workers] all were in agreement that . . . their experience in adoption and young mothers, that this was just a manipulated ploy on this girl's part. She was very immature and she had no intention of keeping the baby. She was just enjoying the limelight for a while." Such reported incidents, I think, reflected deeper cultural doubts about severing a birth bond forever. The conflict of interests rarely appeared on stage, as they had in this case, but the possibility (and occasional occurrence) of such conflicts colored the experience of adoption for most adoptive parents.

Adoptive parents did not have enough information to correct the negative stereotypes. The birthparents who were crucial were often ciphers: girls who had babies by mistake. "No. We don't know anything [about the birthparents]," said one couple, adding: "We didn't want to get involved that much." An adoptive mother told me, somewhat shamefacedly, "I don't even know her age. It's funny because everybody asks you, 'Well, how old was the mother? Was she married?' I have absolutely no interest. . . . It's just like he's ours." Most parents did have a description, with facts considered important for the child: physical traits, ethnicity, an occasional remark about education and hobbies. And reports of these "thumbnail" sketches tended to sound the same from one adoptive parent to the next. They knew about the birthmother—not much, but more than they knew about the father. "I knew hair coloring and height. That was it," said one parent, and another: "We know her age, we know that she's a student at a local university. We know that, we know her ethnic background. She's Italian. We know the father's black and poor. That's all we know. We know that they're about our height."

"It's just like he's ours." That was the point: without the birthparent, the child was a blank slate to be molded by his environment. "And I guess in retrospect, personally now I would just as soon not know," a father remarked. "It's something that you don't, I guess we don't have to deal with. Their personalities, projecting their personalities onto Jill [daughter]. And I guess that would be the reason I would just as soon not know them well." When adoptive parents were able to consider inherited traits an essential element of the child's own nature, the reality of the birthparent faded. Genetic background was then part of the child, not exactly part of the child's "other" family. One adoptive father laughingly told me about his oldest adopted child: "She's very smart. She loves music. I guess she probably inherited that from her birthmother." Mainly, and not surprisingly, adoptive parents put their faith in upbringing: "about 89 percent of the child turns out as they develop after their birth," a father said to me. "I'm not really worried about it."

In the end, too, it was not surprising how little they wanted the other 11 percent. The as-if principle of American adoption was key to being able to assume a "right" to the child that was as strong as that of the birthparent—which meant letting the birthparent "vaporize." On the other hand, a few adoptive parents wanted to know more about the child, without knowing about the parents. And they complained about social workers who knew something they would not tell, about descriptions of a child that left out unappealing information, and about a rushed placement that did not consider a child's temperament. Complaints like this intensified when the child who had been placed was older and had a substantial past. Then adoptive parents reconsidered the routes by which they had chosen the child in the first place and thought about how much information they had had with which to make a choice. One man noted his advantage in having gotten to know the child before he decided to adopt. "I didn't pick him out of a book, so I think I know more about this kid than most adoptive parents know about children that they pick out of a selection process."

One wife and husband remembered the description that had determined their choice. "It had a picture of this little boy with a smile on his face. And it said how he was, the foster family liked him and he was a trustworthy and happy-go-lucky kid and wanted to be adopted. Not very much," they concluded somewhat sadly. Another parent was frankly annoyed at the deceptiveness of a short sketch. "Which I felt, hey, if I'm gonna be considered, tell me what you can. Because I know that abused children come with some kind of problems. . . . Um, when the woman [social worker] wouldn't give me anything, I was like, hey! I know they do their best to sell them but if I'm being considered, don't sell me. Be honest with me. Like we found out more after we got our children than what we were told. A lot more came out." Although he did not say so explicitly, the implication here is that he was caught in a market in which he was not given enough information to be a thoughtful consumer.

Eager to have a child, adoptive parents felt gullible and too-easily persuaded by the social workers who placed children. "And when they really got Sarah placed, you know, in an adoptive home, all this other information began filtering in." Another parent sounded more charitable. "Sometimes, Judith, I think people don't tell you cause they don't know. Or some people are very apple-pie in the sky and every child is nice and good and everything'll be ok." But this parent, in fact, felt especially tricked by the process. "The agency—two most horrible things that happened to us, number one, we had no concept that amoral, delinquent, probably psychotic children were being placed for adoption without telling people what they were getting. And the second most horrifying experience, Judith, was that we never dreamed in a million years of the dishonesty, the cruelty and the downright lack of ethics, the incompetency that existed in public agencies." Like birthparents, she saw adoption as full of lies. And she was not alone. "But we never did find out what the complete story was on that because they withheld information from us for some odd reason."

Mrs. Granger came in for less criticism, and she also told less. "We did not even know the birthday," one mother said, half-jokingly, about her Granger-baby, and they only gradually found out there was diabetes in the family. But Granger adoptions had a different aura: they seemed more natural, and people trusted Mrs. Granger's intuitions about "her" babies. They did not demand facts. In an agency adoption, handled by professionals, people expected to be told the truth—or at least as much of the truth as they thought they needed in order to raise the child. Comments on social workers who "held back" underlined the feeling of not being in control of this way of having children. Such comments also revealed a cultural assumption—that with biological reproduction, a parent did know something about the child and therefore about the relationship. In adoption, the child's nature would emerge only as the child unpacked his or her baggage over time.

Not that risk was antithetical to notions of being a parent. Everyone who had a child took a chance. One adoptive mother ended her summary of what she and her husband knew about their children with: "That's all we know. And to tell you the truth, I don't give a darn. I'll take these children. They're so wonderful, whatever happens, whatever, it happens." Her husband said, "the less you know about them, the less you have to think about it. I mean, if they're going to be your kids, what was in the past is in the past." In general, parenthood was "a gamble, . . . a toss of the dice, more or less"—no more and no less for adoptive than for biological parents.[16]

One mother put together the components of the gamble in being an adoptive parent.

We know enough to know he's not allergic to anything. That he shouldn't be coming up with any surprises physically and medically speaking. I know that his mother, his birthmother, went off to college. I know that on his first birthday, the birth grandmother . . . called the lawyer just to check up on Joshua in a removed sort of way. And on the whole day of Joshua's birthday I was uncomfortable, his first birthday. Because if I had given birth to a child and given it up and it was the first anniversary of that occasion, I know I would have a lot on my mind all day. And I just wanted, I was just afraid she'd pop up on my doorstep or something. I mean I didn't want any intrusions from the parents and I was feeling sorry for her and happy—happy's not the word—grateful to her that she gave Joshua up and worried that she would make some sort of attempt to get him back.

She was happy when the arrangement was legalized. "And it was another crossing over a line for me and I realized that even though I didn't know I was doing it, I was holding back just a tiny bit and I let go after that and he's been completely and totally my son from that moment on because that judge told me he was."

"The last ounce of commitment"

Legalization made the relationship permanent. Under a judge's order, the child became just like one's own. And if adoptive parents did not become just like biological parents, they also no longer had to fear that "blood" would prevail. The child was unconditionally *theirs*. As one adoptive father said, until you know the child is permanently yours, "you don't make that last ounce of commitment."

A parent who had both foster and adopted children characterized real parenthood by comparing the two. "There's a thin [*sic*] line with foster care than there is with adoption. You cannot say those kinds of things—really shouldn't say them anyway, but you're forced to with natural children, you know, adopted children. I call them natural anyway." His wife explained: "Foster parenting is a lot different than adoption. Adoption, if we make a mistake, we admit it to our children and we correct it. Like things that we've had, you know there's been times that I've apologized to our children for things that I've messed up on or forgotten about or thought I've handled it badly." Real parenthood was unconditional: the child was accepted regardless of his or her behavior and the parent kept the child regardless of his or her mistakes. Adoptive parents made a "lifetime commitment to the child," as our CYA handout instructed us; no matter what happened, the bond would not be broken.[17]

The child became a full member of the family, not always immediately after legalization or without a struggle, but always without question. And this was true even when the difference in this kind of kinship was acknowledged. "Even though I love those children as if I had given birth to them, there's still that thing that you won't ever get to experience, that part of it," said an adoptive mother who described "bitterly crying" when she visited a friend who had just given birth. "And of course the mother was there and flew to the hospital and I had to hear, oh, you know, every detail there and I think what triggered that was the feeling that, missing that attention of the same kind—because it's different. It will always be different, the way we get our children, the way they arrive and everything will be a difference and I think that was what was hard there."

And if one ultimately had a biological child, the difference remained. "I could assure them [an adopted and a biological child] that I love them equally because they're both so special because they both came to me in such special ways. I mean, you can't ever match the way Joshua came and you could not have another adoption that was more exciting and more surprising. I mean, to have someone call you up and offer you a baby is just incredible, it's unheard of. And then to want to get pregnant so badly for so long and then to finally achieve that. There's not too much that could surpass that either, but they're entirely different and it makes both of their origins very, very special in their own way."

The burden of being "very, very special" lay heavily on the adoptees I encountered. For them, as I show in the next chapter, permanence was a problematic concept and "fictive" had resonating significance. In a culture in which birth is essential to the parent-child relationship, adoptees had to deal with a "missing" birthparent and no biological ancestry. In a culture that viewed parenthood as unconditional, they had been chosen by one and "unchosen" by another parent.

6

The Chosen Child

Growing Up Adopted

"I ask, 'who am I?'"

An adopted person in the United States grows up learning that he or she has been chosen, specially picked out and a special child. In the words of one adoptee: "When I was growing up everything was cool. It was like the chosen child, read to me from bed." Most adoptees learned about adoption through the "chosen-child story," the origin myth that has guided adoption practice from the post-World War II era until the present. The story tells of a child chosen by parents who really want and love him. The story does not tell about the parent who had to relinquish a child, and for adoptees, cool as the story might be, it left out a crucial piece of their identity. An adoptee has been given away by one and taken in by another parent. This "fact of life" shaped the accounts of growing up adopted for virtually every adoptee I interviewed.

Adoptees viewed being chosen as a burden. The child who was special had to act in certain ways: once "chosen," adoptees said, they might be "unchosen." Adoptive childhood was contingent, a matter of having been picked out by, not *born to,* someone. This was not the ordinary way of coming into a family, and adoptees struggled with the consequences of that difference. The details of the struggle constitute the themes of this chapter. It begins with the experience of being told. "Telling" dominates adoptee memories of childhood and shapes interpretations of fictive kinship. Many had heard the chosen-child story; for those who had not, the story was part of the milieu—an aspect of adoption in American society. The story was a reminder of the disappearance of a birthparent and of the lack of "blood" in their ties to a family. It was also a reminder of the stories adoptees did not have: a mother's rush to the hospital, relatives celebrating the arrival of a newborn, a remarkable and remarked on resemblance to a parent. Some adoptees were more bothered by "missing pieces" and "gaps" than others; all were aware of the changes in adoption policy inspired by those adoptees who demanded more information and, perhaps, a meeting with a birthparent. Some would themselves eventually start down the road of searching, for facts or for family or for both.[1]

Recent publicity about adoption—the controversy over open records, reunion stories—also influence interpretations of growing up adopted. The stories in Betty Jean Lifton's books, and in other personal accounts, provide images and references that "make storyable" the experience of being adopted even for those who only knew these writings second-hand. For some adoptees, being adopted was not a central part of their lives. But they were exposed to the winds of change in adoption and expressed the fact of its nonsignificance differently in the late 1980s than they would have a decade earlier.[2] In volunteering to talk with me, adoptees, too, "came out of the closet" and subjected their kinship to the kind of scrutiny their adoptive parents had had to face and their birthparents had insisted upon undertaking. As they looked back, adoptees like adoptive parents and birthparents redesigned the past in the light of the present. The material in this chapter, then, represents the "retrospective introspection of adults adopted as children" (McWhinnie 1967, 257)—a contribution to the critique of fictive kinship emerging from the triad in the late twentieth century.

I interviewed twenty-eight adoptees whom I met through support groups, agencies, and personal contacts. Of the twenty-eight, twenty-two were female, a ratio that reflects willingness to talk about the subject rather than the ratio of female to male adoptees in the population, which is about equal. Age ranged from a 16-year-old who had been adopted two years earlier to individuals in their 60s. (Two older adoptees had recently learned of their adoptive status.) Other sociodemographic data, like education, economic level, religion, and life-stage, emerged as part of a self-description and I refer to them in that context. Three of the adoptees were birthmothers, two were adoptive parents, and one was a biological parent, an adoptive parent, and a foster parent.

The majority of individuals I interviewed had been adopted as infants. The exceptions included the 16-year-old adopted at 14, a woman who had been adopted once at 4 and again, after a disruption, at 9 and a third who, as she put it, "walked into the house on my own two feet"—she was 3 at the time of her adoption. All were "stranger" adoptions: none had been adopted within a family or by someone already considered a relative.[3] Not all had been told of their adoptions in childhood or by their parents. Several told me they had "suspicions" that led them to ask or otherwise discover the "truth."

"It's something I've always known"

Whether or not they had been told in childhood or by their parents, most adoptees insisted they "always knew" they were adopted. Yet how they actually found out was a key feature of every adoptee's experience. Suddenly at that moment they realized they were different from "everyone else." It seemed, as Lifton put it, that they had never been born.

Adoptees did not always learn from their parents, or did not always like the way their parents told them about adoption.[4] Some families did keep adoption a secret, not telling the child or, if the child knew, not telling anyone else. "My cousins never told me I was adopted and every one of those lousy kids knew it," said a woman who found out from an uncle, when she was an adolescent. "And never once did those stinking kids tell me I was adopted and everyone knew it. I can't believe it. And my [older] brother never told me either." But most did learn from their parents, even if it was mentioned once and never spoken of again. In some families, however, adoption as a piece of information just came and went—nothing extraordinary for the child or, apparently, for the parents. The decade of the adoption did not determine this ease as much as did the "emotional tone" of the family—just as the literature said.

"Ok, from what I understand I was placed with my adoptive parents at age 6 months and whenever I could understand the concept, I was told that I was adopted along with my sister who was not a biological sister, to the best of my knowledge, let's put it that way," said a man who had been adopted in the 1950s. Others had heard the word from "the very beginning," and always knew they were adopted. "I don't remember being told that I was adopted," said a woman in her 20s. "I mean I know that I was adopted and I always knew but it didn't seem to be that big of a thing that I remember the time that they told me. I know I was, I was 5 or younger and I knew at an early stage and I think that's a real appropriate thing to do, the earlier the better."[5] She went on to tell me about how much her father doted on her: "I was always the apple of his eye."

Being adopted could feel like an ordinary part of family life. "I really don't remember when I was told," said another woman. "They told me so young and so I just, it's something I've always known and never considered myself any different just because of that. I really have never—I should have asked my mother just when she told me but I'm not sure she even could remember. I think it was just something that was taken for granted. I do not remember being sat down and told 'you are adopted.' And quite honestly I never gave it much thought as a child, although my parents, six years later, had my brother who was their biological child. But it never occurred to me that there was anything different about he or I [sic]. It was just a fact of life. So however they did it, they did a wonderful job doing it."

"Just a fact of life." Adoptees who were content with the way they had been told tended to feel good about everything in the family. Telling became a measure of how good, or bad, an adoptive family was. "I can't remember the first time I was told, it is as if I was always aware of it. And to be honest, in fact we were friends with a family who, their children were adopted and they weren't told until later on and they got all bent out of shape, and I really can't understand the reason for that. I mean, if your life has been good up to that point, I mean I consider my parents my parents." As this adoptee's anecdotal comparison suggests, a successful telling confirmed the bond between adoptive parent and child; the acknowledgment of difference solidified the relationship for him. Adoptees who were told, in this interpretation, did not doubt where they belonged. "I wouldn't trade for anything."

But a number of adoptees had not learned about adoption from their own parents. They had had suspicions, and growing up adopted meant being sensitive to hints that they were not like everyone else.

As one woman recalled, when her adopted brother was brought home, "I must have had a suspicion at that time, although they never told me, in fact they never told me I was adopted . . . I must have had a suspicion because I thought at that time that I would try very hard to remember what they said about his family so that I could tell him." This woman found out about her own adoption only when she was in college, and then only by "tricking" a man who found her attractive. "There was this fella I knew who was real, he was real on to me, and I didn't really like him but he liked me and I tricked him one time into saying it." His statement confirmed her suspicions; "because of my brother's adoption I had pretty good inklings." And another woman reported: "I suppose I was about ten or so and I had an inkling that something was a little different because of the age difference [between her and her parents] and that."

A few who suspected also asked questions, prompted by an experience or unexpected information. "We were doing a lot of studying in genetics [at the university]," explained an adopted woman, and "there were just too many things that didn't add up. I went home one day and said to my parents, 'I know I'm your daughter but I am not your natural daughter.' [It was] the first time I ever saw my father cry." This confrontation had a happy ending, however. "Then my brother came upstairs. . . . He said, 'What's going on?' And my dad told him. He said, 'So what? She's still my sister.' And I think that explains my feelings about being adopted beautifully."

But not all approaches on the part of a suspicious adoptee were received well by parents. As one woman recalled: "Because I think that subconsciously you know that there is something different about you even though I used to ask if I was adopted and everybody, my mother would say, 'Oh no.' 'Where are my baby pictures?' 'Well, it was during the Depression and we just don't have any.' I thought, gee, that's strange, because there's all these pictures of my brother and no pictures of me." This adoptee eventually did find out the truth, but not from her adoptive parents. "I was in eighth grade and I was sitting in my uncle's dentist chair and he was drilling my teeth and all of a sudden he said, 'Did your mother and father ever find out who your real parents were?' I said 'No' and I started to cry. And he said, 'Boy, you sure are a baby today.' And I said, 'Well, you are hurting me.' And I let it go at that. I didn't tell him that he had told me."

Occasionally the parents themselves could not keep the secret, revealing the adoption at a moment of anger and loss of control. "So I went from 2 to that age of 12 assuming that I was a natural child to these particular parents. And at 12 my knowledge of being not a natural child to the foster parents [she was never legally adopted] came at a dinner table whereby I spilled my milk and the foster, my foster mother said something to the effect of, 'I'm very glad that you don't belong to us because I wouldn't want such a sloppy, awful child being mine.'" This adoptee did not claim that she had had inklings; learning was a complete shock. Another learned when her parents were in the midst of a bitter divorce and adoption, as she put it, was just "one of the cats that came out of the bag." Most adoptees were convinced the news would come out somehow or other and not necessarily at moments of anger or distress. Secrets could not be kept forever.

This was a central argument for adoptee support groups. "The adopted always find out, sooner or later. And even when they are unaware of their status as an adopted member of the family, they do frequently feel different, without knowing why," an ALMA brochure (1988) reminded readers. "Adoptees who are not told somehow know it," said the coordinator of the support group I attended, "something doesn't fit." It was not exactly that clues would inevitably be left around but that adoptees would have a strong sense of their difference from everyone else. With this sense, an incident or glance or slip of the tongue could give the whole story away. Adopted people reported a variety of ways in which they "found out," and then knew the reason for feelings they had "always" had. One woman told me of her discovery: "I remember going to a big formal party at a girl's house. I came home to tell my folks about the girl and she's adopted and I remember the funny look on my folks' face."

Feeling different was a dominant theme in what I heard from adoptees. The manifestations were not always the same, but the strength of the feeling came through in every case. Some put it in terms of loneliness and others in terms of thinking themselves "strange." Some were analytical and others just reminiscent about this aspect of growing up adopted.

"I think, I feel like I knew that my original parents were gone at six weeks. Now some people will tell you that you can't know at six weeks, but I don't know, you can never prove it one way or another. But it's so deep in my consciousness that it was communicated to me in some way or some later date than six weeks." This woman's account of difference was a rather sophisticated version of what others expressed as "pieces missing" or a "feeling of emptiness."[6] But finding out about adoption did not necessarily lead to conversations, adoptees told me.[7] "And I asked her a few questions and she was not really thrilled with answering them," an adoptee remembered confronting her adoptive mother. "But she told me that my parents had been married and were divorced and that if I ever wanted to know anything, she had a friend that knew them. But then I could feel the conversation was over and I knew she didn't want to discuss it and didn't want to be asked about them at all."

"I've known since as little as I can remember that I was an adopted kid. I just put that on the shelf." But putting it on the shelf, this 40-year-old man recalled, had not been his idea. "My parents never talked about us being adopted. We were just their kids." In whole-heartedly accepting the "just-like" principle, his parents managed to suggest that adoption was taboo and ought not be mentioned. "I felt like as a child that there were a whole lot of things that I couldn't talk about. So anyway, I think this is something that's, as I say, it still does in some way affect my difficulty in knowing when I can tell people that I'm adopted." Sometimes the just-like principle had a harsher consequence, banishing the birthmother and the past. "I think I was about 12 when I started, 'Hey, what happened to my mom? My grandma?' And she said, 'what happened before you came in this house is inconsequential, and I am your mother.' And that ended the subject."

The as-if-begotten principle influenced those adoptive parents for whom a "rejection of difference" impulse was strong (Kirk 1984). "But it was never talked about even though it was an open fact that Sonia [the adoptee referred to herself in the third person] was adopted and that Sonia was an adopted child of the Lundstroms and her sister was too and everybody knew in the community. It was nothing that we talked about." Other adoptees were not so tolerant about their parents' secrecies as Sonia was. "There were no brothers or sisters and whenever the, anything concerning adoption came up, the subject was immediately changed. It was, I suppose, thirty years ago and so it wasn't as spoken or as open as we discuss it, as it is now-adays," said a woman, angry in retrospect. She went on: "I tried to talk to mother about it and she got so upset and so embarrassed about it that I never pursued it anymore." An adoptee with a good relation-ship with her adoptive parents told me: "we were close, but the min-ute I mentioned anything about the adoption, she [mother] would get very cool, cold."[8]

One or two adoptees blamed themselves for the lack of discussion. "We just didn't talk about it. I think they wanted to talk about it, but I just never felt that comfortable. But they were always open if I asked questions but I always felt funny asking them too much. I didn't know how they really felt about it."[9] In the end, unlike this woman, most adoptees blamed their parents, not themselves, for the awkward silences. "And that is one of the things that you read about, that you kind of pick up a sense that you are not supposed to do that [ask questions]. It's not that it is ever verbally said. Sometimes it is, 'don't ever ask.' Kids try and they get a real bad response. But sometimes you just know it ahead of time." "That look" on a parent's face warned the adoptee that the subject was uncomfortable. "If the word came up, well it's sort of stigmas, we don't talk about that. It's like you're the bastard child—we don't want to talk about that. And if you begin to raise those questions, then we have to talk about that, about how we feel about bastard children, all the stuff that brings up, and we don't want to have to look at that. So there's all this stuff about 'you can't.'" Talking about adoption meant talking about illegitimacy, sex, infertility, and the decision to have children at all.

"She couldn't have a child of her own"

"I think I could say that—my father is a Catholic and in those days Catholic men had families and my father wasn't able to do that. I truly don't know [exactly why they adopted]," a man in his 40s explained his situation. Most adoptees did not know a great deal about why they were adopted and assumed what everyone else did, that their parents wanted children. "Well, it was brought up almost in passing and, you know, with the understanding that, that my mother couldn't bear children," another man told me what he knew. "You know, that in itself, that, you understood why. You know, very plain and simple because if you take some of my relatives, like my Uncle Joe had seven I believe, another uncle three. There's breeders in this family, let's put it that way."

A few adoptees knew a little more. "And this was a case of a middle-class couple that had had seven, Esther [mother] had had seven miscarriages. She had lost seven children, and she was determined to have a child, absolutely determined, whatever that would cost. And so I became that child," reported a woman. She interpreted her mother's motives as a kind of competitiveness, a need to have what everyone else had rather than a loving gesture or nurturing impulse. "And unfortunately instead of a lot of mothering going on, it seemed more like a care-for situation as you would sort of a pet, or a doll or something that she wanted." Characterization of the adoptive parent as consumer echoed the birthparent viewpoint: those who could not "have" children took them. Adoptees who remembered unhappy childhoods were most likely to frame adoption this way, but they were not alone in being troubled by parents who "got" rather than gave birth to children.

Making "storyable" the experience of growing up adopted accentuated the unnaturalness of a fictive kinship. The interpretation came out in negative characterizations of a mother who was unable to "have a baby," characterizations that if exaggerated also reflected a cultural association between the "physical realities" of pregnancy and birth and the capacity for being a real mother. So even adoptees whose childhoods were apparently placid imposed a stern image on their adoptive parents—specifically, their mothers. This characterization of a stern adoptive mother was then completed by a contrast with an idealized birthmother: a warm, generous, loving, and sexually productive woman. So powerful was this contrast that adoptive mothers who had once been fertile were not spared. "I know she did have a child," one adoptee related. "They had a child and the girl died, I think, when she was 18 months old. But I sort of couldn't discern that there was any connection between that and adopting me." The adoption, as she perceived it, was done to "keep up" with the rest of the family.

The characterization of adoptive mothers had a component of circular reasoning. Adoptive mothers had not had children, adoptees implied, because they were cold and asexual women—unable to give love, they were unable to have a child. Moreover, not only the child but also the father suffered from a mother's coldness and selfishness.[10] "But she wasn't, I mean, for example, the most physicalness I ever saw on my mother and father was shaking hands or a peck on the cheek and that was it," a middle-aged adoptee recalled. "They didn't even hold hands, nothing. It was like ice. When you said goodnight, it was 'goodnight, I'm going to bed.' Everything was ice cold, and it wasn't just with me, I mean their relationship was ice cold. That's why I said he should have been a minister. I think he was living in celibacy anyway [laughing]." Another adoptee blamed her mother not only for putting her father "out" but also for banishing any talk of love and sex from the household. "My father slept on a cot in their little dining room, that was half this size [the room we were in], if you can envision it, this little weak cot, and she had the big bedroom. And that's the way from the time I walked into that house. So I never— and there was no talk what husbands and wives do. Or how babies came to be."

Similarly linking performance as a mother with biology, an adopted man attributed his mother's lack of warmth to the fact that she missed the experience of "conception, creation, gestation, and parturition" (Schneider 1984, 55). "But god knows, at work I hear all the time, you know, women talking about their pregnancies, you know, and how long they were in labor, and how long that and how long this, and how much weight they gained and how their figure never turned out the same and all this stuff. . . . It's war stories. But the adopted mother, the adoptive mother, never has that, if they've never had anything, even a miscarriage, and that's a tough . . ." One way or another, more than one adopted person voiced the view that infertility and emotional stinginess were connected—including one woman who said her mother was so "expressively loving," she ought to have had "many babies." That was unusual; the more common formulation was negative. Explaining her mother's "total inability" to express her feelings, an adoptee said, "She has never ever and never will come to grips with the fact that she couldn't have a child of her own."

One adoptee in her early 20s was more sympathetic while still linking being "fully" a woman with bearing a child. "Cause like my mom, I guess she didn't feel like she was a woman, you know, because she didn't have a child. She has somebody else's child. I think that would be real hard because I think the greatest thing in the world would be having a baby, you know, carrying it and everything." This adoptee also remarked on how hard it must have been when her mother had to say to doctors, "well, I didn't have her but this is my child"—neatly capturing the dilemma of adoptive parenthood. Like other female adoptees, she also talked about having her own children: "Oh, I would love to have children right now if I could."

Female adoptees talked more about their own parenthood than did male adoptees. This would not have been surprising, except that the men I interviewed as frequently as women linked an adoptive mother's personality to her failure to reproduce "naturally." At the same time, considering whether or not they would be biological parents did not frame men's experiences of adoption as thoroughly as it did that of women. For their part, female adoptees frequently compared themselves with two mothers. My adoptive mother, one said, found "everything disgusting—she was made in stone"; but she also knew her other mother's story: pregnant at 14, struggling to keep a child she could not take care of. The concept of "mother," therefore, was split into the dimensions of sexuality, love, and ability to take care of a child—and divided between two mothers.

The kinship terms "mother" and "father" are generally problematic in the adoptive situation. They float free of their conventional attachments to genealogy, to a sexual relationship between parents, and to a "natural" link with the child. Yet they remain the only terms adoptees have for all their parents; consequently an adopted person who thinks about his or her background becomes an analyst of semantics and metaphor. As one expert on adoption put it: " 'Mother' (or 'parents') may now [when the adoptee learns about adoption] undergo a change in semantic status for the child, becoming more abstract and denoting some ill-defined qualities shared by his own 'mother' and an unknown person" (Nickman 1986, 371; cf. Triseliotis 1973, 161). The adoptees I interviewed worked out the difficulty by making the concept of "mother" concrete, through a contrast of one mother with another. Furthermore, it was around motherhood and not fatherhood—which remained abstract—that adoptees played out the distinctiveness of their parentage and did their best to define the terms they had to use. In the process of contrasting a birth with an adoptive mother, adoptees also (inadvertently) brought forward the central paradox of American adoption: a loving mother gives away the child to whom she is naturally, passionately, devoted.

"Knowing my mother gave me away"

However little adoptees knew about why their parents had adopted, they knew even less about why their other parents had surrendered. They did have bits of information: the sketch of physical traits, educational background, and hobbies that their adoptive parents had (usually) been given. From these details, and a contrast with the parents they knew, adoptees constructed a picture of parents who had had to give away a child. And just as a mother was the focus of the adoptive relationship, so, too, a mother was the focus of the imagined genealogical relationship. It did not matter that biological was in fact *sexual* reproduction; motherhood was the issue and fathers only secondarily significant.[11]

As one adoptee said, "I'd come up with questions once in a while and the answers were, 'we don't have any information and the only information we have is that your mother was 100 percent Welsh.'" And another: "Well, just that she was seventeen years old, she was Sicilian. The doctor said she was a beautiful young girl, that type of thing. But that's really basically it. Brownish hair, that's it." The information most adoptees had was all their parents knew—or wanted to tell. Adoptees also made things up; fantasies were a part of growing up adopted. "And I think that would make a difference, don't you? Growing up knowing something," a middle-aged woman said sadly. "But it was like I had a nightmare that never stopped and a dream that would never go away." And another: "To have nothing, it's like fantasizing around the paper." Like birthparents, adoptees used the word paper to represent the non-blood and, by extension, insubstantial aspects of adoptive kinship. "Paper" stood for a (precariously) contracted rather than a (permanently) consanguineal relationship. A blank paper also gave rein to an imagined relationship.

The available literature on adoption has a good deal to say about fantasy. So did adoptees themselves.[12] "And you know the fantasies that you had, I think every adopted kid has a fantasy about what their natural parents are like, and intellectually they know, they may know that their mother might be rich and, you know, married to some rich guy in the suburbs or whatever. I don't know, I don't care about that particularly," one man explained to me. A few minutes later he referred to the imagined birthmother again: "Maybe she's not this happy, serene, wonderful, warm, caring, you know, together person that you always wished your adoptive mother was. Which is the other thing, cause when you're adopted you always could wish that you had this, you could always have this fantasy of this other one out there that was better." He added: "Most natural kids have these fantasies at one point or another that they're adopted. Which is essentially the same fantasy, out there there is somebody better. Well, adopted kids have that, you know, I mean it's not only a fantasy, but it's, there's more of a possibility there is someone else out there, it's not something that you just toss away."

Fantasies were not just about a "better" parent but, as this man suggests, specifically about a mother who gave away a child. The problem became one of reconciling the image of a warm, caring, and "together person" with a woman who rejected her child. One adoptee solved this for himself. "I've just had a fantasy for a number of years, I don't mean in any real way, just sort of like the only loving person that I had in my life was the Nanny that I had for years. And the fantasy was that she was my real [birth] mother, without family and penurious and so my other mother would keep her on, but she was looking out for me whereas my real [adoptive] mother didn't." But he said this mockingly; like other adoptees, he knew he had been "given away."

"Let it here be remembered that every adoptee, as child and as adult, has to come to grips with having once been given up by biological parents" (Kirk 1983, xiv). "I think it just always bothered me, knowing my mother gave me away," an adopted person told me. Adoptees wanted to know about the surrender, a story the adoptive parents did not always know (at least until recently) and often were reluctant to repeat if they did.[13] A few adoptees (especially younger ones) had heard anecdotes. "And like she was flown into Memphis to have a baby and I guess apparently flown back. My mom [birthmother], she was 5' 7", green hair, oh god, green eyes and brown hair and my dad was 6' 4" with blond hair and blue eyes. He was going to college and she was just a, I guess she worked in a town or wherever they lived. She didn't do anything, I think. My dad was 19 and she was 18. I guess then if somebody was going to have a baby, uh-oh. They just like moved her away for a little bit." Most adoptees would probably also have agreed with the woman who said: "it was just, you know, just a lot of shadowy-type stories that didn't make a lot of sense to me."[14]

These stories rang changes on the conventional account of a surrender. "My mother's youngest sister, in a conversation with me along the line, I imagine I was maybe 12 or so, told me that I was the oldest child of an improvident musician who couldn't keep me, and a very good family. Which is a very typical thing that gets said," this woman pointed out.[15] "And that was an interesting story for me and I believed her." Others also accepted what they had been told—perhaps until they brought it up with me. And even then the conventional story was persuasive, as for this man: "I understood the reasons why, what for, I was put up for adoption. In 1953 an unwed mother does not normally keep the baby. I mean, history dictates that." Another adoptee added a note of admiration in repeating a similar interpretation of surrender. "I can also say that I have a lot of respect for my biological mother because back then [1950s], I assume she was not married, and back then to have a kid out of wedlock was sort of taboo and it took a lot of guts."

The coordinator of the adoptee support group I attended applauded such positive stories and did not let her audience blame the birthmother. Unwed mothers, she reminded us, had no social or economic support—and this probably did cover the circumstances under which most ASG members had been relinquished. "You have to stop and realize that today maybe you can get on mother's assistance and maybe there is something to help you, but back when you [hypothetical adoptee] were born—they were born 18, 20, 30, 40 years ago and there was nothing. When I was a child there was absolutely nothing but Depression. And women didn't even work then except for as baby governesses or waitresses or things like that." She continued: "Plus the fact that 18–20 years ago it was something that just was not done. The family was ostracized and it was usually the family that made you do it, made you give up the child."

Adoptees who talked with me ended up chafing at the conventional stories during their interviews; they wanted to know specifics, not just the social circumstances of a surrender. The adoptee who fantasized that his Nanny was his mother also had his own surrender story. "It would blow me away, for example, if the two of them were actually together. That would be a real trip and a half. The worst scenario would be if, that I had been the kid who missed the train. That in fact he had come back from the war and that I had been adopted and they couldn't find out who I was—. And they went on and got married and had a wonderful, happy life and had three other kids." The thought that relinquishment might not have been necessary troubled other adoptees as well: the kid who just missed being with his real parents seemed even more a "stranger" in the adoptive family. This adoptee also had a version of the mistake that led to his birth: "What I call the Fuck Story, which is how I got conceived. I mean I have actually gone back, I was born in July, so I have to have been conceived whatever nine months before that is—something like November—and a cold winter's night, and my mother being real young and my father sort of being a sailor and going off to war and 'this is our last chance, honey, and we can't get married now, but we will when I get back and this is the way that you will show that you really love me' and all that stuff. So I have that."

Still, an unexpected pregnancy did not completely explain giving up a child. Nor did the chosen-child story, which so strenuously emphasized being wanted that not being wanted was left unresolved.

"I'm adopted, I'm chosen"

"I was a little kid, I guess. I was told when I was really little the story about they picked me out and I was special. So that makes you feel good." Since the 1940s, the chosen-child story, emphasizing the parents' desire for a child and the child's special qualities, has been the standard way of explaining adoption to a child.

The story appears in adoptive parent manuals decade after decade, little changed in its basic thrust.[16] The gist of the story is: two people wanted a baby and could not give birth to one, so they went to an agency (or individual) and chose a "very special" baby, bringing it home to be a full member of their family. Simple and generous in many ways, the chosen-child story yielded interpretations of parenthood, love, belonging, identity, and relatedness that did not always sit well with the adoptees who heard it as their origin myth. Besides leaving out the other set of parents, the notion of being chosen brought its own particular burden. Does a "picked-out" person really belong to his or her parents, especially in a culture that assumes people come inevitably and naturally into the family? Not only did choice seem unnaturally arbitrary, but for some adoptees the whole notion of choice in adoption itself was a lie.

"When I was growing up everything was cool," said one man. "It was like the chosen child [story], read to me from bed. My sister and I used to sit on my mother's bed, you know, and have the chosen child read to us from as early as I can remember. And if it's as early as I can remember then it's earlier than my sister can remember. So, and we used to brag that we were adopted and we used to go around the neighborhood, 'I'm adopted, I'm chosen, you weren't, ha ha.' And the, you know, and it was always something to brag about." Confidence gained from being chosen was exactly the effect adoption experts wanted the story to have, and it worked—from time to time. "So what," an adoptee responded to a friend who mentioned adoption, "my mom and dad picked me, your mom and dad are stuck with you." As a new girl, another adoptee remembered, "one of the ways that I got some status in the community was to tell my story because that was different from everything else that came up among the children in the neighborhood."[17]

At various points in their lives, adoptees had turned, or tried to turn, the chosen-child story to their advantage. The gesture was a way of exploiting rather than succumbing to a sense of difference. "I always considered myself somewhat unique being adopted," a man assured me, with incomplete modesty. "But yes, I've always considered it just another unique quality. That and being born on Friday the 13th." "Like I said," he repeated later, "I have always considered it a unique quality. And being adopted, you know that my parents, they wanted me. I was a wanted child, which was a good feeling, too."

Because their parents viewed them as special, adoptees said, they were given especially indulgent attention. And if not actually spoiled by that indulgence, adoptees certainly had advantages in the family. "I think maybe they bent over backwards for me sometimes. I thought they yelled at her more," said a woman, comparing herself with her sister, a biological child. "I thought they were nicer to me because they didn't want to hurt my feelings or anything, but they treated us really good." Like birthparents, adoptees understood adoption in terms of moving a child from a "disadvantaged" mother to a well-off couple, and put it in terms of getting everything they wanted. But there was something more here: an insight into the thinness of a contracted bond that might be "fleshed out" with special attentions to the child. "I was treated real nice and . . . had everything I wanted, ballet lessons, piano lessons, all these one-week courses that the other kids [had to ask for]—'I have to have these, mom, I have to have ballet and I have to learn piano.'"

Some adoptees described the negative side of indulgence. "It was like the whole time I was growing up I got whatever I wanted but I wasn't a brat—do you know what I'm saying? So when I got old enough they said, 'we are going to let you go with your freedom until you mess up.' Well, when I messed up they didn't want to admit it." In her 20s, she had messed up with drugs and by her account was never reprimanded by her parents. Devotion was a mixed business: on the one hand, confirming a child's place in the family and, on the other, underlining the adoptee's difference from everybody else. This adoptee also remembered, with ambivalence, an overly fond grandmother. "Yeah, and my Gram, my God, forget it. She loves me more than she loves any of them [cousins]. When my grandfather died she said to the priest, 'this is Andrea and she is adopted and we love her more than, we love her more than we love our other grandchildren,' in front of the whole family."

In other words, they were *too* special, which brought with it its own problems. Preeminently, they expected to have to fulfill the promise of having been chosen and that was what they thought their parents wanted. "I was told that I was chosen, that I was the best person in the world," a participant at a support group meeting told us, and described the tension of having to be a "good girl." "What they told me was, they looked in the nursery and they saw hundreds of babies in the nursery and the social worker let them pick the very prettiest baby." So a woman began her story about choice and, by implication, un-choice. "And they picked me because I was pretty and because I had long fingers, and mom wanted a baby that could play the piano well. And then, all of a sudden—I was a very pretty baby, I'll show you some pictures, I was a beautiful baby—I became very ugly, ugly duckling. I did. So I think, 'I let them down. They chose me because I'm pretty and I let them down, I'm an ugly duckling.' Then I started to take piano lessons and I bombed out. . . . I wouldn't practice, I never got anywhere and they [adoptive parents] made me quit. Here these long beautiful fingers that I had, they didn't do what they were supposed to do and that's what they picked me out for. I let them down."

The swan who became an ugly duckling appeared in other accounts. "Again, part of it feels like I am the duck in a group of swans." This adoptee also linked the image to his version of the chosen-child story. How good did you have to be to belong? Only now, the adoptee said, at nearly 50 years old had he settled some of the childhood issue: "which leaves me with like 3 percent of my old stuff of like I'll never be good enough. But it's really only 3 percent. I am willing to go to my grave with that 3 percent."

The burden of being "good enough" persisted into adulthood for those adoptees who felt this consequence of being chosen. As the coordinator of ASG, who identified perfectionism as the adoptee's problem in general, said: "I was about 38 years old . . . and I lost control of my perfect household. And I couldn't handle it because I was striving for perfection. And when the kids [her children] all hit their teenage years there was just no more perfection, gone with the wind!" An adoptee had to prove him- or herself worthy. A woman I interviewed put the problem bluntly: my "whole life," she said, "was spent trying to somehow show my adoptive parents I was worth adopting. I was worth—as one, as my dad's business partner said, 'you're lucky that they pulled you out of the gutter.' So that, you know, what does that do to your self-esteem?"

Being "rescued" confused the meaning of being "wanted," and the confusion wove through more than one adoptee's memories of childhood. "So then you're in a situation of inability to deal," another person remarked. "It's really easy to take that personally and say, 'Oh, I am a bad person again, what did I do wrong?' And in fact you don't even have a clue." I reminded this adoptee of her current success. "Well, that's the old overachiever. Like keep busy and if I do enough good things I will finally get approval from the outside world."

Some adoptees rejected the idea of choice altogether. They had not been selected, but placed. Adoption, as one adoptee said, "is really a lottery. It's a fucking lottery is what it is." Nor, in their view, did their parents have any choice. Another adoptee regarded the chosen-child story as one more lie in adoption. "Oh well, number one, when you find out that you're, you find out you weren't chosen and adoption is all a bunch of lies, secrecy, secret lies, and secrecy or one or the other or both. And I wasn't chosen, they took whoever happened to come along. I just happened to be born and they got whatever baby that sister [her birthmother] happened to get." Social workers placed babies without rhyme, reason, or sensitivity—though maybe swayed by "market forces." One man mocked agency policies: "But it's kind of like, 'well, we only have five [babies] in here now.' I mean, it's like when I was in retailing, it's like, 'here, we've got five here, which one goes to that folks, which one goes to this folks,' and stuff like that." Like him, few of the adoptees I met were angry at their parents so much as at a system that made their origins a lie and belonging to a family a matter of contingency.

Being chosen simply did not fit with cultural assumptions about parenthood. Selection made a tenuous bond, a frail basis for what was supposed to be a nonconditional, enduring relationship. In talking about choice, and whether or not their parents had chosen them, adoptees also identified signs of commitment in their parents. Said one woman: "Then like right after they adopted me, I was like a little over a year old when they adopted me legally in court, right after that I got deathly sick and they thought I was going to die and they were like, 'we just got you, please don't do this.'" After the near tragedy, she continued, there was no question but that she belonged to the family. Hers was a happy understanding of "belonging." Other adoptees did not share that understanding. Some, accentuating (as birth-parents did) the "possessiveness" the word also connoted, described a different sort of belonging.

"It was something you wanted," said an adoptee about her mother's decision to adopt a baby. "You went out and bought it or purchased it and you dressed it up and fed it and clothed it." Later, she told me how strenuously her mother had objected to her marriage. "It was like, 'this is my possession' and no matter who it would have been—." And she provided her own image of the connection. "There was just no way that she's ever, she was ever going to cut a nonumbilical cord, I mean, to use that kind of expression. There was just no way that she was going to ever cut a cord because I guess she felt that through her blood, sweat, tears, money, or whatever—she's really money-minded, money meant a lot to her—that she had made a *purchase,* that she wasn't about to let somebody else take her purchase."

The most comfortable sign of belonging was involvement in a whole family. Then the connection between parent and child gained texture and solidity from the other connections; the more people, the more related one was—as if extending also intensified kinship. "But yes, it's a close-knit family on my mother's side, with the kids, and I have one special aunt and uncle, my Auntie Bea and my Uncle Dave. They have four children of their own and I am godparent of their youngest child, Dylan, and we're very close. And there's other cousins and other aunts and uncles around, and we're close too." In his statement, "close" replaced the symbolism of blood. An older adoptee, from a quite different background, pointed to the same "closeness": "So, of course, my cousin and I, well I'm two years older than he is. But, so we kind of grew up as brother and sister . . . we're close, a close relationship."

Not being close meant being distant and, precisely, being different. For adoptees, the foremost sign of difference was not looking like anyone else in the family. And if they did resemble a person in the adoptive family—which was perfectly possible, given the policy of matching—this was not entirely comfortable. One woman told me: "I look like my mom, you know, I don't look like my dad. . . . We have the same color hair and the same color eyes. But nobody, if you looked at us, nobody would say, you don't really look alike. I don't look like the Gordon side of the family, they have these little skinny legs and these big stomachs and I don't look like that and their dark hair. But I look like my mom's side." Then she launched into a description of the fights she and her mother had because, as she explained, "we think so differently."

"I look like my mother. Since I was knee-high people would say it." This adoptee, a man, went on to emphasize that the resemblance was all in the eye of the beholder, a "trick" played on the outside world. Physical likenesses, he implied, were superficial—perceived by people who assumed that parent and child "naturally" shared features. People, another adoptee remembered, "would pinch your cheek and say what a wonderful little darling child you were and how much you looked like your mother and I knew that that wasn't true. So my suspicions of what people tell me—and I was real suspicious for a long period of time, it's not quite as bad anymore."

In many cases, adoptive parents encouraged the fiction that an adopted child looked like someone in the adoptive family. It was understandable: "looking-like" signals genuine kinship in American culture. "Of course, when I was growing up in my family, in my adoptive family and probably lots of families, people talk about who do you look like," a woman remembered. "And so, in a sense, my parents pretended that I looked like my adoptive father since he was dark and . . . so that's what they said. But . . . this always gave me a certain, you know, falseness." As with an amended birth certificate, the very contrivance here also caused some distress. "And of course, yes, I don't look like my family. . . . And they built me an identity," another woman commented. "I was supposed to look like, take after, resemble, everything of my Aunt Flora. She was an old maid, overweight, looked like the Buddha, put henna on her hair. I thought for sure when I got old I was going to look like that. And that was a problem."

As with an amended birth certificate, too, a contrived resemblance reminded people of the real similarities between relatives. "I want to see a face that has similar genes to mine," an adoptee said, arguing that she lacked what "everyone else" had. Another adoptee shared this view: "There's almost some innate understandings among biological parents and siblings that is not there among adoptive parents and siblings. Because my temperament is just so different than either my mother or my father." For adoptees, creatures of their culture, blood was thicker, and showed up more truly, than water. The conviction came out especially when adoptees talked about having their own, biological, children. "When people do point out the characteristics about my children that have come from me, which may be mannerisms or voice tone or style or something, I am pleased," an adoptee admitted. "I am kind of amused that I am a fast driver and I have got a son who drives just like me. You know, I think, you know it's not marvelous, but it's funny that it's true." The significance of biology was so persuasive that she did not consider a similar voice or the same driving habits superficial: "They all sound alike and they're related to me."

When there was a genealogical bond, resemblance was not just in the eye of the beholder. "And of course I notice this in particular with my own daughter, you know . . . I think she looks like me and other people think that she looks like me—a little bit like my husband, but probably more like me. And you know, I think that it is, well, I can see that in some ways it's sort of reassuring to feel that you look like people in your family," said another adoptee about her daughter. She linked this kind of kinship to her experiences growing up adopted. "I remember feeling before I had my daughter that I wanted to have the experience of living with somebody who was biologically connected to me. And, as I said, I do like the idea that in her case I can see this resemblance."

The need to feel connected was strong, and for a number of adoptees did seem to be missing from a contrived and contracted relationship. There was no one with "genes like mine," not knowing who you looked like, in a sense, meant not knowing who you were.

"A thousand identities—and yet none"

"Because of this big hole, and you have to jump over it every single day, cause there's a whole big gap in your lives." Like this woman, adoptees talked about a gap or void in their lives that came from not knowing where they came from or who they looked like. People at meetings commonly said, "adoptees don't even know where they originated." As Lifton (1979, 5) has written: "Unlike the *real* orphan who still carries his family name, the Adoptee is cut off completely from his past." The implication of not knowing where you came from, of being cut off from a past, was poignantly felt. The adoptee did not have a complete identity. The "gap" would have to be filled.

What was missing, of course, was "biological background," a physical map of one's self. Hartman (1984, 51) is succinct on this point: "And no matter how early the adoption or how total the cut off from that [birth] family, an important part of an adoptee's identity is deeply rooted in that biological system." An adoptee said to me, "I think heredity has got a lot to do with you and the way you are. It seems like it anyway." Because in the absence of this "core of identity," there is a sense of "isolation, vacuum or emptiness," as Triseliotis (1973, 81) has put it, adoptees need to have information about their biological background "to complete their self-image." One adoptee was as precise: "There's something about feeling that you are centered within yourself, that the people who you are calling your relatives are in a biological sense your relatives. You hear little clips about how blood is thicker than water. I can't relate to that. I don't have blood as far as I know. They are out there somewhere." When you have biological relatives, she continued, "you are a whole person. That part is missing [for the adopted person]. There's a basic physical aspect of our lives that's missing. . . . There is some relation that pumps through a blood line and that is gone [for the adoptee], completely gone."

Another adoptee described how it felt to be without blood, finding no reflection of oneself in anyone else. "I know with me, too, 'who do I look like?' [was important]. I always looked in, I remember . . . just looking up in the clouds. And it's just kind of a blank. I see a body, except that the face was completely blank and trying to get the clouds to make a figure, almost ordering the clouds, go there and make a figure, show me what the face looks like." There was no one with "genes" like hers. The adopted person, Betty Jean Lifton (1979, 72) wrote, "looks in the mirror and wonders whose eyes are looking back at him."[18]

Adoptees were certain they would know the real resemblances; those *showed*. "Mostly all my cousins looked like their sisters and brothers," said an adoptee. "You know, I can *see* who looks like who." Similarities in the adoptive family were counterfeit or "secondary," as one man put it. "And it's interesting that my dad and I have both identical secondary hair characteristics, right down to the bald of the head, down to the hair on the chest, and the beards, almost identical. And, you know, that's just a fluke obviously." Moreover, perceived or arranged resemblances obscured the real likeness with a birth relative. "It used to bother me when people would say, people have said, when I worked at my [adoptive] Dad's store, people would come in, 'oh, you're Harry's daughter, well, I should have known, you look just like him.' And it kinda hurt me." She explained why: "But still, gee, maybe I do look like my father [birthfather] somewhere."

Real likenesses told a person not only who they were in the present but also what they would become in the future. Adoptees lacked such maps, and could not predict whether they would be fat, alcoholic, talented, happy, or sad. "And if that's there and my [adoptive] parents don't drink a thing I still may be an alcoholic or a foodaholic," a man in his 30s said. "Plus the fact your tendency to heart disease, your tendency to diabetes, you know, it's in your genes and no one can change that environment." His context, and the material in adoption literature, supported his point. "And though he has 'psychological' parenting in the adoptive home," wrote Lifton (1979, 5), "he suffers a severe physical deprivation in being cut off from anyone whose body might serve as a model for both the wondrous and fearsome possibilities of his own." At an ASG meeting, a young adoptee said, "You don't even know if your baby is going to be black or white."

Without a past, a person has no future. As an ASG *Newsletter* stated, without a past a person is "rootless." Adoptees embraced this popular concept and linked it to another symbol in American culture, the family tree. "Everybody goes back and looks in their family tree and I can't," an adoptee in her mid-20s said, remembering a class assignment. "Everybody says, we looked back in our family tree and our parents came from Italy and everybody says, 'Bonnaccio, you must be really Italian.' I don't know, yeah, I guess so, I guess I was." Elements of their identity jumbled together as adoptees bemoaned what was "missing." "And people talk about their nationality and who do they look like and pictures and all that kind of—it's very common and I didn't really look like anybody on either side of the family." She solved the problem uncertainly: "my adoptive parent's background, I guess."

The concept of a tree reminded the adoptee that she was not really rooted in a family. "Because I am the part that is grafted, not at the bottom," an older adopted woman reported sadly. Just placed, an adoptee could be moved from here to there, attached to one and then another person. The phrase in adoption literature for the resulting confusion is "genealogical bewilderment."[19] According to this theory, without a firm point of attachment, the adoptee struggles endlessly for an identity. Lifton (1979, 29) put it eloquently: "Everyone identifies with the hero who must go forth into the world alone to search out his origins, but in the Adoptee's case this is a literal quest. At times he feels that he too has a thousand faces, a thousand identities— and yet none."[20] Discovery of origins, then, is crucial to establishing a sense of identity—and not just any origins, but specifically a biological ancestry.

In some ways contradictory to adoption policy, in other ways the claim suits an emphasis on the importance of "heredity" that those who arrange adoptions no longer ignore—and never really did. The coordinator of ASG reminded us that adoptees had "two sets of *real* parents," and went on to argue that, therefore, an adoptee ought to know as much about the "birth" as about the "legal" set.[21] An adoptee carried the argument further when she assured me that adoptees who know something about a birthparent "feel very confident of who they are. If you say, 'who is your mother and father,' of a picture, you know, if you picture everybody, and they know who their birthmother is and you say, 'who is your mother and father?' 'That's my mother and that's my father.' 'And who's this?' 'This is the woman who gave birth to me.'" Adoptees who know nothing feel "lost" and "unreal." "To have some sense of reality is what I wanted and I presume most people want," another adoptee concluded.

Knowing birth relatives and attaining a "sense of reality" underline the physical dimensions considered fundamental to self-identity. The adoptee view was a variation on, not a rejection of, cultural conventions. "An optimal sense of identity," wrote Erik Erikson (1968, 165), "is experienced merely as a sense of psychosocial well-being. Its most obvious concomitants are a feeling of being at home in one's body, a sense of 'knowing where one is going,' and an inner assuredness of anticipated recognition from those who count." Implicit in this definition of identity was the notion of physical continuity over generations. Adoptees missed these elements and found support in published autobiographies. Jean Paton (1968, 241), for example, writes: "The question arises: How does a person reared without immediate signs of kinship acquire the aspects of character which come from a sense of kinship, a sense of belonging to the race, of being continuous with generations past and to come, of being 'on the rope' and not alone on the mountain of Nature's deep and inescapable claim?" The need to find one's place "on the rope," in order to achieve an identity, underlies the movement for change in adoption policy.

Preoccupation with the biological basis of identity also indicates the parameters around artificial kinship in American culture. Different from marriage, the other presumably permanent but chosen relationship, a contracted parent-child bond seems inherently contradictory; culturally, parenthood is inevitable, not arranged. Qualms about an amended birth certificate occur in that context: how could a fact of nature really be rewritten? As an adoptee put it, "whatever the color of your eyes . . . that can't be changed."

In response to a notion of as-if-born, a number of adoptees demand an original birth certificate and the "visibility" of a birthparent. Filling in the pieces, from this point of view, requires facts of birth as well as papers of adoption. These same adoptees do not necessarily want to *meet* the relatives to whom they are attached by blood; they want, as one adoptee told me, "what everybody else has. They [other people] know who they are and they know who they're related to. And there's something about that."

"What everybody else has" constituted an interpretation of growing up adopted and of fictive kinship. The phrase also acknowledged the distinctiveness of a quest for identity when one was *chosen by* rather than *born into* a family. But for some adoptees wanting what everybody else has meant embarking on a search for real birthparents. They are the adoptees who are not satisfied with discovering who they take after from a file or who they look like from a photograph. They need to see "a face with genes like mine" and, in some cases, establish an ongoing relationship with a birthparent. These adoptees form the core of the search movement that blossomed in the 1970s. They are the subject of the next chapter.

PART THREE

The Revision of Adoptive Kinship

7

Just My Truth

The Adoptee Search for a Birth Family

"All those why's"

"I'm not looking for a family. I'm looking for roots. That's so important." That was how one adoptee explained her search to me. "Roots," she continued, means "where we came from, who looks like me. . . . It's completing the circle to have it." She wanted more than the information she had on paper; she wanted to know the person who had given birth to her. But she also made a distinction between meeting a parent and getting a new family. She was not looking for relatives, she said, but for the source of her own identity. A birthparent represented her origins, telling her who she really was.

This was the missing piece, the "gap" an adoptee described as part of the experience of growing up adopted. This was the quest Lifton also described in her books, using an Eriksonian notion of identity and of an identity crisis to justify looking for another set of parents. Decisions to search, accounts of the process, and reactions to a meeting are the subject of this chapter. Adoptee searches—their causes and effects—have had an enormous impact on American adoption policy in the past decade. They will have an equally great impact on cultural notions of kinship.

Searches have already had an impact on the American public. Dramatized on television and reported in newspapers, reunions between long-lost kin resonate to Western literary and religious traditions.[1] The sight of a child embracing a parent she has never known stirs the imagination, and also compels a reconsideration of love, parenthood, and relationship. "Reunion," however, both covers and confuses the event: *is* this a family that is being reunited? If people who watched or read about a reunion reconsidered the meaning of kin terms, those who experienced a reunion tested those meanings in *practice*. And, as I show in this chapter, it was not easy: what they were doing was "wrong" and the meanings they challenged were "natural." In searching, adoptees violated a central premise of American adoption, that birth child and birthparent were not kin but "strangers."

"Search" actually refers to a range of behaviors. Sometimes the word is applied to a request for information and for more background material than an adoptee has. The word can also refer to an attempt to find a birthparent or, perhaps, another member of the birth family. Taking the first definition, all adoptees may be said to be searching, and some adoptee organizations make that claim (ALMA 1988). Taking the second, a relatively small number of adoptees are actually looking for a birthparent.[2] The importance of the search does not lie in numbers but in its commentary on the institution of adoption and, specifically, on the as-if-begotten principle. For adoptees, growing up adopted increasingly involves finding roots and drawing a "real" family tree. From their point of view, this is perfectly normal, not crazy or neurotic or bewildered.[3]

Wanting to know does not inevitably prompt an adoptee into action. Some just wonder and do nothing about it; others do begin the process—moving step by step closer to the mother who gave up a child, to a family in which someone might "look like me," and to a kinship with a stranger. Those who do act may be more curious, more uncertain about their identity, more insecure, or simply caught by the fashion of the moment. No one really knows, and experts use the same words adoptees do: to relieve "a sense of emptiness" (McRoy, Grotevant, and White 1988, 7).[4]

The twenty-eight adoptees I interviewed talked about searching as a personal quest and as an aspect of adoption. Yet not all were searching. A few said they were "mildly curious" about their birthparents while others had requested birth and medical records. Ten had established some kind of a relationship with a birth family.[5] No one said they thought searching was bad. Those who did not want to find any more information were convinced that all adoptees had a "right to know." Four told me they would never consider searching. "I would never go looking for her [birthmother] or my father. It just isn't something I consider important enough for me to—in the first place, she could have passed away." One admitted that he had a "burning curiosity," but considered it would be "a selfish move on my part" to find out anything further. Another who said she had no "desire to go looking," added, "I wish I could see a photograph of my parents without meeting them." A fourth said, in an uncertain tone of voice, "maybe I am just not curious enough."

The idea of knowing a birthparent was powerful even when adoptees claimed they would not take any steps to find out. "But I do understand," as one insisted, "I understand why people do it, it's just not something I would do." Another adoptee gave her version. "I mean, how can you walk back?" She hesitated: "It's just, I just don't feel for me that it's necessary. Yes, it would be interesting. Yes, it would be interesting to know why I had gray hair at sixteen and why—all those why's and where does this come from, and that sort of thing. But it's not something that I have to have to continue to live." Yet the idea *was* tantalizing, and with the spread of adoptee search groups it was available to almost every adoptee.

"They can never seal our minds"

In the mid-1970s, Janet, an adopted woman in her 60s, decided to contact other adopted people and start a local support group. The decision was prompted by her desire to search; the group was modeled on the consciousness-raising groups that flourished in that period.[6] Hers was the group I joined and where I met most of the adoptees I interviewed. Janet had taken her first step by getting in touch with Jean Paton, who encouraged her search and the founding of a group.[7] Janet's philosophy can best be represented by a statement made in an ALMA newsletter: "They sealed our records. *They can never seal our minds.*"

Like other adoptees who thought about searching, Janet had read Betty Jean Lifton's books, *Twice Born* (1977) and *Lost and Found* (1979); these were on display, along with other books, at every meeting I attended. Lifton did not discuss the organization of a support group, but she certainly provided justification for searching. "I ask,

'Who am I?' Looking into the mirror my eyes searched for clues. There were none. Nor were there likely to be. For I am adopted," begins *Twice Born* (1977, 3). The group Janet started had as a primary goal "mutual support," but virtually everyone came to talk about searching. People learned about ASG by word of mouth and, after awhile, from its presence in the adoption community. Janet is now a significant figure in the politics of reform in the state.

ASG claims adoptees are oppressed, accorded second-class citizenship, and denied their rights. "The date of May 1 [1991] again coincides with National Law Day to point out that the laws of most states still discriminate against 30 million Americans because of their triad status" (ASG *Newsletter*, January 1991). The recurrent usage, "adopted child," supported the claim: an adoptee never grew up, in the eyes of others and in the words of the press. The people who came to ASG ranged in age—some were in early adolescence, thus adopted at a more liberal time, and others were in their 50s and 60s, adopted when the arrangement was kept secret. Some were not even sure they had been legally adopted. All came because they were intrigued by the idea of unsealing their records; at least, they wanted to learn *how* to do that—and the possible consequences.[8]

Instructions on searching were conveyed through personal stories. People described the steps they had taken, how they had persuaded social workers or lawyers to "relent," and how they had learned to plumb government documents for personal facts. Members of ASG also talked about state laws and the possibilities for bending the law, about the legislators who were sympathetic, and the judges who might grant a "court order."[9] Sometimes discussion focused on political action—writing letters, lobbying legislators—and sometimes the whole afternoon was devoted to an exchange of reunion stories. Janet could turn a highly personal narrative into a platform in ASG's agenda for change. It would have been hard to walk out of a meeting and not be convinced that searching made sense.

But searching was not advocated broadscale. ASG, like other adoptee groups, advised caution for those under 21—and that they consult their adoptive parents before doing anything. Members were reminded of a birthparent's rights, and that an encounter could result in "another rejection." Janet told her own search story to illustrate the ups and downs of the process, to emphasize the importance of restraint and, ultimately, to show the value of searching. "I completed my search when I was 48 and it was as if the weight of the world was lifted from my shoulders," she wrote in the newsletter (January 1991). The details of a quest were fascinating, and held the attention of the group: the unexpected cooperation of a cop who knew an address, the slip of a tongue by a rigid social worker, the clue in a small-town newspaper. We learned less about how to make a post-reunion relationship work.

The newsletter captured the tone of meetings. "The birthday [the adoptee's] was around the corner so I studied the marriage license again. The sister married a man whose father was a farmer in another small town so I ordered a phone book and it only took a week to get here. Found a number right away and hit the jackpot!" (ASG *Newsletter*, October 1988). There was a pervasive tone of excitement in the newsletter: "For a long time, I wondered if I had any family, like a brother, or sister, or maybe both. I was really happy to find out that the feeling that I had was genuine, that there was somebody else. I received a letter from Janet, and it said that she had found my younger brother. I called her, and she confirmed it. I still couldn't believe it! . . . It just goes to show you that if you wish for something hard enough, it will come true" (ASG *Newsletter*, May 1986).

Once given the idea or a piece of information, adoptees found it hard *not* to pursue the quest. "It's like getting on an express train—there's no turning back" (Allen 1983, 28). "There comes the time in your pursuit of information when you become more and more involved in your search—nothing or no one can deter you" (Askin 1982, 26). Adoptees were propelled forward with an irresistible momentum, regardless of why they had begun the search in the first place.

"Because I don't know who I am"

"The step of enquiring and searching was not taken lightly by most adoptees. The final step usually came at the end of a fair amount of deliberation and usually at a stage when it could not be put off any longer" (Triseliotis 1973, 92). Adoptees decided to search for a variety of reasons. Some did see it as a step taken after long deliberation; others claimed they acted instantly, after hearing that other people did this—from a television program or a newspaper article or a friend. A woman explained: "And then I saw an article in the paper and I took it out and I stuck it on the board [at the office]. And then

I found out my boss was adopted and had found her mother. That was what did it." Everyone who searched said they had *always* wanted to know their origins. What was new was taking action.

Adoptees had also known that wanting to find a birthparent was taboo. Secrecy was the norm, anonymity the foundation of American adoption, and "sealed records" the phrase adoptees grew up with—whatever the era of their adoptions. The birthparent had not been part of family discussions and adoptees were reluctant to bring her (or him) into the family, even when they were past childhood. And while what prompted individuals actually to take the risk varied, all remembered exactly when they did take it.[10]

Birthdays pushed adoptees into doing something; so did sickness, the anticipated birth of a child, or, often, just a chance discovery. "I started searching on my birthday," said an 18-year-old adoptee. Janet wrote in one newsletter: "I made a promise that maybe she would be ASG's 500th complete search. Her birthday was about to arrive and you know adoptee's [*sic*] and birthdays" (ASG *Newsletter*, October 1988).

One adoptee just found himself on the "train" of searching. He and his mother dropped in at the bank and "went to the safe deposit box and she said, 'here is your Baptismal certificate, here are your adoption papers,' here's your this, here is your that, take this, take that, take this. No thought about it at all, you know." He paused, then continued:

No, no I didn't look at them at all, there was the envelope . . . and it was really just clean-out-the-safe-deposit-day, you know, it wasn't anything else. And I went back to my mother's house and threw the envelope in a suitcase and got in my car and went to Beach Shore for a couple days and then got in the car and drove back to this city. So then it was September 6th, my birthday, 30 years old, you know, four days later, I'm 30 years old, I'm back in this city. About 2:30 in the afternoon, I happened to be born at 2:35, I'm sitting in my apartment and no one else is there and I hadn't emptied out my suitcase, I kind of just dropped it on the floor and . . . I say to myself, oh, I have this envelope . . . what's in it? So 30 years, almost to the minute that I was born, I open up this envelope and I see adoption papers, so I open them up and I find out my natural mother's name is on the adoption papers.

It was rare to find a name. But it was not at all uncommon to associate a birthday with the move from wondering to doing something—after all, birthdays were a natural time to think about a birthparent. Celebration of the day reminded adoptees that they really had been born, not just chosen, and that they had an essential connection with blood as well as legal kin. "Then I wondered how much my mom weighed when she had me, you know, and stuff like that." Birthdays explained and justified a desire to search. No one questioned that— and people at ASG added to this conviction the assumption that a birthparent thought of her or his child especially on that day: a parent's feelings of attachment were also awakened. Searching, then, was not an intrusion, but an affirmation of existing bonds.[11]

Adoptees also began to think about searching when they gave birth. As a woman in her late 30s put it: "I really don't know but I think that after I had Peter, I started thinking about it. I think I asked my dad to give me my papers, my adoption papers. And he gave them to me." Beyond identifying with the mother who gave birth to her, she was curious about her child's looks, what his temperament might be like, whether he would grow up to be red-headed or fat. The answers lay with a birth and not an adoptive parent. The lack of knowledge about one's own body also came up when adoptees talked about sickness. One woman captured the feeling: "It is so embarrassing when you are lying on a hospital bed and you can't tell anything about your own family."

Another woman remembered when she started to think about searching: "[It was] when I nearly died, that was nine years ago. And the surgeon sat on my bed and wanted to know, 'ok, what did your mother have, what did your father have, what did your sister have?' I am sitting there with this blank look on my face saying, 'I can't tell you anything because I am adopted.'" She decided then that she had to know more; "I need to find out who I am." Many adoptees who talked about medical reasons for searching recognized this as a relatively acceptable reason; court orders to open records often respond to medical crises. But a few adoptees themselves were convinced this was an especially sensible reason, and they translated the search into a purely practical affair. Not a confused identity or an awakened self-consciousness, but simply the need for data drove them on.

"I was having lower back trouble and I was seeking different doctors to find out why and what from, and it was told to me that I have, in the lower part of my body, I do not know the technical name but three vertebrae are not totally formed, ok, which sometime will put pressure on the spinal cord and they said this is a genetic trait, and that just made me—questioning that," said a man in his 30s. He offered another, also sensible, reason. "And . . . with the advent of my wife's pregnancy, what exact genetic code am I giving to my children?" He may not have been untypical in turning the search into a quest for knowledge, but he went farther than most adoptees in eliminating the emotional content. "Man has always been interested in the unknown," he told me.

More often, curiosity went along with a passionate desire to find out about one's other parents.[12] Without an emotional component, curiosity could seem selfish, an unnecessary indulgence on the part of the adoptee that might hurt others—particularly an adoptive parent. "I was always rather a curious type . . . I wanted to know," said a woman who decided against searching. "But I think rather than embarrassing mother, who was getting on in years, I felt I wouldn't do it [search] when she was around." In these cases, thinking about a search solidified bonds with the parents who were "real" because they had raised and loved the adopted child. "Besides I'm sure it [searching] would hurt my parents and I just don't think—that's a lot of hurt to inflict on a lot of people just for 'why do I have a musical talent?'" On the other hand, an adoptee did not have to talk about searching, and since most were adults, not living with their parents, they could conduct the search in secret. Many did.

Whatever prompted the quest, adoptees entered the terrain cautiously, aware of the risks in breaking rules and violating conventions. "It was really frightening," an adopted woman told me. "Like I said, when we started it, we were all just scared, like we shouldn't be doing it because everybody always told you that since you're adopted you just don't have any rights [to know]." Adoptees also heard they were crazy, neurotic, ungrateful for initiating their quest—and, like the unknown birthparent, irresponsible and impulsive. For some adoptees, it was a no-win game: "feeling like we've done something wrong and that we're criminals for having just been born." This woman continued: "And on bad days, I still feel like that and it's all my fault that all this happened because I got conceived and caused all these problems and I am not allowed to know." Like adoptive parents, once they "did something," they ran into obstacles and "hoops" set up by others who "called the shots." Like their parents, too, adoptees found satisfaction in successfully jumping—or circumventing—the hoops. "I guess it's the idea that when you are not supposed to do something or you don't have access to do something, maybe that's when you want to do it more. There's a secret somewhere and you want to know what it is," as one adoptee said.

The energy to continue in their quests, despite the opposition they encountered, paradoxically came from feeling "somebody else" made the important decisions in their lives. "Yeah, and then the more people that tell you you can't do it, you get mad," an adoptee admitted. "I went to a lawyer down in the city one day before I got very far and I told him what I wanted to do and he gave me a big lecture how I should go home and just be happy with my family and don't be selfish and think this is important. It shouldn't be important, I have little kids. Well, I was crying when I left, he made me feel like a monster." Being defined as less than adult and not in control of one's own life course was not unique to searching adoptees, but it was certainly part of their experience. "I really thought I was crazy," the coordinator of ASG told us, "and I told, they told my brother that he was crazy. Any longing, any adoptee that has a longing about some missing relative or a birthparent that has a longing, you're crazy. You need psychological help."

A few adoptees considered taking greater advantage of this designation. "I could get a psychiatrist to say that I am looney-tunes and we need the records and I could get doctors to say that there's a health problem and we need to get records." This woman spoke sarcastically, as if had she been seriously tempted by the idea, she would have rejected such complicity in a system that (also according to her) denied adoptees the dignity of having "honest" requests granted. Other adoptees agreed and, instead of trying to deceive those who had information, decided to convince social workers and judges that a person had a *right* to information about him- or herself. A particularly forceful woman told me: "So I drove up to get them [records] and I got up there and I saw the judge and he goes, 'I can't give you this.' And I just, that was the hardest thing, was to be a good adoptee when you're trying to pursue all this stuff but—make sure everyone knows that you are a logical, rational person."[13] Eventually, after insisting on her rights, she prevailed and the judge succumbed to the logic of her argument.

In some cases, whether by mistake or by accident, information came easily. In moving her aging adoptive parents to a nursing home, a woman found some papers lying around. "At first I didn't think about it too much and then it did get into my mind, they don't throw anything away and what have they got put away?" She and her brother then "got in and we really cleaned the closet out and sure enough . . . we found a lot on me." Yet such information, appearing faster than a person was prepared for, could present problems. Searches, as ASG told us, were supposed to be under the adoptee's control. This woman whose first effort was unexpectedly fruitful decided to wait. "I didn't want to put my time and resources that way, not yet," she told me.

The content as much as the amount of information could be overwhelming. "Well, the most heavy thing is that I found a little note written in pencil by my original mother about me, after I had been born, that she had written and that really, I look at it sometimes and sometimes I don't." This adoptee learned what few others knew: the story of her mother's pregnancy and relinquishment. "So my natural mother had gone, this is someone, she was writing this little note, she had gone back to Raleigh, after I was born, to whatever home she was working at. . . . They, apparently my adoptive parents had sent her a package with some money or something through the social worker, and she's writing to the social worker and she is saying thank you and how she cried when she got it. . . . There's this description in there about my original father, about my birthfather, as energetic and intelligent, kind of a rising young executive. That's the description about him and pretty well-thought of around town and he got himself transferred." In fact, this was enough to halt her search, at least for the while. "So I found all that . . . and I don't know if I have it all processed yet."

Stops and starts were presumed to be part of the process. There was no timetable for a search; one proceeded as one saw fit. "I started in 1970 and it took me to 1976 to really get there. So it was six years of fooling around, writing a few letters and then quitting," said one adoptee. It might be "rhythms" or fear or simply the trouble it took to look for clues when adoptions had been closed for decades. Another woman admitted somewhat shamefacedly: "I didn't pursue it actively and I kind of had to, you know, say to the Lord, 'Well, if my parents want to find me, I guess they'll have to come find me, I can't go find them. It's too hard.'" After her children were married, this woman started again—her interest "peaked" and she had the time during weekends to do "investigative work."

Of course, the search could be halted utterly because the end was unknown and the impact of finding unpredictable. One adoptee compared searching to writing a dissertation: "very similar-type projects. And with all the same different kind of ambivalences, and things like that. Oh my god, you know, on a dissertation, 'oh my god when I finish this I have to grow up and do something in the real world, oh my god.' And the same thing with the search, it's like, 'oh my god, what happens when I finish this, I, you know, all of a sudden I have another parent, or another set of parents.' There's a lot of ambivalence around the whole search process." The challenge of beating the system pulled a doubtful adoptee through; so did the triumph of finding clues no one wanted to give. The detective story, not the dissertation, framed the accounts I heard; members of ASG became skillful private investigators.[14] "But it's amazing when you go in a small town, and maybe when you go in a big town, you go in a small town and you just mention a couple things, people tell you more than you ever would have wanted to know," said an adoptee who had been searching for years.[15] At these moments, a search took on a momentum of its own: clue followed upon clue, and preoccupation with the means forced the end from mind. People prided themselves on their powers of discovery, on being rational, careful, and conscientious.

"So it [court microfilm] came around and it indicated that a young woman named Deidre Cox had been abandoned by an unnamed person and had taken refuge in the Dolly Madison Maternity Home where a baby was born who had stayed there for something like five months and then was adopted by these two older people. So I had a name and my mother had a name and it was just truly filling a space." But she did not stop there. "So I then got the original birth certificate and found that my mother had been 30 years old and was born in Black Knife, Kentucky." The more this adoptee had, the more she wanted to know. "So I wanted to know the rest of the story. I really wanted to know how she could possibly have gotten there, what was the story, whether I had siblings. Who was the person who fathered me? All of those things."

Minor characters along the way provided clues and help. And some major characters gave things away with a slip of the tongue—or indirectly, if they wanted to help and it was against the law or agency policy to provide information. As one man explained: "She's not allowed to say where you're born but we got talking about the search business and there is a thing there, a listing of books like *Searching in California, Searching in Indiana, Searching in Wisconsin,* and *Searching in Ohio,* and I kind of read the list and went, '*Searching in California,*

Searching in Indiana,' and she said, 'Yes, that's the one you want.' So things like that, she couldn't say you were born in Indiana, but she could say you want this book." Still, the social worker's hint did not give him enough data; he ultimately turned elsewhere. "So it's really beneficial having a search consultant and that's what she's called, because she does it, . . . literally she does the search. And all the money I've given her is $75 to really cover phone expenses and you know the $5 and $10 here, the $5 to get a birth certificate or $10 to get a that. So really, I mean $75 is nothing."

A search consultant was a kind of expert, someone who knew the tricks and could do the legwork.[16] But the tricks were not always comfortable for the adoptees who hired a consultant. "At first I hated it. I hate lying. But it's the only way to beat the system," said an adoptee whose searcher tried everything to get information. Another adoptee explained the lies to me. "There's a lot of little fibs, and as people in the networks, you know, the whole adoption network call them, little lies, and some real underground connections, people who have connection to the motor vehicle computer bases, data bases, and stuff like that. So that when you get a name, nationally you can search it under a motor vehicle check or things like that . . . you know, it's not unethical. I don't think it's unethical, well, I don't think it's immoral, maybe it's unethical. I definitely don't think it's immoral, it might be unethical but I don't, I see it as a legitimate breach of ethics, if there is such a thing." And a searcher herself put it: "I don't believe in doing illegal things but I certainly do cover every aspect and use every source and contact that I can find to help, because if you go to the agencies, they're limited."

A searcher could also become one of the obstacles, another difficulty in the adoptee's way. "She was so cold," a young woman complained about her searcher, "I fired her." The searcher, another adoptee reported, "is real helpful with searches but she is a little bonkers herself and had some, I don't know what you want to call it, but certain times when I would call her up I would just catch her at a bad time and she would take it out on me." Searching was an aspect of being adopted that adoptees could control, and though a searcher helped, she also took away the autonomy of a search. On the other hand, coming to ASG meetings provided help without depriving the adoptee of control. "I don't think anybody—anybody who does a search by themselves loses something," said an adoptee who later became a search consultant. "I recommend a group or to work with somebody knowledgeable, but to try because a lot of times people close up things, because asking the wrong question or being too open—. You can't say, 'I'm adopted, I want this and I want that.' They'll just tell you where to go. You have to be a little subtle and tell them a little fib here and there." ASG also advised working with a group. "You will do your own search with our help." This was followed by warnings: "Do not use the word adoption when you search! Do not make contact without calling ASG first! Make sure you let us know when your search is complete! We will do our best to help you!" (ASG note to new members).

Support groups provided instructions and reassurance, but advised the adoptee to make her own decisions along the way. "Although it may be possible for an individual to undertake a search without having to deal with the highs and lows others face, I have yet to meet such an individual. You will need support from someone right from the beginning," urged a search manual (Askin 1982, 21). At ASG, Janet managed a delicate balance between preparing an adopted person, letting him or her act on his own, and offering emotional support for whatever happened along the way. She did this, in part, by exploring her own search and its consequences.

The first step, receiving an unamended birth certificate, was thrilling. "And just to be able to know your name, even if you don't know your biological mother's name or your biological father's name," she remembered. "Just to have 'I was born, and I was born with this name' helped me tremendously." Janet grew skillful at reading government documents, persuading clerks to give up information, and moving from one clue to another—until she found the name of a cousin. She made a phone call. "And I said, 'does the name Janet sound familiar to you?' And she said, 'oh yes. Oh my goodness, that's my cousin.' I said, 'Well, I'm Janet' and could we come over and talk to her." Next she met her birth sister, and then at last her mother. "My search," Janet assured us, "was the best thing I ever did."

"Just to complete your history"

Janet also argued that searching was primarily for *oneself* and not for another family. "I think that it [searching] was something that I had to do for me and if it was selfish, I am sorry. It has done me more good than anything else in the whole world." Finding a birthparent meant filling in the missing piece of one's identity; it ought not be threatening to anyone else. Once contact was made, however, it was hard to stop. Adoptees wanted to know more about the mother who had given away a baby and, often, more about that person's whole family. The need for "biological ancestry" rationalized the curiosity, but the curiosity led in all sorts of directions—including a reunion and an ongoing relationship. As long as actions could be covered by a quest for identity, they did not seem wrong. "[But] if you're searching just to complete your history, it's ok," continued Janet.

Like Janet, as their first action, most adoptees requested the unamended birth certificate; they needed that proof.[17] Lifton (1979, 20) provided the axiom: "But the Adoptee says: 'I'm not sure I ever was born.' . . . Without the original birth certificate, he has no proof." The request for a birth certificate was significant in another way: it was an action against the state, and for many adoptees a bold move. Demanding recognition of the "right to know" brought a personal quest into a public arena; an identity crisis became intertwined with bureaucratic procedures, law, and customary policy. People at ASG encouraged each other in this move by condemning a system that denied a person his facts and kept him the adopted *child* forever. They also joined forces, verbally if not actually, with other oppressed groups— much as birthparent groups did.[18] "The denial of an adult human being's right to *the truth of his origin* creates a scar which is imbedded in his soul forever" (ALMA brochure; italics in original).

Adoptee arguments about the denial of rights were neither unreasonable nor unsupported by lawyers and social workers. "It is the thesis of this Note that the adult adoptee has a great psychological need for and should receive access to his original birth certificate. The first amendment right to receive information and the constitutional right of privacy mandate the availability of this information" ("The Adult Adoptee's Constitutional Right to Know His Origins," 1975, 1197).[19] "It's infuriating that in some way you can't say, 'Yes, I want the records,'" an adopted man complained. "And could you let the person know who is my birthmother that I would like to have that information at least, and if there is a waiver to be signed, if she happens to be wealthy, I don't want the money, I don't want, you know—," and he trailed off, leaving unspoken his anger at the assumption that he would be exploitative. Confronting the state, adoptees spoke of waivers and contract—an emotionally appropriate if not always accurate rhetoric.

"But they make this agreement between the adoption agency and the adoptive parents that the adoptive parents are not going to go find the natural parents which is the unlikely thing anyhow," an adoptee began his comment on the legal constraints, which also kept the "natural parents" from finding the "natural kid." "The hard and cruel fact," he continued, "is that the one person who is not consulted in this whole thing is the kid. Now, you know, once again, how could the kid be consulted, the kid is an infant. But the fact is the kid didn't have a choice in the matter. And so when the kid becomes of an age where he or she wants to know what their biological roots are, they just, they are then essentially, I hate the word victimized because I think it's overused, but in a sense they are victimized by a system that they had no part in. Yeah, they're bound by a contract that they didn't sign."

Adoptive parents who made the contract could break the seal of secrecy by providing whatever information they had—which usually did not include the name of a birthparent. "And I did talk about it with my [adoptive] mother more and she did start to give me a little more information and eventually gave me the papers that she had from my adoption records. She gave me enough information that I could start getting public records," a woman in her 40s told me. Another man, in his 30s, found his adoptive mother's involvement a bit daunting. "She [adoptive mother] seemed real wrapped up in it, too. I was inbetween more or less, like yes and no, kind of easy going." Still, if depending upon a parent opened the records, adoptees were willing to make this concession. It did not have to mean a loss of control—and if finding a birthname was the result, it could, as Janet remarked, be thrilling. Some adoptees stopped right there.[20]

"'Oh, by the way,'" a social worker reportedly had said to one adoptee, "'did I tell you your name at birth?' And I said, 'no.' And she said it was Anna Jo, but she didn't say what the last name was, but I saw Anna Jo Walsh—I saw the last name. So I was pretty sure about that and I regret I didn't take a tape recorder to that session and I wished I had because you're so excited about getting all that information that it's not sinking in, you're hearing it but you don't remember all of it." A birthname did make the birth real, and confirmed the connection with another family. Knowing a parent gave a name before giving away her child changed this adoptee's view of the surrender. "I didn't realize that [adopted] people had names when they were born and that they never changed. I didn't know that and they didn't know that—my [adoptive] mom and dad didn't know that." "Knowing that you were named," another adoptee told me, "makes you feel less like a thing."

A few adoptees used the discovered birthname, in one way or another. "No, I use my married name for everything except that my name never changed from Janet, even though Ann is the name my husband calls me by. When I was adopted they added the Ann in front of it." There was something powerful about being called what you were called at birth; it counteracted the amendment of a birth certificate and proved that a blood bond could not be absolutely severed. One adoptee talked about another: "She gave her daughter her birthname, which was Marilyn. But she said, 'I can't use it, but I don't want to lose that name.' So she gave it to her daughter."

A name represented an essential connection, as tangible, real, and confirming as looking like another person. In addition, a name was a tantalizing clue to the person who had bestowed it in the first place. Having a name, a number of adoptees were not content with just relishing it. Armed with the information an agency or state had been reluctant to provide, feeling triumphant in the quest, adoptees moved on to the next stage, though not always with deliberate speed. Whether honestly come by—the ultimate cooperation of a court or social worker—or the end of a trail of little fibs, the name brought out of her obscurity the mother who had once "unchosen" a child and might again.

It also resulted in a reinterpretation of the contrast between a "lawful" and a "natural" mother that had been part of growing up adopted. Contemplating meeting another parent, adoptees acknowledged the warmth, generosity, and commitment of the parents who had raised them. "Like we always talked about it," said a woman in her early 20s, "but when I did it and when I said, 'okay, this is step one,' my mom was like 'uh-oh' and my dad was like good, great, whatever you want is what I want. Which is really nice. I don't think I could do anything without my mom and dad being behind me." By report, adoptive mothers were transformed by the presence of a natural mother, even if she just appeared on paper. "And my [adoptive] mother had never done that [expressed her feelings] either until her ground was shaken with my search. And after I completed it she became much more open with her feelings."

In more than one instance, the adoptive mother, remembered as cold and stingy, was portrayed as "opening up" after the search. The adoptee herself changed. Satisfied in her quest for the missing parent, she moved closer to the parent she had always known. "[I] feel I appreciate her [adoptive mother] more in a way. That is, feeling that there wasn't this other ideal family that I would have been happier in. So that improved the relationship. So the extent to which she could be open-minded about my searching is another thing that could have improved the relationship."

A rearrangement of the childhood contrast also altered the "good" versus "bad" adoptive parent configuration. In one or two cases, after the adoptee learned about her birthparents, the adoptive parent who had been loving turned cold and withdrawn—possibly, though adoptees did not say so, as a result of feeling betrayed. "It bothers me when I think about my [adoptive] dad because the last few years if I'm going to talk to anybody, we've become a lot closer and if I'm going to talk to anybody it's my dad that I'm going to talk to and he hasn't said 'boo' about it at all. And there have been a couple of times when the three of us have been out to dinner and my mom says, 'well, have you talked to Marsha [birthmother] lately?' and I say 'yeah' and it's like I'm talking to my mom and dad isn't even there. And he hasn't said anything or asked any questions."

"It's hard for me to call them Mom and Dad"

This woman's search had the familiar stops and starts. "And then I went over—I was working at Youth Emergency Service and at a PDQ store and I just had an hour break so I thought, well, I'll go over there and relax and just mellow out and get psyched up for work. And a friend comes in and asks me, 'well, where are you in your search?' and I go, 'I have a name' and she said, 'what are you sitting there for?' I go, 'and I know where she lives too.' And she just couldn't believe that I was being so calm and trying to absorb it and trying to decide what to do. . . . However, after talking for a while we decided or I decided that I would call there to see if Marsha lives there to make sure I still have the right person and that if she answered and it was her, I was going to hang up and then, if she didn't answer or if she wasn't there, then it was no big deal." Often, even if they had moved fairly quickly before, adoptees stopped just before taking the final step of a meeting.

A younger adoptee drove all the way to her mother's town, and then back and forth in front of the trailer she knew her mother lived in. "And it was a very nice trailer, it had a barbecue and all these curtains in the window and plants all nice and taken care of, very pretty. So did I go up to the door and knock? No, we went all the way back [home]." Then a few days later: "And so finally Liz and I were sitting there one day and she was telling me, reading me a letter and I was crying. She said, call, call. I said, like, no, no. 'I'm going to call, I'm going to get the damn number. What do you think, I don't know the area code down there.' So she called up and got the telephone number." But here the adoptee took over her own quest; with instructions from ASG lying by her side, she made the first phone call.[21] "Then I say, 'May I speak with Mrs. Sarah Nolan?' And this guy answered and I was all excited, it was like this young sounding guy, not like a father. Oh, maybe I have a brother, and I'm like, 'is Mrs. Sarah Nolan there?' 'Sarah, oh, no, she's out for the evening.' And I'm like [incomprehensible excited noises]. I said, 'ok, can I leave a message? Oh, no, that's ok, I'll call back,' slam."

Two days later, her mother was at home when she called, "'Does the date June 9, 1964 mean anything to you?' There is the digital clock going and going, going and going, for two minutes nothing was said. . . . There was this big, long pause. I thought she was going to hang up, and then she didn't hang up after a minute and she's like crying, 'I never forgot about you, I've always loved you, I can't believe you called, I can't believe you found me, I'm so happy.'" Weeks later, the actual meeting between mother and daughter was as exhilarating as the phone call for the adoptee.

A first phone call could also be casual and cool, as the adoptee or the birthmother or both avoided rushing into unfamiliar territory. One morning, an adoptee told me, he "simply" picked up his office phone and dialed his birthmother's number. "Oh, my god," she reportedly said. "This is just like the Donahue show." This was followed by: "How are you?" "I'm fine, thank you." "Are you happy?" "Yes, I'm very happy." After several more informational phone calls, they arranged to meet in a city that was conveniently half-way between their homes. He did not mind the relatively distant phone conversations, especially in retrospect; the actual meeting had been exciting—"we stayed up all night talking," he told me. "Her love for me was unconditional, so much so that she loved me without ever having seen me."

Other adoptees were disappointed by lack of warmth on the part of a birthparent. "I said, 'are you busy? If you are busy, I can call back.' I said my name and I asked her if she remembered last year when the lawyer called, and she said, 'yes.' And I said, 'well, he was calling for me and I thought I would just like to talk to you,'" she paused, then continued. "So about two months later, I went up and met her for about an hour." The phone call set the tone for subsequent contact, which was lackadaisical and sporadic. "So it's not the greatest relationship, but it's better than nothing. I am just glad that I found her."

An unemotional encounter was easier if the adoptee found in it a sign of the similarity between him and his new kin. One man recalled his first meeting: "It wasn't, you know, hug and kiss and all this kind of stuff. It was, you know, I guess—well, they're the same way [as me]. I guess it's blood. They felt you out a little bit and I felt them out a little bit type of thing. You know, cause you don't know what's going, I didn't know what was going through their mind and I didn't know what to think. I was sitting on the plane, I didn't know what to say, what to do, just see what happens." But the ideal was an outpouring—of talk if not of feelings. "Our reunion went very well and we talked for hours. She told me many personal things pertaining to my adoption. We both had many questions answered. It is such a good feeling to know that you were and are loved. It is a special kind of love that neither time nor separation can diminish."

A meeting also allows the fortunate adoptee to see at last the "face with genes like mine." "I mean it was real interesting because when I walked into the nursing home [where her birthmother lived], I really didn't know who she was and one of the counselors came up and said, 'Oh, you must be Maria's daughter or sister because you look just like her.' And it was just a real, it was a given, there was no way that—. And then in seeing my father, too, I could see some characteristics that he had. And talking to people I could see a lot of, I don't know, characteristics that I have picked up, similar ones that he had had." As they knew from growing up adopted, features were not as significant as similarities that lay beneath the skin and emerged over time. "I was kind of disappointed because I thought we would look more alike," said a woman about meeting her birthmother. "Joe [husband] said we did and now that I am older I can see that we do look more alike. My hair was a lot lighter and I was pretty thin then, about ten years ago. I was real thin so I didn't see any resemblance. But now I think there is more."

If the adoptee did not look like the birthmother, even after time and scrutiny, she might look like other blood kin. "Well, both my brother and I look like that father. I have his dark eyes. William has the blue eyes of the mother. Other than that we're the father, bones, the whole structure is dad, not mom. The only thing we both got is this [pointing], the high forehead." Looking from a mother to a father extended this new family "naturally." "I guess I look a little bit like my natural mother. I think I look a little more like him [birthfather]. You know, they're ethnically very different, in that he's Jewish. I'm not sure if he's German Jewish or from which other, in which other country. She is a mixture of Scandinavian and Norwegian. This is the Norwegian, German, and English fair-skinned. Her hair was a reddish before it turned grey, her hair style, probably her face shape is something similar to mine. But my color is more like his." Tracing resemblances, adoptees extended their blood ties beyond the parent-child relationship. If the search was not for a family, it was for a network of kin—a "biological ancestry," as adoptees said, not just an individual.

Janet discovered the person she really looked like was her grandmother. "Where if you are 48, like I was, grandma was gone. The one I look like was gone, never to see her, never to know her. I accepted looking at the picture. I know doggone well if we wore those little house dresses and those little laced-up Oxfords that that's what I would look like exactly. And that's exciting too." Resilient, she extended the resemblances through her several families. "The picture of Robert [her son] and then I have a picture of Lance, my nephew, and they look so alike." With a happier outcome, another adoptee told me the person she most resembled was her birth sister. "And she comes through the door and my boyfriend's like trying to pay attention and trying to not fall asleep . . . , and so he was sort of like semiconscious. He went, 'oh my god, what—' and he's shaking me. . . . Pictures we don't look alike but face to face we look alike."

Most of the adoptees I interviewed did not want just to look like but also to *be* like the found parent; this closeness differed from the "superficial" similarities that came from matching or from chance. "My [adoptive] mom is real outgoing and she loves to drive and she would get in the car and go anywhere. Like she would drive to Florida. I would go up to the store, but I don't really—. And Joan [birthmother], she's the same way. . . . She doesn't like to drive. And I can't sew worth a darn and my mother is a really good seamstress and she made all of our clothes when we were kids. And I can't even sew buttons on. And Joan said she's not good at that. She said she can sew but she's not good and she's not mechanical, which I'm not either." Closeness with a birthparent also provided the "bodily" map an adopted person did not otherwise have. "So I didn't know that I had both grandfathers who had died [young] and that kind of disturbed me."

Still, there was the problem of interaction, not prescribed by even the most astounding resemblances. The "child" was an adult, and could not act childlike; the parent had no role to play either. One adoptee half-jokingly told me how her mother "closeted" the relationship. "My mother is still in the closet. When I go to Chicago, if she meets someone she knows down the street, she'll introduce me as her friend from Colorado because she's not able to face it. Now if any, if you were to walk up to us on a street corner even without knowing you would automatically assume that we were mother and daughter. I mean, it's, you know, pale complexion and same eyes, same nose. And my sister same way. And it's very hard to, to not accept somebody that looks like you." This sort of compromise, accepting kin while denying the kinship, was rare but understandable. The two had not shared a household or a past, and they were often closer in age than the "normal" parent and child. The genealogical relationship was not accompanied by the expected generational span.

Adoptees, in fact, exploited the unusual nearness in age to emphasize how close they were to their birthparents. Several told me they "could have been twins," occasionally showing me photographs to underline the point. The idea of twins extended beyond age to looks and likeness in general; it also was a way of asserting the importance of nature over nurture. As twin studies claimed, people who were separated by time, space, and experiences could still be "stunningly alike." At the same time, the concept of twins further confused the parent-child relationship by its insistent denial of difference—allowing the birthparent to seem, and act, like a peer rather than a parent.

Yet adoptees almost always wanted more than friendship; they wanted something from a *parent*, unclear though that concept was in this situation. Most searched for a mother and expected the behaviors associated with a female parent. Those who searched for and found a father also puzzled about how to interact with a parent who was a "familiar stranger" and barely of another generation. One woman told me about her meeting with her birthfather: "I was prepared [for his questions], but then every five questions he just kept saying, 'well, I'm not admitting anything and I'm not denying it.' I was getting real anxious towards the end of that hour because I wanted him to say it." But it took awhile before he would declare his parenthood. "So that was about it and then my birthday came around in August and I didn't get a card from him and I was really angry about that. . . . And then I got three cards. They were late, but I got three cards, and he said 'this is to make up for the ones that I missed and then this is for your birthday now and then this is for the ones after this.' That was neat."

So she had her father. The texture of the relationship, however, sounded more like a friendship than a father-daughter relationship. "When we'd go out to dinner alone it would be more intimate discussions and learning more about each other. But just the fact that he was willing to socialize and learn more about my life, other parts of my life—," she trailed off. Then she concluded with a slightly cynical remark: "Of course, the happier that I was, the less risk of me wanting to latch on to him as a father."

Birthday cards seemed to be a convenient way of acknowledging the tie of birth without having to take on a *performed* parent-child relationship. A card sent, a card received: no one had to do anything more. "And another exciting thing is to have your birthday come and get a whole batch of cards in the mail and they are from both your mothers, and your sister, and both your brothers," the ASG coordinator told me. "And I sit and read each side by side and that is the most exciting thing. It is just marvelous." When people actually interacted, the thinness of a purely biological relationship became apparent. "You know, you come upon the scene and you want to do everything you can to prolong their life and make them comfortable on their final days and all those kinds of things. And it was like I didn't know what to do," said an adoptee who found a sickly birthparent. "So I didn't have a lot of choice since I wasn't in charge. I was really nobody legally, in a sense."

Occasionally birthparents acted more parental than the adoptee wanted. "You know, she comes here and tells me what to do and what not to do. And I can handle it for a few days but I go to her house and she does indeed live that way. I mean, watches cartoons for breakfast, a bowl of cereal and a cup of coffee and I'm used to eating more—you know, just little things." But the adoptee was philosophical about it. "A lot of people have oddities, so it's not something I find a problem with. We write and talk to each other and I hope and

pray she doesn't say, 'Oh, we're coming to California for a week.'"
This sounds like any grown child complaining about a parent, and
hers was an unusually accommodating attitude. Other adoptees did
not easily add a third or fourth parent to the set they already had,
chafing at having to do double filial duties.

"But I'm sure she—at one point she said, 'you can come visit us for
Thanksgiving,' you know, she was really—at first especially when exactly how this was going to work out, she wasn't really, I think, clear. I
think she was really thinking about sort of welcoming me back as a
family member who would be there as often as any of her, any of the
boys she had raised. She did think about, 'Well, how am I going to introduce her when I bring her to church?'" This adoptee resolved the
problem of how she would be a "child" in the family by identifying
with one of her birthmother's sons. "He's the second oldest and I see
him as not only potentially more broad-minded but also perhaps more
interested in intellectual things." And she made sure the relationship
would continue down a generation. My daughter "does have pictures
from that trip [to visit the birth family] and so she knows my natural
mother is Grandma Josephine to her. And the other grandmas have
their other names and she has lots of grandmothers. So I expect that
eventually I will explain this to her and she'll probably visit them on
some other occasion or occasions."

A few adoptees refused to have a relationship after the initial meeting. "I didn't think I wanted a relationship, just my truth," said one,
and another: "I don't think that people have to establish intimate relationships with the people they find." The quest, these adoptees asserted, was not for another parent but for oneself. "It doesn't feel like
I'm looking for a mother, that's real clear to me," a man in his 40s
commented about his search. He went on to imagine an acceptable
relationship. "I think that if I had a birthmom who was real, real together—in some sense like an Auntie Mame—just 'you go on with
your life and boy, do I wish you well.' And we'll meet occasionally at
the Black Stone and have a drink and we'll talk about our lunatic lives.
That might be a lot of fun."

They already had parents. "My adoptive mother is my real mother.
She raised me." That was the gist of the search, even for those adoptees who did not stop at "knowing" but went on to a reunion. They
wanted to find birthparents, and especially a birthmother, because
"birth" represented the missing piece of their identity. Once a mother
was encountered, however, the term lost its abstract, flexible quality;

it was not an empty concept into which an adoptee could pour meanings of his or her choice. "Mother" called up conventions about acting like a child to a parent. The concept remained linked to behaviors even if the birthmother turned out to be more like Auntie Mame than one's adoptive mother. "So my adoptive mother is also needy and I can't do everything for her [birthmother] that ideally she would like a daughter to do and ideally that somebody could do. But at some point I just have to recognize my limitations and I have more responsibility to her than I do to my natural mother."

"So you don't want to neglect one for the other and it's, you know, it ain't as easy as it sounds," said an adoptee, who was working hard to manage two sets of real parents. "I'm telling you, all of everything worked out real good. Sometimes you sort of hate to, I don't know, sometimes I don't like to bring it [birth family] up when we're all together but a lot of times they [adoptive parents] ask." Later he added: "It seems like the last six months or so they've been on, they've been on my mind more than they ever have. You know, just the family in general, sometimes I'm thinking of Mom, thinking of Dad"—without clarifying which Mom, which Dad.

The coordinator of ASG reminded us that all family relationships need work, including those that came after a search. "Some people's relationships go by the way side," she said. "But you have to work at them. If you don't work at it, if both of you don't work at it, it's going to fall apart. If everybody doesn't work at being a family, then that's going to fall apart too." She concluded: "I would never search my whole life for somebody and then let it go by the way side." By implication, there was no such thing as natural, untended love; even the "unconditional" love between mother and child required conscious, reciprocal effort.

"I've got two brothers, both named Jim"

Janet loved getting birthday cards from both her mothers and all her brothers. She also wanted them to meet. "And to me, the ideal situation would be to have both parents meet one another. And I can't understand why not, except my [adoptive] mother is 88 and she has never ever, and never will come to grips with the fact that she couldn't have a child of her own." Although a "blending" of families was the ideal goal of a reunion, it happened rarely.

But it did happen. One 24-year-old I met had contacted her birth-mother and was quickly incorporated into the birth family. The situation was unusual: she had medical problems, was more vulnerable than most people her age, and had met a mother who had simultaneously been searching for her. The birthmother and the adoptive mother came to know each other through conversations about "their" daughter's well-being. But it was not all smooth sailing. The adoptee liked her birthmother better, she told me, and she told her birthmother that she wanted to be "re-adopted" into that family. Failing that, the adoptee used kin terms to solidify and legitimize the new relationship. She was the only one who called her mother's husband "Dad." The other children (her half-siblings) called him by his first name.

The problem of conduct in this case had been overcome by concerns for the adoptee's health. She needed a parent's attention, and the birthmother willingly gave it. And so far the adoptive mother, appreciative of the help her daughter was receiving, did not seem to be threatened.[22] But it was a precarious arrangement, one that might not last after the adoptee grew healthy and mature. I talked with another adoptee, a vigorous man in his mid-30s, who had maintained a post-reunion relationship for nearly four years. As he said, "it ain't as easy as it sounds." And he laughed: "I've got two brothers, both named Jim. It's funny to explain." That *was* easy.

What was not easy was reconsidering the meaning of "parent." Meeting his birthmother made him realize how special his adoptive mother was; without her, he would not be where he was. At the same time, he did not minimize the significance of a mother by birth; she represented his place on the "rope of life"—she symbolized his flesh-and-blood reality. And of course they each merited the appropriate kinship term, compounding the difficulties he already mentioned. "You know, see it's hard for me to call them [birthparents] Mom and Dad in front of Mom and Dad. But as far as I'm concerned they're [adoptive parents] my Mom and Dad. But now, but when I'm with my real [birth] Mom and Dad I call them Mom and Dad. Because they are. What am I going to call them? Mr. and Mrs. Blackman? You know, I mean, that's not, to me, that's not respectful."[23] My brackets illustrate what was for him a pragmatic, and continual, problem: there were not enough kin terms for his relationships.

Few adoptees plunged wholeheartedly into such blended families. Appealing in the abstract, blended families were almost impossible to manage in concrete, day-to-day interactions. It was one thing to blend two mothers as aspects of one's own identity, and quite another to invite them both to a wedding or Thanksgiving celebration. The ideal solution might be to sever "parent" from a notion of family, and treat all mothers and fathers as distinct individuals. "And I tried to go in with an open mind and also look for the good in each parent, respective parent, and tried to find that. And I really did. Yes, it made me feel a lot better, it really did. There was a lot of healing and a lot of sadness to say that, wow, out of four people, couldn't any of them have been normal? [laughing]. Because they were all really different kinds of people." Removing "mother" and "father" from an association with "family" would, of course, make adoption an even more "funny kind of kinship"—in the words of one adoptee—than it already was.

But those who searched and met a birthparent were willing to put up with the consequent confusions in terminology, symbols, and conventions of kinship. "I would never change anything," Janet insisted after she met her birthmother. And in some profound sense, she did not change anything: her real mother was the person who adopted, raised, and loved her. "I would never want a different mother than I have. I mean, she's my mother." This did not, however, mean relinquishing her mother by birth. "But then again I would never want to go back and not know my birthmother either, ever. Because the last ten years have been emotionally the happiest of my life. Through all the problems that I had, that could keep me going. The joy of having—it's unbelievable."

Adoptees initiated a search movement and birthparents followed, with their own expectations and definitions of being a parent. No relationship entered into by an adopted person was free of the feelings and interpretations a birthparent brought to the encounter. A "lost" child is as much a challenge to notions of kinship as a "found" parent.

8

Lost to Adoption

The Birthparent Search
for a Relinquished Child

"I need to know whether she's alive"

"I went back to work, getting there late, and this really has to do with coming out of the closet. . . . Well, I went in to see my boss. . . . Then I told him that I had a daughter that I had given up for adoption and that I was inquiring about my records" (CUB *Communicator*, 10–11/82: 15). In this chapter I focus on birthparents who decide to find a relinquished child, for whom coming out of the closet was only the first step—the next, a reunion. After that, for some, lay the possibility of an ongoing and enduring relationship. But what that relationship could be, especially if the found child was grown up, was problematic for everyone who undertook a search.

Like adoptees, birthparents borrowed from the rhetoric that was developed at support group meetings and published in birthparent newsletters in order to "make storyable" a private experience. "Reunion," with all its cultural connotations, resonated for birthparents much as it did for adoptees who were looking for long-lost relatives. "Reunion" implies a family and a meeting of people who, while perhaps strangers in daily life, are still profoundly familiar. Yet the concept of a reunion does not contain instructions for subsequent behaviors. Birthparents' use of the word was significant, but the consequences of an actual reunion with a child "lost to adoption" remained unclear.

Increasingly throughout the 1970s, birthparents demanded information about their relinquished children and the opening of adoption records. "I need to know whether she is alive, whether she had a happy childhood, what she is doing now," a birthparent told me. These demands gained strength from the existence of support groups, and I will discuss here the complex influence of birthparent organizations on the actions taken by individual birthparents. Media stories also had an impact: dramatic presentations of meetings between long-lost kin encouraged birthparents to look for a long-lost child. They were reminded that they had not "turned back the clock," that the child really existed, and that a relationship might be established. They learned from the adoptee movement to plead the urgency of their own case. "As a group, birthparents too need and deserve open records not only because we need to know whether our children are among the murder victims on the shrouded stretchers, but also because we're panicked that they need us, but have doors and file cabinets slammed closed in their faces if they try to contact us" (Birthparent Search Group [BSG] *Newsletter,* 7–8/90: 13).[1]

But birthparents had a harder time than adoptees. Social workers and lawyers were not as sympathetic to the parent who seemed to be changing her mind as they were to an adoptee looking for his or her "roots." The appearance of a birthparent might not be in the child's best interests, these experts noted, and it certainly violated the confidentiality they had promised adopting couples. Birthparents struggled against this point of view, and in their battles against the system recalled the earlier time of surrendering a child. In this chapter, then, I show the way in which reference to surrender framed the steps and justified a search.

Not all the birthparents I met wanted to find a relinquished child. Of those who did search, several had already had a reunion and five had established a relationship that, by the time of the interview, had lasted for over four years. Of the twenty birthparents I interviewed, four did not want to search. "I do not want to disrupt his life. I know he is happy," said one, who added: "I feel that he is living somewhere south of me." Another described searching as "throwing a monkey wrench into the soup." And two mothers had relinquished so recently that they concentrated on that rather than on the future. One of them did say, "I just can't wait, I just can't wait until eighteen years has zoomed by, whenever she's out, I want to see her, I really do. I just can't wait." A few had just recently encountered the child; reporting their ecstasy, they also wondered where the relationship would go next. And those who had actually established a relationship continued to feel "perplexed" about what map it should follow. There is no model for "love between acquaintances" (Hanssen, *Coping with Rejection*, n.d.).

The differences between those who searched and those who did not is hard to pinpoint. Existing studies of birthparents do not (yet) offer reliable data. Like birthparents themselves, these studies emphasize the naturalness of wanting to know, the obstacles to getting information, and the challenge of parenthood when the child is a virtual stranger. A 1984 article, for example, reported: "We evaluated several personal, demographic, and historic variables relevant to the surrendering parent, the surrendered child, and the process of surrender, to determine whether any were associated with subsequent search activity." These researchers found that only "the primary reason for surrender [pressured by others] and the elapsed time [c. 12 years] since surrender were significantly related to subsequent search activity" (Deykin, Campbell, and Patti 1984, 271).[2]

Birthparents knew that whatever the reason they decided to search, their behavior was likely to be condemned—that they would be considered certainly irresponsible (again) and probably "crazy." Support groups like Concerned United Birthparents provided reassurance and solidarity. As one birthparent said: "When I got going with CUB and I found out I wasn't that crazy, that a lot of people have this yearning, they don't want to cause trouble, that everyone mentions that—'I don't want to cause trouble, I don't want to hurt anybody'—that's the first thing they say. And then they say, 'but I have this horrible longing just to know if she's ok, if she's even alive.'" CUB persuaded a birthparent that wanting to know a child was "natural." "The desire to search for one's child lost to adoption is pretty much a universal one" (Hanssen, *Before You Search*, n.d.). But even CUB literature could not determine the relationship that came after a reunion; that, too, would be another kind of kinship—one created after the series of steps described in this chapter.

"CUB is a M.A.S.H unit"

In 1976, a Massachusetts woman, Lee Campbell, placed a notice in the *Boston Globe* asking for responses from individuals who had relinquished a child to adoption and wanted to talk about their experiences. Among those who answered, several agreed to meet on a regular basis. "Four of us met in my house on the Cape," Campbell said, and created Concerned United Birthparents. From that original group, CUB has grown to include approximately 3,000 people, scattered across the United States.[3] Membership includes birthparents, adoptees, and adoptive parents, though the great majority are birthparents and of these, the largest number are birthmothers.

Established as a support group, CUB added to that an educational purpose. "CUB is a M.A.S.H unit (mutual aid, self help)" and "has been able to educate the public to the trauma of family separation by adoption," those who joined were told (Concerned United Birthparents, *New Member Information*, n.d., 5). In its early years, CUB did not encourage searching or tell people how to do a search, though local groups were permitted to "host" search workshops. "No subject is taboo at CUB meetings or in the newsletter (with the exception of actual search methods)," a brief CUB pamphlet reminded new members. The newsletter, the CUB *Communicator,* publishes a list of "search buddies," a directory of search groups, and information about CUB's reunion registry, along with articles and letters from readers.[4]

The *Communicator* borrows rhetoric from various social movements, often confusing as much as clarifying CUB's position. "Coming out of the closet" is a persistent and popular expression for declaring birthparent status, but gay rights are not part of the newsletter pages. Similarly, the use of M.I.A. for "missing in adoption" captures an emotion rather than makes a political point; the presumption is that not knowing whether a person is alive or dead is worse than knowing the truth. Most notably, CUB rhetoric is dominated by language and imagery stemming from the women's liberation and civil rights movements of the 1960s: birthparents are said to have been oppressed and subordinated, denied their rights as adults, and deprived of information crucial to their lives.

Lee Campbell's story appeared in several publications, including the *Communicator,* and presented a persuasive argument for becoming "conscious" and deciding to search. The overall emphasis in birthparent literature, however, was on individual timing and control. "Our support of you includes the recognition that you alone have the right to make your own carefully considered decisions about search and to control it from beginning to end" (Concerned United Birthparents, *Hosting a Search Workshop*, n.d., 1). Nevertheless, Campbell's story remained an important guide for CUB members, and one to which they accommodated their own experiences. There was a tension, both at meetings and in the newsletter, between following her example and making "your own" decision from beginning to end. Given the stigma attached to looking for a surrendered child, other people's stories offered comfort: as at ASG, personal accounts were the primary content of CUB meetings.

CUB has changed since its founding, and search has become a prominent subject at meetings and in publications. Local branches distribute instructions for searching and propose amendments to state and federal laws that will open records and waive confidentiality at the request of a birthparent. CUB belongs to the American Adoption Congress (AAC) and with other member organizations supports the movement to "humanize adoption" by permitting individuals to have input into the terms of an adoption. "The American Adoption Congress believes that growth, responsibility and respect for self and others develop best in lives that are rooted in truth. The American Adoption Congress is therefor [*sic*] committed to achieving changes in attitudes, policies and legislation that will guarantee the availability of and access to identifying information concerning one another to all adoptees and their birth and adoptive families" (quoted in CUB *Communicator*, 7–8/89: 19).

There is agreement on the issue of opening records and ending secrecy. Within CUB, however, disputes persist over the role of birthfathers, both as members and as figures in the triad. Some people claim that birthparenthood is a woman's issue and that the significance of motherhood should guide decisions about children. "We have walked in a land you have never seen, that no man has ever seen, the mysterious landscape of pregnancy and birth" (CUB *Communicator*, 4/83: 7). Others argue for inclusion of men and a broad definition of birthparenthood. "It is sexist and unreasonable to think that one birthparent is somehow more responsible, more equal and more loving than the other by virtue of their sex. It's also an insult to men to suggest that their biological connection with their children is not important," wrote a birthmother (CUB *Communicator*, 11–12/84: 7).[5]

CUB has also become increasingly anti-adoption. The July 1990 issue of the *Communicator* quoted with approval a report demanding "sweeping changes," so that birthparents were insured of continuing "connection" with the child. "Open adoption, which we helped pioneer, is not a solution to the problems inherent in adoption. Without legal sanction, open adoption is an unenforceable agreement at the whim of the adoptive parents. Instead, a form of guardianship adoption would be in the best interests of all concerned, with special benefits for the adoptee. It decreases the abandonment/rejection issue and permits the child to know that the birthparents cared but could not raise him" (CUB *Communicator*, 7/90: 3). Editorials oppose adoption in an even more uncompromising tone.

Changes in the interpretation of the group's logo, a bear, symbolize the shifts in content and purpose CUB has recently undergone. Between 1976 and 1982, the bear was transformed from a mother nuzzling her cub into Artemis, the bear goddess, confident of her strength and her ability to conquer enemies. "Artemis represented the wild self, the power to be your own person, free, uncaged, with permission to growl and protect. As the myth went, those who invoked Artemis awakened the integrity of self that upholds the right to be different, to be the people we are and to walk the path we do" (CUB *Communicator*, 6/83: 23). The image of Artemis conveyed the individuality of a quest as well as the importance of control, confidence, and assertiveness. "And I did not consciously deal with the impact of the surrender until more than a decade had passed—until a time when my life was secure enough that I could allow the suffering to surface" (Campbell 1979, 26). The bear is still on the cover of the *Communicator*, a symbol of strength combined with nurturance; inside the pages, bearlike qualities are directed toward fighting the institution of adoption and ending the oppression of birthmothers. A recent column entitled "A White Bear" (referring to a Tolstoy story "Try not to think of a white bear") concluded: "The only way to conquer obsession is by facing our fears, searching and finding" (CUB *Communicator*, 7–8/89: 25).

CUB rhetoric influenced the language and content of search stories told by birthparents who had not joined a group. They defined the search in terms of gaining strength, coming out of the closet, and "unsealing" the little box of memories; search was a moment of confidence for birthparents, not a moment of tribulation. Moreover, they were convinced that looking for one's own child was only "natural."

"It is against the laws of nature to sever a mother from her child in such a final way!" (CUB *Communicator,* 1/83: 10). Wanting to know the fate of one's child was part of being a parent.

"The buzzer will go off"

Birthparents always wondered about the child they surrendered; searching came out of a "constant longing" to know how the child was. "To never know your birthchild is to spend a lifetime in the anguish of forever wondering, a punishment disproportionate to the 'crime' of giving birth" (Concerned United Birthparents, *The Birthparent's Perspective,* n.d.). At some point, a person moved from longing to acting. And, as with adoptees, the particular prompting varied; there were few common threads to what pushed a birthparent over into beginning the process. It might have been a television program, or hearing that someone else had found a child, or realizing that one's child was an adult. Birthparents tended not to emphasize a moment of decision, underlining instead the constancy of their interest in the child. That was the meaning of being a parent. Yet the instant of knowing you would search was also significant.

"I always knew I would find Heather," a birthmother said, not untypically. "I always knew I would get in touch with her." Another told me her reason: "I think all I want is to have a chance to talk to her and explain why I did what I did or just find out how she feels about it." Searching related directly to surrendering. "And I knew I had to see them just once in person and tell them that I love them. Just deliver that message. Tell them that I really felt terrible about what happened and that I hadn't forgotten them, and that I loved them."[6] Feelings of guilt, confusion, and love were stronger at some times than others, but that did not necessarily turn a person into an active searcher. In an early book bringing the birthparent side of the adoption story to light, the authors note: "The mothers reported that their sense of loss fluctuates and is typically felt most severely on the relinquished child's birthday, on the birth of subsequent children and on the attainment of certain milestones" (Winkler and van Keppel 1984, 67).

Those were the things birthparents said: birthdays of the relinquished child were difficult, and the birth of another child brought up memories of a first child. "The birth of my second son ten years later brought forth the tremendous impact of realizing just how much I had lost" (in Rillera 1982, 37). Birthfathers who had "come out" said exactly the same thing as birthmothers; the birth of another child had an equally powerful, and physical, impact. "The first time I think the full impact of what I had done hit me was when my next daughter was born and the nurse at the hospital basically laid her in my arms and right away I knew there were two. And I knew that when the situation was right that we would begin to search earnestly and that we would find her" (Birthfather, *Today Show*, 4/86). But when was the situation right?

"Finally when Julie's 18th birthday approached, I really began [to search] in earnest" (Birthfather, *Today Show*, 4/86). That was when the child was an adult; she could search for her parent and she could handle the disruption if a birthparent arrived on the scene; by convention, an adult was free to decide about relationships and by law the adoptee was no longer a minor. "I can't believe it has been seventeen years," a birthmother considered the situation out loud. "I remember when she was five and thinking, boy, can't I ever wait until she was seventeen and [I] could find her." Even the child's adulthood, however, was not always enough to push a birthparent over the line: it might take something "out of the blue."

"I was unprepared for it," said a birthmother about a call from an adoptee. "I had no earthly idea. And this girl was trying to get me to remember anything I could remember of her mother. And see, I was the only living person who had seen her mother, that she had ever talked to. . . . And actually [I] was able to remember her mother's name which was really, really unusual because I could not remember anybody's name and I finally came up out of the deep with her mother's name, what she looked like, and what her personality was like, and what it was like for all of us living in that home [for unwed mothers]. . . . And just saying those things out loud, you know, to somebody really rocks the boat here. And I still didn't have an idea that I was gonna search for her, for Lorna. I just felt like all confused and stuff."

But the phone call, as she wrote later for a birthparent newsletter, was a turning point. "All I could feel was the return of a nightmare I had been trying to erase. 'Coming out of the closet' is a shattering experience at first, because it brings the dark shadows of the past into present reality without hope for the future. All of a sudden, old memories took voice, again causing me to relive the tears, the terrors, the lies, the manipulations, the tearing away and apart, the loneliness and despair. And, through another voice, my own daughter was calling to me" (BSG *Newsletter*, 11–12/89: 5). Still, one more thing was necessary before she actually decided to search. "And I was telling Tony [husband] about the conversation and at the end of our conversation he said, 'have you ever thought about, would you like to see your daughter?' And I said, 'well, I would give my right arm to see my daughter.' And he said, 'well, what are you waiting for?' I said, 'what do you mean, what am I waiting for? You seriously think I should do this?' And he said, 'of course.'"

Whatever the prompting and encouragement from outside, birthparents emphasized that the final decision was their own. "And I know that when the time is right for me, the buzzer will go off and I'll either pick up the phone, get on a plane or write a letter. Or something" (Concerned United Birthparents, *Biennial Report*, 1983, 40). Like CUB, BSG told its members: "We believe in the capacity of each individual to choose how, when or whether to search," adding, somewhat pedantically, "Search should only be undertaken when an individual is prepared to accept the commitments reunion entails" (BSG *Newsletter*, 1–2/90: 2). The decision to search came at a moment of strength and self-confidence. "Much to my surprise, I also realized that I was beginning to stand taller inside," a woman wrote to the newsletter. "It was like a rolling stone that gathers a momentum of strength, courage and hope for dreams that just might become true" (BSG *Newsletter*, 11–12/89: 6).

They had to feel strong; numerous obstacles stood in the way for a searching birthparent. "In our efforts we are not unlike 'Pac-Man' in that we travel the maze hoping to eliminate all opposition, gobbling our enemies one by one" (CUB *Communicator*, 10–11/82: 14). For most birthparents, however, being confident about searching was not enough—they had to discover how to begin.

A few started with the relatively safe method of registering. A member of ASG[7] told me she had not planned to search for her relinquished daughter until she accidentally heard about Soundex. "But you know I just thought that it [waiver of confidentiality] should get to the child and that there should be some way that the child could know that the parent wanted to be contacted so that they wouldn't be afraid to try to contact them, for fear that you're being rejected or something like that. I never knew there was anything like that until my aunt saw a thing in the paper for Soundex and she cut it out for me. And I thought that was a good idea, so I signed up for that." Her daughter had also registered and a meeting occurred in less than six months.

One birthmother joined a support group only to meet, the first time she went, a nurse who had been in the delivery room and remembered the relinquishment. Later this birthmother told me: "So I attended a meeting with ASG and it turned out, at the very first meeting, I met Susie and she talked to me and she worked at County General when the baby was born and she knew Dr. King and he had handled a lot of adoptions. And she thought that she remembered Dr. King saying that she was a very lucky baby because she was going to be adopted. When she told me that, maybe it was wishful thinking or whatever, but that was it. And the whole coincidence—" propelled her, she implied, into searching.[8] Usually, however, joining a support group was a way of gaining reassurance—knowing, as adoptees also said, "you weren't crazy." "LEAF [an adoptee support group] was the first place that I could really share my feelings and my needs. Really tell someone 'I need this' and they understood. They didn't look down on you and they didn't tell you, 'but this or that,'" said a birthmother whose search began slowly. "But CUB is where I really knew that people understood exactly what I was feeling."

By the mid-1980s, support groups also provided specific instructions for conducting a search. The first step involved "coming out" and declaring one's parenthood in front of the others. This was the step, too, that counteracted the invisibility the surrender was supposed to have brought—unfreezing memories and claiming the child's place in a birthparent's present life. "Well, I was secure enough to be able to let those feelings out from being a birthparent and all the years that I had thought about my twin daughters. And my husband is really understanding," said one woman. In fact, he also had "lost" a child: "he had his children but he had lost one, or one of his oldest daughters went with his wife," after a divorce. Tony, mentioned above, had another reason for supporting his wife's search. "He was the one who said that my brothers had a sist—uh, my sons had a sister, had that ever crossed my mind?"—her slip of the tongue mixing up generations anticipated the blurring of age difference a reunion would bring. "It hadn't crossed my mind. I don't think everybody gets support from their husbands the way I got. He just, being Italian he just thinks blood is the most important thing in the world [laughing]."

Still, she had to face "Pac-Man" on her own, and that was not easy.

Birthparents could not petition to have adoption records opened and could only get a name if a social worker or lawyer were willing to help. And that was rare. Few professionals are wholeheartedly enthusiastic about birthparent searches, and for good reason: such searches intrude into the promised privacy of the adoptive family and do not seem necessarily in the best interests of a child. At ASG, the gossip was that the only sympathetic social worker was the social worker who was herself a "closet" birthmother.[9]

Searching birthparents did not have an easy time with social workers. "So she definitely was leaning more toward the side where I don't have any rights," a birthmother described the social worker she consulted. "Or she kept on saying, 'it's not a good idea. It's not a good idea to open business up.' I asked her if she would at least contact them [adoptive parents] for me and tell them that I am interested and if they would please contact me anonymously. Just call me, tell me some general, talk to me, you know, make me feel that they don't think I am not good enough to give them a baby. So I pleaded with her and she kept on saying, 'no, no, it was not a good idea.' And I pleaded and I cried, and she finally said 'alright, I will do that for you. I'll give the message but I can't promise anything.' Well, I never heard anything from them. I don't know what she did or what."

The only help seemed to come by accident. "Oh, then she [social worker] had sent me to this other social worker who had known the family supposedly, because I said I want to know what they are like as people. I don't care if they were 5 feet 4, and so anyway this other social worker knew them as people and—" catching herself, "I don't think she really did. She had met them once. Yeah, but I caught her off guard this one day. I mean, it was just a quirk of fate and, well, the first day I didn't talk to her, in fact, and to this other social worker and she accidentally said the name. Oh, my toes curled and I could not believe my ears and she couldn't believe her mouth. She started talking twelve miles an hour about this and that and this and that and said, had said it really fast, the name, and I was frightened and trying to figure out all different ways that you could spell it and stuff."

Or, in the one or two cases where a social worker was cooperative, birthparents found that too involved a struggle. "That's the Child Welfare Service, Ann is in charge of that department [requests for information]. I called Ann and felt that, well, initially I felt hopeful and then after several months—I contacted once a month. I wrote her letters once a month. And I don't know whether she was trying to see if

I was real sincere or whether she was extremely busy as she said; I don't want to judge her. But every time I would call her, it was 'I don't have any information for you yet but I'll get back to you.'" The birthparent began exerting more pressure on the social worker and developing techniques of her own. "So I contacted this person [friend] and I said, 'I am going to ask you to do something illegal for me. And I know you will because you really care.' I said, 'in your computer work, is there any way you can find out marriage license applications if you don't have a name?' . . . She came up with like 700 pages, which I never got because in the meantime everything transpired the way it should have." That is, she heard from the social worker, who had contacted the adoptive parents about her request for information and for contact if they were willing.

Birthfathers, of course, had a harder time. No one really understood a man's desire to contact a child he had never seen: in cultural terms, "childless father" made even less sense than "childless mother." By report, fathers confronted more obstacles and more outright condemnation than birthmothers. "They were amazed that a birthfather would call," said a man at an ASG meeting. He was given no help by the social worker. He hired a search consultant, but with no more satisfaction than he got from the agency: "I can't get anything, not for money or anything. They keep telling one lie upon another." "$2,500 and no results," he complained at another meeting.

For either birthparent, taking over the search oneself was often the only option. The birthmother who accidentally learned the adoptive family name continued her story. After a delay of three years, "I drove by their house once and it was funny, in my dreams I could always see green. But their house is on a hill, surrounded by trees." She took the next step more quickly. "Sonia [search consultant] did go with me, because she went into the high school. I figured out what high school district they would be in and I saw a picture in the yearbook. . . . We both went into the high school and you know her, she is tiny like you, she looked like a teenager and so we went into the library and she got the yearbook and we found the pictures. And I was on cloud nine. I saw that they probably were a great family and had a stable life." But then she waited again before making contact, four more years, until the children "were of age."

"Anyway, it turned out that Margo's neighbor had a daughter that attended the same private school," said a birthmother who was pursuing her own search. "And Margo borrowed the yearbook on some pretence that some friend of hers from out of state wanted to, was moving back here and wanted to send her daughter there and they wanted to see a yearbook. . . . She called me the minute she got it; she says, 'I have the yearbook here,' and within forty-five minutes I was at her house, you know." This birthparent did not wait. "And at that time, right around that time, is when I decided that I was going to see her [relinquished child]." Once a birthmother had a name and an address, she might well find it hard to resist taking the next step. "So I sat down and I wrote her [child] a forty-page letter, describing my whole family, everybody, you know, everybody's birth dates, who they were married to, how many children they had, what had become of them, what they were doing, everything. And I enclosed a picture of Ralph [husband] and I [sic] and at that time we had two kids and I put it in, and if she ever came [to the agency], I wanted her to have that—that went to the agency."

By depositing the letter, this birthmother had in effect created her own registry. And in fact the daughter did come to the agency for information. "So I shot off a six-page letter to her boss, to the adoption, post-adoption supervisor, sending a carbon copy to my caseworker and said, you know, 'what the hell's going on here and I want a meeting arranged. Too, I believe that if my daughter came into the agency, she wants to meet me and I want to meet her.' So after a couple of phone calls the caseworker called me back and said, 'how about Monday?' and you know I about dropped my teeth. I, all the years that I've yearned for that thing to come up, how about Monday was really a shocker." Then there was another hitch. "So come Monday morning the caseworker called me and says, 'gee, I haven't been able to get a hold of your daughter,' and I said, 'my God, I haven't been sleeping for three days, you know, I've been so anxious I've been flying and now you call me an hour before I'm supposed to leave the house and tell me you haven't gotten a hold of her, you know, what the hell are you doing? You're playing with my life.' You know, just no regard. So then she called back an hour later and did get a hold of Candy and I said 'yeah' and here Candy is going to school in Woodmont where I'm from."

A major aspect of searching involved rejecting the image of passivity and vulnerability that went with surrendering a child. "And Barbara [social worker] had tentatively set up a meeting at the agency for the following Monday, so that she could be the intermediary. I guess she wanted to see the happy reunion or whatever. We took that away from her," by meeting before the scheduled time. The adoptee called and said, "why do we have to wait until Monday?' I said, 'well, I don't know, I guess I just assumed that was the way we had to do it.' Here I am again, you know, this is what you'll do and ok, fine, I'll do it."

Birthparents did not see any contradiction between taking control of a search and being utterly overwhelmed by the first phone call. "The first phone call was like having to experience the entire range of emotions all in one fell swoop," said a birthmother who was still excited several months later. "I don't think I've experienced it to that degree before, when you're terrified, you're exuberant, it's like a real true dream that comes true, like a fairy tale that never happens but in your life it's really happening." And with dream versus reality still a theme, she went on to say: "On the other hand, I felt like I was doing something extremely real where everything else was kind of blurred. My memories were blurred, I would try to think 'did I do that, did I not do that?' All of a sudden what I was doing seemed real, like I was—there was some real thing that was happening in my life about this situation. And it made it present and then it was fixing things somehow, fixing them in the sense of truly ending a chapter and being done with this blurry feeling that you carry with you."

A few birthparents skipped the phone call entirely and went to look at the child before arranging a meeting. "So that same vehicle that I had seen that girl in, a gold one, sat in the school parking lot every time I went there and I kept thinking, 'that's it.'" Hers was a moderate response to the first sight of a lost child, at least compared with the accounts published in birthparent literature. "On the way home I would vary from laughing and babbling about the wonder and joy of finding, to having to stop the car so I could vomit" (in Rillera 1982, 15). But moderation disappeared when there was an actual meeting. "And we talked for, I mean the first couple of minutes was a little shaky, but after that it was like we were never separated."

"I felt as if my body was turned inside out"

Meeting a child who had been relinquished and raised by other parents was the climax of a birthparent search. But there was little way of knowing what to expect or what to do during such a meeting. Birthparent literature described the encounter as joyous, ecstatic, unbelievable, but did not provide "maps" for how to act with a totally unfamiliar child—a child, moreover, who had grown up.

"I felt as if my body was turned inside out. We met, hugged, kissed, held hands and cried together," a birthparent wrote to the CUB newsletter (*Communicator*, 11–12/84: 4). "I was filled only with joy equal to the day I gave birth to him" (in Rillera 1982, 48). The exhilaration that had been suppressed by "signing away" a baby came out at this sight of the child. "And the first thing that, the first meeting was so, oh, it was just—," a birthparent breathlessly began her account to me. "I went home, I was crying, I was laughing, I was screaming in the car. It was just too good to be true!" And another: "So we met on September 14, it will be a year. And when we saw each other we just looked and opened our arms to each other and held on and bawled and bawled and bawled. That's all we did, we just hugged and cried."

There were love-at-first-sight meetings like Diana's: "And when I got off the plane we, neither of us had any problem recognizing each other. And we stood in the middle of the aisle, all the people are still trying to get, you know, the aisle just as you get out the gate. And people had to go around us. And we stood there and cried, for a long time. With our arms around each other. And it was the most wonderful tears I ever shed in my life. The most wonderful, unashamed—." But there were also awkward and uneasy meetings. As one woman expressed it: "Well, the first part was awful. I didn't know what to, how to introduce myself. I guess I am kind of sensitive about how she would feel about it if I would have said, 'this is your mother,' because her adoptive mother is her mother. So I just told her my name. I felt so stupid. 'Hi. This is Eleanor McKay.'" "I couldn't touch them," said another woman who found her relinquished twins. "But I just kept looking at them. I tried not to be awkward, but I was just so pleased to see their faces."

The awkward, like the ecstatic, encounters ultimately testified to the strength of the bond between parent and child. "And I said, 'hi.' And she says, 'hi.' And she was looking at me real puzzled, and I says, 'you don't know me,' I says, 'but—.' But then I just blurted out, I says, 'I'm the woman that gave birth to you eighteen years ago,'" carefully avoiding the term "mother." "And I started crying. I was like, you know, I was real emotional and she just like looked at me, her mouth dropped open, she says, 'oh my God!' And I says, 'if you don't want to talk to me, tell me and I'll walk away, I'll leave you alone right now.' She says, 'no, no, please don't.' And what ended up, we spent two or two and a half hours standing there in the parking lot, talking." Talk meant more than exchanging information: talking made the bond tangible, almost physical. By and large, parents met adult adoptees and touching was not an easy option; being a *mother* altogether was not an easy option.

"We didn't get into everything, not in great depth anyway," said one birthmother. "It was hard to get, like I said I have a problem and it's hard to talk about those kinds of things. That situation, I just kind of felt awkward. So it was really unreal. Like I know she's my daughter but I don't have any of these motherly feelings. And I don't know how to act like a mother because I have never been a mother. If I had other children and had been a mother to them, I would kind of had a motherly attitude. So it was like we ended up talking like two college roommates or something instead of like mother and daughter."

"She's my daughter but I've never been a mother" captures the paradox of these reunions. Birthparents who were "mothers" discovered other complications as well. "And I realized afterwards that what I wanted to find was this cute, cuddly, needing little baby who was going to say 'mother,' you know, after all these years. Because that's what I had wanted and that need, although I had two sons, was never filled. I still had this baby somewhere that was taken from me and so when I saw her I wanted to hold her and cuddle her and buy her things and take her shopping and shower her with my love and attention and affection and move in and 'anything, anything you want, I'll lay down and die, anything.' " Not every birthparent was this explicit or, perhaps, this honest about the appeal of a baby. And it was not exactly that anyone *did* want a baby. Rather, the image of a baby who could be hugged and cuddled rationalized—and normalized— the "gush of feeling" a birthparent experienced upon meeting an adult-child.

Thinking about a baby helped to distance the passion from that experienced between peers—which could have sexual overtones. "My every thought was of him. I now knew what the term Magnificent Obsession meant," wrote a birthmother, expressing the strength of her love with a term that evokes an overwhelming, romantic attachment (CUB *Communicator,* 4/87: 10). For some birthparents, analogies to the power of a sexual attraction best captured the quality of this meeting.

One birthparent in her mid-30s went to San Francisco with her college-age son: staying in the hotel together, she said, had been a "lovely adventure." When she came home from that trip, she enrolled in parenting classes—an effort to channel the intensity of her feelings. That they were missing the generational differences and the patterns of conduct that ordinarily regulate parental emotions was not lost on birthparents.[10] The BSG newsletter reassured its readers about too-passionate feelings: "As time passed and we discussed the subject more, we found this was happening to a great number of newly re-united people; not only mothers and sons, but daughters and fathers, sisters and brothers and even mothers and daughters and brothers with brothers. This was a relief to know because it really meant it was more than sexual. It was more of a need of physical bonding that was taking place" (BSG *Newsletter*, 3–4/90: 7).

As adoptees did in their reunions with members of a birth family, birthparents transferred the intense feeling of closeness into an appre-ciation of the "remarkable resemblances" they discovered.[11] Such a merging of two people was, in their eyes, appropriate to parenthood.

A birthmother showed me some pictures. "I just want to see if you can, that was the yearbook that Margo had. See if you can pick her out." I laughed, uncertain about what I would see. "It's awkward to ask," she admitted. "My family could pick her right out." And later, "This is her sixteenth birthday. Now that one, I have a picture almost identical to that with my hair flat and pulled back. We do look a lot alike." As we went through the album, she commented: "It just seemed real natural for me to think of her as my daughter." These natural connections came out in all sorts of similarities. "They had things, all the things that I love I could see in their room," a woman told me. "And I took that, I don't know if it's right or not, that's my characteristic." The significance of shared nature also came out when a birthparent had the bad luck of finding a spoiled child, her nature "ruined," or at least molded into something alien, by the adoptive parents. "She is 6 feet tall, beautiful, and sweet, but she is also a spoiled rotten brat who is vain, materialistic, doesn't help with chores, and doesn't have the words 'thank you' in her vocabulary," one birth-mother said after her daughter came to visit.

"We are in two separate worlds," another mother reported sadly. "And that's a lot, part of the problem with her, too, is she is very spoiled. She was never, I mean, she's never done a dish. She's never made her own bed, you know, that type of thing. She went off to col-lege and didn't even know how to run a washing machine. So we're in two different worlds that way." Spoiled, I realized after hearing it so much, had powerful resonance for a birthparent: the concept represented the consequences of moving a child out of her natural setting. "She is, I mean to me, my husband and I were talking last night, and it's like she's this 2-year-old child who thinks the universe still rotates around herself, and she doesn't—. She can take terrific but she doesn't know that she should give something back."

Spoiled was equivalent to unnatural in another sense as well. Brought up in an adoptive family, relinquished children learned to be restrained, not emotional and expressive, as birthparents described themselves. "And I was crying, which really didn't help matters at all, and I kept apologizing for being so emotional and I tried to explain everything and they [adoptive parents] just looked at me. They were really controlled emotionally, and I wish I could be that way but that's not the way I am." Her birthdaughters, she said, had learned to be like their adoptive parents. "But she [adoptive mother] has a really strong personality and like I said they [daughters] are both really controlled emotionally. They grew up learning this, and they are like their adoptive parents in that way. They can talk about things and not cry or get emotional and I can't." But one daughter changed after the contact. "I got a wonderful letter from Lizzie just a couple of weeks ago and she said 'I love you a lot' and at the end—. It was the first letter that I know she cares about me. There's something real special between me and Liz, a special bond and I could feel it the first time I looked at her. I knew she could feel it, too, even though we didn't really talk."

Reunions recalled the contrast that had been established during relinquishment: the unemotional, materialistic, and selfish adoptive parent versus the loving and expressive biological parent. The contrast was imposed upon the details birthparents heard about a child's upbringing. "She says that they [the adoptive family] don't even see each other—even when she was in high school, they barely saw each other. Everybody went their own way. Her mother and dad went golfing every weekend. Little things like that bother me, too. Things about her father especially bother me, when you—when you're told you're giving your child to this ideal family, when I hear about him being so narrow-minded and—, that bothers me," said a birthmother who had recently found her daughter. Just as during the relinquishment, in searching birthparents emphasized the attachment that persists beneath the superficial arrangement of an adoption. "[B]ecause what we have exists just because of who we are to each other," a birthmother explained to me. "And it's really special. For no other reason this love exists, that's because of who we are and it's really beautiful I think."

Still, if the meeting turned into an ongoing relationship, enduring love did not provide a map for everyday interactions. "I don't have any role models. It's like a virgin field, so I don't know what I'm supposed to expect and what I'm not supposed to expect. There's no map. Even if I were to say to myself, am I supposed to be really involved with her in her life like a real mother, and if I were to say yes, I would have to tell you that—I don't know that I can do that. Because I wasn't her parent. That makes a big difference on things, you know. I also think that would be very freeing, though, if an adoptive person [parent] could understand that. That just like nothing can change the fact that someone else gave birth to their child, nothing can change the fact that they parented that child."

"I am perplexed about where we go now"

"The glow has worn off." After the reunion, birthparents faced the challenge of establishing an ongoing, enduring relationship with a child they had not known. In most cases as well, this was not a baby or even a child at all, but an adult who had ideas of his or her own about parenthood, family, and kinship—and about the behavior associated with these concepts. Whatever the quality of the reunion, it did not carry either person through the ordeal of learning how to act with a stranger you were supposed to love. "Post-search," said the coordinator of BSG, "is a whole new chapter."

Birthparents tried a variety of models, including friendship, extended kinship (becoming another member of the family), genealogical parenthood (a tie of biology, not of conduct), and social parenthood (involvement in the adopted person's life). Always, however, the practical details of establishing a relationship compelled a reconsideration of the meaning of parenthood: how *is* love linked to behavior? *Do* resemblances create solidarity? How familiar *ought* a child really be? Most birthparents claimed they loved the child unconditionally; few were sure about the expressions and the obligations this love entailed.

"Michael and I have established an affectionate bond between us that does not replace any previously existing ones. What has been replaced, he and I agree, is the pain and the fantasy," wrote Lee Campbell, founder of CUB, in a published version of her story (1979, 27). Affection, as she used the word, represented a modification of the initial intensity of feeling between parent and child. As she told the story, in the first "glow" of reunion she had been introduced to the adoptive family, invited to family gatherings, and treated like a special kind of relative. Then, suddenly, the adoptive parents rejected her. "The most difficult areas have been interacting with the adoptive parents and with the birthfather and his family," Campbell commented in an article she wrote three years after meeting her son (1982, 23). In response to the change, she turned the relationship with her son into a friendship. Casual and less demanding, friendship avoided the presence of any of her son's other parents while allowing her to stay in touch with her child.

By and large, birthparents did not find friendship a satisfactory model. Being friends with a found child was discordant with the interpretation of parenthood that had prompted a search in the first place. And it was too "cool" an aftermath to the excitement of a reunion. "'I don't want to be your pal, I want to be your mother,'" one birthmother told her 19-year-old daughter. "But if she doesn't want me to be her mother, then forget it. I don't want to be her friend, although I told people I just wanted to be a friend, but that really wasn't true. Some people say that they want to be their friend and I think that they really believe it, but I didn't." This birthmother added: "I feel like I am her mom. I mean I know I'm her mom, I mean, for God's sake I gave birth to her and I don't want to be called anything else. I am her mom. She's got two moms." She inserted herself into the family, warning her daughter's boyfriend that he would have two mothers-in-law. By insisting on "mom," she meant to have a role as well as a status.

This birthmother had definite ideas about what a mother-child relationship meant. But so did her daughter. "I call every week and I write to her and then letters, would you know, the first letter came after a week and then it was three weeks and then a month and then, 'I'll talk to you later.'" The daughter was not responsive. "You know, I felt this distance growing and everybody told me to back off, which I found really difficult to do." Four years later the birthmother reported to me: "But nothing has changed. Nothing has changed." The daughter continued to be withdrawn. "And it's real hard to continue that relationship, you know, because I feel like I'm—I mean, I write her very emotional, loving letters and tell her what the relationship means to me or what she means to me or how important the adoption movement is and what I'm doing, and she writes back and says, you know, 'the weather's nice and we're real busy and we went to the football game' and she doesn't respond. And I'm thinking, I feel like I'm batting my head against the wall sometimes, that she's not giving me the response that I want and so I get angry sometimes. And then I say, well, hey, she was raised by other people and I have no control over how they raised her, and I might not approve of it and I might not like it. I don't—you know, she's never really shared her feelings about her family."

The wall she was batting her head against was another person's definition of the parent-child relationship—a grown-up person, raised by other people who, moreover, did not need another mother. "Our children may someday allow us to be their friends but we cannot be their mothers," a CUB pamphlet warned CUB members (Anderson 1980, 2).[12] A birthmother told me her daughter was a "friend, definitely. Close and sometimes more, you know. Like you would—a sister-type thing. . . . You know it was never any question that, whether she would call me 'mom' or anything. It's always sort of a little awkward." No longer a childless mother, the birthparent was not a "mom" either. Yet the pull after reunions was almost always toward a relationship based on notions of motherhood, even for birthfathers who contacted a child.

But they could not do it without cooperation at the other end; "motherhood" was not simply a set of traits but also, clearly, a pattern of behavior. A birthparent commented to me: "There was still something missing. I can't even explain it, I didn't—I started feeling like she was communicating with me and bothering with me like an obligation, but there really wasn't any need or desire there. And I started feeling like she doesn't really have time for me in her life." Even a crisis did not necessarily alter the relinquished child's behavior or create a role for the birthparent. "And a few days prior to this my husband and the kids and I had all been out to Pizza Hut and we were talking about Candy [birthdaughter] and I said, for some reason, 'I could be a grandmother for all I know.' And then two days later she called me and told me that I was a grandmother. And that she realized that she had dumped on me and she said that her parents weren't speaking to her, they were very angry, they were very upset. 'But now,' she says, 'I understand what you went through when you were pregnant.' And I thought, oh, finally now we can have a relationship." But in fact nothing changed.

I heard the same thing from another parent whose daughter called unexpectedly. "It was in the middle of the afternoon and she sounded very upset. And I said, 'Katy, what's the matter?' And she says, 'nothing, it's just really been a bad week. I've just had a lot of problems.' And I said, I sensed that she wanted to talk, why would she call me, you know, and I kept saying, 'what's the matter? what's the matter?'. . . And I thought, 'here we go, she's going to tell me she wants to just break this whole thing off.' So instead she proceeds to tell me she's pregnant. I could not believe it. She said she just really needed somebody to talk to and she knew that I could understand where she was coming from and that I could relate to her. But she wanted to tell me, she didn't want to tell me. So she's pregnant now." After a pause, this birthmother said to me: "She would rather die than her parents find out." But still her own role was not clear. She did not think she could do anything, though she was struck by the fact that her daughter now shared *her* experience. "It was just like history repeating itself. It was—I got to feel what my mother felt when I went through it. It was different circumstances. I didn't raise Katy but it really, I mean, knowing it's your blood and—."

The uncertainty about how to act came from her, prompted perhaps by the daughter's ambivalence; she wanted to, she didn't want to. "I want to be with her but I don't," said the mother, echoing the daughter. Powerful as the model of motherhood was, birthparents recognized how firmly being a mother was grounded in raising a child. "But the funny thing is, you know, when you're not the mother, when you're not the parent—that's a better word, because I am the mother. But when you're not the parent and you weren't involved in parenting, you just have to sit back and wait and let those things take care of themselves."

One way of getting around this was to involve the birthchild in an extended family, embedding one relationship in others—whose rules were known and familiar. Katy's mother brought the grandmother into the picture. "And I took her up to the car and introduced her to my mom and that was another emotional exchange." This three-generational relationship had familiar components, like rivalry over being a good mother. "And my mother told me, at the end of the conversation she says that she sort of resents Katy because of the way she treats me. She doesn't feel that she—she's thinking as a mother, she feels protective of me, and she thinks that I'm being hurt by Katy, that Katy's not responding to me the way I'd like her to." The birthmother responded just like a mother: "And I said, 'I understand how you feel.' Then I get real protective of Katy too, you know."

It was even more desirable to draw the child into a family that included siblings, cousins, aunts, and uncles. (The strategy recalled the adoptee's conviction that kinship was more solid the more people were involved.) This demanded a commitment to working out the intricacies of a new kind of kinship. Margo, Danielle's birthmother, undertook this task, describing Danielle's arrival in the house. "She walked in and I said, 'this is your brother Alan and this is your sister Elizabeth.' It was like they knew each other. It was no problem. Then Tammy came over, she was at school or something, and she came over later that day and she met her. And it was a non-stop weekend and I was totally exhausted when it was over. Then she spent the next three or four weekends here. Danielle was a very demanding person with all of the problems that she has." Danielle also had her own kinship priorities. "She calls him 'Dad.' All the other kids call him Smitty. . . . But Danielle calls him 'Dad.' She asked if it was alright if I call you Dad. She calls me 'Mom.'" The adoptee wanted all this to be permanent. "Well, she even said to me, 'can you re-adopt me?' I said no. I said what is on her legal document means nothing. The bond we have between each other is what is important."

The bond went beyond nature, and Margo became as much a "mom" as a mother to Danielle. But this was an unusual situation; Danielle had medical problems that required a good deal of care and attention. Danielle was babyish in her frailty, and that made it easier for Margo to be maternal. The birthmother took on her tasks willingly and, as far as I knew, the adoptive mother willingly relinquished her role in at least that part of Danielle's life. Margo depended on the support of her husband and other children, and fit her role as parent to Danielle into established family patterns.

Margo's husband was not unique in embracing the child of his wife, and adding his role to hers. Even if the husband gained from an unspoken comparison with the vanished birthfather, still a number of husbands seemed remarkably open to the strange new relative. Another birthmother reported about her husband, "and he said that he was totally unprepared for what happened to him when he met her.

That he thought he was going to be very gracious, he had made up his mind that he would probably love her as my daughter. But he said something really funny happened about half way through the week. He said, 'she wasn't your daughter any more, she was mine, too.' And so that was a wonderful, wonderful thing." The sons, however, were not overjoyed; one was irritated, "constantly probably feeling that we expect him to act like a brother or to do that or the other thing." But these sibling rivalries gave an air of normalcy to the relationship. "The one, the oldest one [of her children at home] is 5 and the other one's 3. He doesn't really, you know, know anything. But the older one, he's answered the phone a couple of times when she's called and he said, 'Mommy, it's your daughter.'" This little boy also asked, "How come we've never been to her house? When is she going to come to our house?"

A big family party could be the best way of incorporating a new child. "And it happened to be that this is the weekend that I had planned the shower and so Candy [birthdaughter] got to meet all the female members of the family, all her cousins, her grandma—not the real grandmother, my father remarried, my mother died, so kind of a grandma, stepgrandma—and my sister that wanted to keep her and my sisters. And she met Ralph [husband] and her brothers, so she met everybody. But her and my one niece about the same age . . . , her and Candy have developed a friendship." Thus, this birthmother underlined Candy's place in a whole family. "So I was just real flattered that she would come two and a half hours to visit and I hugged her, I was so happy to see her and we took pictures and all this kind of stuff, and she was warmer, I could feel warmth."

There was also another birth family—the family of the child's father. How did this parent fit into the postreunion picture? With one exception, the birthmothers I interviewed were not hostile to their child's father, but few were certain about whether to introduce him into this chapter of their lives.[13] Some did, however, and in various ways. A few scrupulously described the father to the child they met. "So I was very honest with her about how I got pregnant—oh, the first time we talked on the phone she wanted to know that. And who he was. And I told her as much about him as I could," said one birthmother. Another brought the child to meet the father's family. "So I sent a picture of Candy and [said] that his mother was a great-grandmother. So of course they wanted to get together. So Easter we all went out and had breakfast together. So there was the grandmother, the great-grandchild, the sister, the daughter-in-laws, and we all sat at this huge table in this restaurant and it was really nice."

And if a birthmother were willing, the father himself might become part of the re-created family. "I called him before I met them [twins], it was after I found them, I decided I wanted to talk to him," a birthmother told me. "So I was setting everything up in my mind how it was going to work and if they asked to see him, which I assumed they probably would, would he be open to it and how did he feel about it." Contact with the twins' father tangled her further in the past. "I was so glad that I talked to him because we brought up so many loose ends from before and I learned that he did grieve and he did care and a lot of things I never realized he felt." She learned a good deal about their relationship. "And I wasn't sure that he loved me either at that time and I wanted to make sure in my own mind that they [twins] were born in love. Because I felt that I loved him, but the more I learned that guys use women a lot or, you know, they give love to get sex and girls give sex to get love. And so finally it was really a good talk and I was so glad we did it. And he said, 'you bet I loved you.'"

But things were not entirely resolved. Contact with the man she had not seen for eighteen years had an unanticipated impact: "It's funny," she laughed, "there are still feelings there." But she was careful about those feelings, and tried to make them as familial as possible.[14] The twins "got a real kick out of seeing us together and I could almost feel them imagining what we were like twenty years before because we are still kind of silly. I'm silly because I still have feelings for him and I'm not afraid to hug or kiss him on the cheek, that's the way I feel." And though her husband seemed not to mind, she suspected there were risks in the arrangement. "It was really so nice. It did feel like you were cheating though, it really did, it was really nice—."

Still, the birthparents and the two grown-up children spent time together. "It was the strangest thing because we all just had the same grin. We were all sitting there looking at each other and realizing this is our family or a second or different family. This would have been our family and they'd look at me and look at Andy—." Andy also told his daughters how he felt: "I was really proud of Andy because he can't express his feelings at all and he said, 'there's one thing I want you to say or to know,' to the girls, 'that you know I feel real bad about what happened.'" This second family had been reunited for more than four years when I interviewed the birthmother, and she was beginning to realize there were also risks in a "fantasy" family. Real and fictive could get confused once again.

"It would be fun to get together once in a while but that is a dream that didn't come true and there is no way we can go over and make it come true," she told me, with regret in her voice. "We are not, we are a family but not in the real world, in a special world that we, the four of us will always have but it's outside of the real world." During the interview, this woman gave further thought to the unrealized birth family. "So we won't ever have a family but we will always have something really special and it is special and it can exist in this real world. When I write to Lizzie [one twin], I put myself outside of this world because I love her so much and like when I got this picture blown up, they had given me a wallet-size one and I wanted to get a big one, but by this time I could sense some little things around here in my excitement. And it made me realize you had better stop being so excited when you think about them because other little people [her own children] are beginning to feel not so important." This birthmother continued to explore the significance of biological ties, her obligations to the children living with her, and the possibility of acting on her several parental attachments.

Even less intricate postreunion relationships were not easy. One woman, whose found daughter looked very much like her, was uncomfortable about how attached her husband had become to the girl. "He just fell in love with her. There are times I think he fell in love with a younger version of me, maybe, or something." A re-created parent-child relationship was not just like a real one, even for a birthmother. "And you know what's funny?" she continued. "I don't feel her absence at the holidays, it's the strangest, craziest feeling. I would die if one of my sons weren't with me during those times, but I don't feel that with her." And it could be less like a parent-child relationship for the adopted person.

"I can't really expect her to feel that way either," a birthmother recognized about her birthdaughter. "I don't know if *I* would. That's what my mom said to me, she said, 'ok, just think if you or I, or if I raised you all these years and even if you knew you were adopted and all of a sudden this strange woman comes up and says, "hi, I'm your mom."' She says, 'do you think that you would feel this instant love for this woman?' And I, you know, no. And you know, even if it's curiosity or an interest, I don't think I could fall in love with some-body that easy. So I imagine it is totally different from that [adoptee] point of view. Whereas, you know, she's not—all these years I've loved her and thought of her."

"You never have too many relatives"

The adoptee's understandings of parent, family, and rel-atives shaped the birthparent's experience of reunion and subsequent visits. "Heather has to lie when she comes to visit me," a birthmother told me, convinced the adoptee could not tell her adoptive parents about the reunion and the new relationship she had.

Birthparents blamed adoptive parents for the lies adopted children told. "And she told me that when she broke the news to her parents they were very upset. The mother, mostly, felt that I betrayed her." This birthmother went on to explain why such deceptions occurred. "And, in turn, Katy felt that her allegiance should be to her parents—I guess they gave her the guilt, I don't know. She never really said that in words, but they went to extremes, like they were trying to get her to go see some type of, get some therapy or some type of help." As birthparents portrayed it, adoptive parents' reaction to a reunion con-firmed what they suspected, that adoptive parents were not interested in the child's own nature. Another birthparent put it poignantly, per-haps recalling her own earlier invisibility. "But Lorna's [adoptive] mother doesn't ask her any questions about this experience. I mean truly it is like total silence."

On the whole, birthparents mapped the terms of relinquishment onto present adoptive parent behavior, contrasting a parent who could give, and share, with one who took, and kept, a child. "The adoptive mother and I share something. She has the raising of him but I went through the conception, pregnancy, and birth," said one birthmother. A birthfather, just as forceful in his notion of sharing, remarked: "And to me, if her parents love her they shouldn't fear me. I love her too. I don't want to hurt her, can't we all love her together, you know? And I think adoption as it is now is just really ridiculous; I don't know why it can't be an open and loving and sharing relationship." In the con-ventional language of adoption, birthparents argued that "more love" was in the child's best interests. "I just kept explaining to her [social worker], 'I am not here to take away from Danielle's life, I want to add to her life.'" Nor were they there to take the child. As one birth-father explained: "I don't think there's anything wrong with that child sharing their love with their birthparents as well as their adoptive parents. You can love people in many, many different ways. I found that adoptive parents, their initial reaction is constantly one of extreme fear that we are going to come and steal the child away. And yet I have never known any of us to feel that way" (*Today Show*, 4/86).

On the other hand, the very basis of a search—the strength of a biological bond—might rightly prompt adoptive parent concern. A birthmother put it this way: "I mean their parents, they did not feel guilty about Andy [birthfather] or the grandparents or Francis [birthmother's husband]. They were really open and warm and playful and really let them know they liked them, but with me they held back. . . . They would not be threatened by Andy, but the mother they are. That's because birth is such a special, special thing."

"And they are right, in a way," she added. "There is a special bond [between birthparent and child] but it can never wipe out what they gave them. What they gave them is just as special as what I gave them—more. No, it's not more, but their love is more because they've known each other for so many more years. Geez, it will take me 22 years before—, and by that time their folks will have 40 years. Their folks don't have anything to worry about. I mean, love is so wonderful that nothing can break that." That was the dichotomy adoptive kinship created: a mother who was real because she gave birth to the child and another mother who was equally real because she raised the child. One birthparent echoed another; their themes were similar: "I said 'I'm not disrupting their life,' you know. I mean they've had twenty years to establish their relationship." A different birthmother described adoption. "Do you think that her knowing me is going to make any difference, is she gonna call me mom before she calls her mom? No way, you know. She was there for the mumps and the measles and the report cards. You can't destroy that." The solution might be, as yet another birthmother put it, to be "another relative. I can't be a mother. You never have too many relatives."

Birthparents needed to make up time and make up rules. "In many—you know when you push yourself, push too much, you are just defeating the purpose," a birthmother explained her decision to go slowly. "A lot of people that are having reunions that I know, that's what they tried to do and they alienate. It is a built in thing, it is, we are—they are part of our family but, and we are a part of theirs, but we've never known each other." The work required being flexible about kin terms, their meanings, and the conduct they implied. "It's the weirdest feeling. Because it's not a friend, it's much more than a friend. It's a connection that's not going to go away, even if we have a fight and don't speak for ten years, it's done, the connection's been made. So I have no earthly idea," a birthmother told me, continuing: "I don't feel like an aunt. I don't feel like a sister, cause I don't feel like I'm in her age and in her world. I have no earthly idea. I'll have to make a new one."

"I felt whole again"

The goal of searching was to find the child who may have been given away but was not therefore forgotten or unloved. Birthparents also, like adoptees, talked about a "quest for self" and a "gap" that could only be filled by meeting the child. "The birthmother gets reunited with herself—not only with the child. . . . And become[s] a whole person" (*Boston Phoenix*, 6/8/82: 6). As one birthmother related, "I have a calm now that I never had about it before." From the perspective of a quest for identity, then, no search was unsuccessful for a birthparent any more than for an adoptee. Another birthparent said: "I can't tell you what a relief it's been. Even, even if she right now told me she wanted to put everything on hold, I could live with that."

Yet that sentiment struggled against the wish to have some response from the child, to have him or her act like a "real" child, not (just) a birth child. "And is she just being, you know, she is really sweet with me and is she just feeling like, 'I owe this woman something because she went to so much trouble to find me,'" wondered a young birthmother who was disappointed at her 18-year-old daughter's behavior. "But she's never really said to me things like 'wow, that makes me really feel good that you looked for me.'" Being a mother, she also knew that children mature. "I keep thinking . . . that over the years things'll start looking, things'll start clicking, we'll get closer. But I do think now, right now, her priorities are totally friends, social life."

So despite their discouragement, birthparents worked at not just *being* but *acting like* parents.[15] "I'll just say things like, 'Katy, what are you doing about homework? Or are you getting enough sleep?' 'Oh, who cares about that stuff?' And I'll just jokingly say things to her, but I know I don't have any rights to," admitted the same birthmother. Yet acting like a "real" parent with the unfamiliar child did not come naturally. This woman added: "Then I witnessed my sister with her daughter. They went through some rough times, but they're real close in age, being she had her so young too. And I really envy the relationship that they have, you know."

Birthparents who anticipated awkwardness said the urgency overcame the cautions. "I couldn't live with not knowing. I couldn't live with this blank picture in my head"; thus a birthmother recalled the beginning of her search. "And everybody kept telling me, 'you're gonna get hurt, you're gonna get hurt,' if I proceeded and met her and she rejected me. I really did feel that no matter what the outcome was it had to be better than the way I was living in limbo. And since, like the first couple of meetings, I was still feeling real anxious and then—but it seems to be like now . . . I feel more at peace than I did for a long time without her." The concept of wholeness was not simply a rationalization for unconventional behavior; it was also a reference to reclaiming a piece of one's "self." Another woman explained: "I had come to the point where it would be extremely healthy for me and for her, even if she chose to hate me and never, never see me again, that it still was going to finalize and complete a chapter." Birthparents did not want a child back; they did want to reinsert a chapter in their lives.

"I think meeting Candy was by far the most nerve-wracking and the most beautiful and the most memorable experience in my whole life," one birthmother began her assessment of reunion. "And after handling that I was so, you know, after all those years of waiting for it and driving to Woodmont that day and being so scared and so happy and the emotions that I had, anything following that is inconsequential." She concluded, "I feel very at ease with my maturity or my growth or the way that I contemplate my life." Four years after the first meeting, she was working on the relationship—making up for lost time. "I feel like I had nineteen years without her, not nineteen, let's see now, sixteen, I married when I was what, 21? So all that number of years on one side, then I have to wait until I have that many years knowing her before it equals out and then, I think, then I'll look at it and see where we have come."

Ironically, only "years" could make the birthparent as much a parent as the adoptive parent had become. Reunions between blood kin showed the importance of cultivated parent-child ties: of *doing* something. However, at the same time and as I show in the next chapter, the genealogical model remained the most powerful one for adoptive parents engaged in creating a social kinship.

9

A Child of One's Own

Being an Adoptive Parent

"This kid's mine!"

Adoptive parents had qualified, and been accepted, as parents. Yet their understanding of how to be a parent still took its strongest guideline from a model based on the "physical realities" of birth. "It was just like I had him," a mother said to me; and a father: "This kid's mine!" When the child was actually there, in the family, the abstract *as-if* premise became concrete, problematic, and precarious. Adoptive parents in the late twentieth century find it hard to uphold the premise in the face of the emphasis on telling the child about adoption and explaining as much as possible about his or her past. Adoptive parents have to create a bond as strong as that of blood, while not denying the origin of the relationship in law. In this chapter, then, I discuss how adoptive parents interpret the "fictive" in their kinship as they engage in the task of bringing up a child.

The first challenge involved transforming a *deliberated* (by them) and a *designated* (by someone else) parenthood into a "destined" parenthood. A bond that was as sure as birth was a bond as unpremeditated as nature. Adoptive parents talked about knowing "instinctively" the child was theirs. They also talked about falling in love with the child. It was not far from that to the analogy of adoption with marriage, an analogy that focused initially on the honeymoon but lost its persuasiveness when carried much beyond that. The second challenge involved "naturalizing" their parenthood, which adoptive parents did by identifying with their own parents; the parent-child relationship was an inherited one. Like their own parents, they were not perfect, just average and ordinary parents. They would not work "miracles," but let the child's nature "unfold." As I show, the unfamiliarity of the child's nature made this an extra-ordinary task.

The third, and central, challenge is *telling*, as significant to the parent as to the child. An adoptive parent confronts the dilemma of making a child unconditionally "one's own" while reminding the child of his or her "other" family. The child is at once "yours" and "not yours." This affected what people *did* as parents, and how they interpreted concepts of love, permanence, and commitment. For the parents I met, the dilemma was further exacerbated by the possibility of contact with a birthparent, either by letter or in person. For most, the chance of a reunion lay in the future; while admitting a child's right to know, they did not have to (yet) actually interact with a birthparent. I met only one adoptive mother who knew her now-adult son's birthparents. Over the course of our conversation, the difficulty of the relationship became clear: she had no script for this kinship and no terms for her new relatives. Like the birthparents I met who had had reunions, the adoptive mother had to make her way without a map. I end the chapter with her experiences, and with her conviction that while the meeting had been good for her son, the shared parenting of an open adoption would not have been.

"Like a long labor"

They had been designated parents, by experts and by the law. Yet adoptive parents remained persuaded of the strength of the biological bond—haunted by the fact that they had "someone else's child." One adoptive mother described her feelings: "I was frantic! That was another thing that was hard on me. Bringing home a new baby all of a sudden, and here I am. I'm sure that he could feel my tension because every time there was a knock on the door you'd wonder, is it today? Is somebody going to knock on the door and say they want this baby?" And she admitted: "I really felt that I had kidnapped a baby."[1]

That was not a good way to begin parenthood. Adoptive parents had, as social workers put it, to develop a feeling of "entitlement" to the child.[2] But this was a hard word, one that left out the kind of emotion that seemed appropriate to having a baby, or a new child, in the family. "To adopt is to take as one's own; to adopt a child is to make of that child one's own child. When we think of adoption, that is what comes to mind: the waiting arms, the welcoming parents" (Rothman 1989, 126). Ideally, "taking as one's own" was accompanied by the nervous excitement and anticipation that is associated with pregnancy and birth; then adoptive parenthood began as much like real parenthood as possible. Although, as Bowlby (1963, 441) noted, "the intense emotional experience of a parent who adopts a baby is often overlooked," it was not overlooked by the parents I met.

"I was numb, unbelieving, and excited and calm. All of the above," said one mother, waiting for the arrival of her child. "Thursday I waited. I sat by the phone, I could hardly breathe all day," remembered a woman who had adopted in the 1950s. "About four or four-thirty I couldn't stand it any longer and I had to have—, no call. So I called them. And they said, 'Oh, Mrs. MacMillan, Sister so-and-so would love to, wants to speak to you.' And she got on the phone and she said, 'Mrs. MacMillan, I want you to know you have a baby boy!' I was in total shock!" The implied comparison with pregnancy and birth in these comments was explicit in others: "And then she [Mrs. Granger] called back and said that day the girl was in labor. So we went wild and went around saying, 'I'm in labor' and we went out that night and bought a crib and had dinner out. 'Guess what, we're—,' you know! And that was the day she had the baby and we went out that whole night and told everybody we saw."[3]

Carrying this further, one adoptive mother made her transition into parenthood by vicariously experiencing the labor of the birthmothers of her children. "Whenever—this is really strange—whenever all three women [birthmothers] went into labor, I was completely, completely sick. All three times I knew, I didn't know, but with Sean and every time something changed with Wendy [birthmother], in Wendy's life. . . . And it happened with Nathaniel the entire time. You know, like severe cramping and just terrible things. . . . Like the only time

I felt—isn't that strange? To talk about instincts, how an adoptive mother can't—. And I mean I am dead serious. And it was the same with Nathaniel, whenever I would get completely, I mean really, like keyed up or nervous, or I mean that real sick feeling." Unusual in extent, her feelings captured the spirit of undertaking adoptive parenthood. Other parents talked to me about nervous excitement and about a desperate rush to get everything ready: they were "unprepared" for the exact arrival of their child. Or, as one mother said, they had done "just enough." "I had prepared enough things that at least when a new baby came we weren't without bottles and a few things. Not that we had a lot, but that's kind of how Jill came in."

Social workers and adoption manuals encouraged parents to liken their experiences to pregnancy and birth. One social worker told me: "I try to put in as much as I can there [discussions with potential parents] on things that they need to do for themselves in the bonding. The adoptive pregnancy, too, is psychological. . . . You know, they do the study, then they need to wait a while until they get a baby, but through the county they get on the state registry and they could wait anywhere from a couple of months, to five years or more. So then what happens is they get anxious over the years and call you at certain times—it's usually seasons, certain seasons that they usually feel—. Then you call them up and see—they have a baby!" And it was not just women who responded to the advice; in adoption, a man could feel just as pregnant as his wife. According to one father: "I guess for us it was like a long labor, like you were in labor for years, you know, trying to give birth to this child." Another adoptive father, a writer, published his feelings: "The change is expressed in an unobtrusive transition between your thinking of him as 'the child' at first and 'my child' later. The change is indeed like a pregnancy; you will find to your embarrassment that you are showing exactly the same symptoms of mood and behavior. Hours of idle dreaming; total and constant preoccupation with the little life now so tenuously and mysteriously joined with your own" (de Hartog 1969, 21).

But gender stereotypes did not disappear. Adoptive mothers claimed their feelings came naturally; they had to help the new father feel parental. "I had planned it then, when it came time to pick him [baby] up, I let Rob pick him up first. So he picked him up first. He tried to get me to do it. I said, 'no, you go right ahead. I want you to pick him up first.' And I think he was pretty much like me. He fell right into it. He just sat down and held him in his lap and we were just in awe of how tiny he was. He was just such a little guy and had no neck muscles yet. His head was still flopping around. He was real good-looking. He had a red sheen to his head. It looked like he was going to have red hair. He is now, well, it still looks red there, doesn't it?"

The same kind of emphasis on a mother's natural ability to be nurturing and tender came up even when the adoptee was older, no longer an infant. Then, too, the mother knew what to do, was "closer" to the child, had a different relationship from the more awkward or, sometimes, less committed father.[4] One man remembered the first days with their adolescent son. "He wanted Mom there. Then that's exactly what he'd do, come in and crawl in bed. So really we had a teenager, but we went through a lot of child things, too, with him."

Acting motherly did not depend on the age of the child, but it did help if the older child seemed vulnerable, of tender temperament if not of tender age. "I think the image of Joey that will always stay with me from that weekend is he carried that pumpkin with him everywhere," a mother recalled about the 11-year-old they had adopted. "And he put all of his little toys and stuff in it and he carried it with him. We would drive up and he would be looking out the window with his little pumpkin. Or he'd be seated on the front step with his little pumpkin." By the same token, a too big and apparently invulnerable child could dampen motherly feelings, as in this woman. "I'm small, I'm petite and here's this big, dangling kid. I don't feel like I could nurture her. I don't feel any kind of bond or sym—you know, I don't take to her at all." It took effort to act motherly. "And what I try to do to show her some affection, in the morning when I wake her up, you know, I kiss her and I try to put my arms—she's so big, I couldn't possibly cuddle her like I could a smaller child."

The physical closeness assumed to come naturally, then, did not inevitably come with adoption. "Matching," as social workers suspected, made a difference. "I feel close to Kevin because his body confirmation is like mine," a mother told me, distinguishing Kevin from another child in the household. But matching was not crucial. "And all this stuff that you go through about this color situation and is she going to be like us," said the father of a biracial baby, "and is she going to be smart? Or is she—you know, all the stuff disappears when she comes in your arms. It's just forgotten." A "gush of feeling" carried people into parenthood, and this could be as true for a father as for a mother. Passion "sealed" the parenthood: this child is mine.

"Love at first sight"

"The feeling, it's hard to describe, the feeling inside. I mean, nobody can know another person's feelings inside. It's real hard. I just fell in love with that little girl," reported an adoptive father. The overwhelming certainty that this was the right child compensated for all the forms and applications, questions and answers, it had taken to become parents. Falling in love also suggested that other contracted relationship in American culture: marriage. The most powerful aspect of that analogy, which crops up continually in writings on adoption, was the honeymoon. As portrayed, the honeymoon celebrated what had come before: the intensity of feeling that cemented a relationship. That a honeymoon came after a marriage ceremony and, generally, before an adoption was legalized did not weaken the analogy. The term, in both cases, referred to a sensuous, physical, and absorbing union.

"Whatever may be true in other emotional relationships, love at first sight is real enough between foster [i.e., adoptive] parents and children," an early adoption manual put it. "And you may not fall in love according to plan, even though the plan is yours" (Lockridge 1947, 43). The implications of this—spontaneous, uncalculated emotion—are still part of adoption literature, and still represent the "best" beginning of an adoptive relationship. The phrase may not be "love at first sight," but the spirit is the same, evoking the inevitability of a relationship—not made by plan or cast by lottery.

"We were there to observe, we were there to be friends of the caseworker's," began a parent's description of her first encounter with the sibling group she eventually adopted. "We observed them, fell in love with them watching them there and everything."[5] An intuitive certainty that the child "belonged" served the same purpose. Her husband, this woman said, saw pictures of the children and knew: "And he said, 'These are *our* children.'" Another adoptive father also remembered looking through the photographs of available children an agency provided. "It's strange—it's sort of a feeling, something that seems to come through from the picture and the commentary." The actual meeting was even more powerful. "So we went and stood at the window, [and] waited and waited and finally a car pulled up and we could see that there was a boy in it with a caseworker. And it was like, how can you explain it? It was instant—like, you *know.* I don't want to say 'love' but it was instant, you could tell."

People who did not want to say "love" talked about destiny and fate: the child was *meant* to be theirs, beyond the criteria of a placement process. "I sincerely believe that this is the way things are supposed to happen," an adoptive parent assured me. "It was so right, it happened so right, and I can remember the next day we brought Lyle home on a late Saturday night."[6] Some parents gave an even stronger interpretation to the sense of inevitability. "We wanted to adopt, we wanted to adopt. And when we finally gave up [because nothing was happening] and said, 'God, you take over here, now you're the leader, you let it happen for us!'"

However expressed, the intensity of attachment and the feeling that the child "belonged" were crucial to the beginning of this relationship. At some point, the process was no longer under anyone's control—it just happened. A father said: "It was just like I got a feeling inside that hey, maybe this kid might work." Such feelings made the tedious autobiographical statements and the examination of one's home life go away. Such feelings, too, were appropriate to the idea of a honeymoon. "It was like, you know, everyone's dream what they wanted, all happy. So, it just seemed like he fit in so well," another parent told me. A honeymoon involved a little bit of luck and a little bit of effort. "I think any adoptive parent during the first few months after they receive the child, walks on eggs," a mother explained. "You know, they have what they call the 'honeymoon period' where both sides are on their best behavior." But that did not make it less delightful—or less important to the work of being a parent that followed. Still recalling marriage, the word "honeymoon" came up repeatedly to indicate the solid foundation for the often painful, subsequent period of adjustment.[7] "So when the three of them got together it was, 'let's see how rotten we can be. And we're just gonna have a good old time here' and it was havoc." Thus an adoptive mother described the end of the honeymoon in her household.

At the same time, a struggle with a recalcitrant child indicated how thoroughly parenthood had set in. "And then I knew I bonded with Kenneth the time when he was in one of his, had been sent to his room because he was running around the house like a nut and wouldn't stop. So I sent him to his room until he could calm himself down and he told me he hated me. And I looked at him and I said, 'That's ok, I still love you with all my heart.' And he broke down and cried. And from then on he's been, you know, he's still rotten but I could tell at that point was when I bonded with him." This mother's love, though she did not use the words, was unconditional and absolute: no matter what Kenneth did, she was there. Another parent found a similar silver lining in the annoying hours she spent feeding a baby who did not want to eat. "But it was just getting to know each other. It was such a wonderful timing because I was on vacation from work. . . . It was really good because we were really in a groove by the time I went back to work."

The aftermath of falling in love, and a honeymoon, brought the work of making a relationship last. With an older child, that was a two-way process. "I guess the most important thing to me in an adoptive child is the fact that the child wants it as much as I do," a single father said. "It's like a marriage. If both sides don't work at it, especially with an older child as old as Raoul, if both sides don't work at it, it isn't going to happen." People did not find the notion of work contradictory but rather consistent with love. "And I think that's what I can attribute his ease into the adoption," remarked a different parent with the same idea. "He knew that's what he wanted, that he was going to make it work no matter how hard it was. He knew he was gonna make it work." Nor did it seem to distinguish their parenthood from everyone else's; all "love," a parent wrote on her adoptive application form, must be "earned."

That this kind of worked-on love took time was something adoptive parents valued: the *experience* of being a parent. If they were instantly attached, they were not instantly sure of how to interact with a child.[8] "Oh yes, you fall in love with the baby the minute they place that baby in your arms but I do believe that it takes time, lots and lots of growing. Experience," an adoptive parent said to me. And that, too, was reciprocal, in the way adoptive parents understood an adoptive relationship. "He writes a note if he, he always comes home from school and he goes back out playing or something, he'll write a note saying where he's at. He'll always sign it 'Love Lyle.' I really feel that he has accepted us as parents, and he's proud to have parents and he's willing to make something of himself now. I think we've made him feel good enough about himself to know that you can, it's ok to work hard and make something of yourself." Lyle had become not only a full but a responsible member of the family. Parenting involved nurturing, loving, and *bringing up* a child.

"We're not going to be perfect parents"

"Not only that, you passed the test other parents do not have to, so when you get that baby you know that you are going to know, to do everything right, you're perfect, you're set up," said an adoptive mother with irony. "I laugh about it," she added. On reflection, the tests seemed mainly to suggest that adoptive parents, like the adoptee, had been specially chosen for special traits. They had a standard to meet, with no certain sense of how to do it. The adoption books they might read—and many did—confused the issue, veering between portraying adoptive parents as exceptional, gifted, especially expressive, and suggesting they were only average members of the community.[9]

Social workers also gave mixed messages, saying, as one did to me, that "there's so many different types of parenting and who's to say that one is better than the other" and that "a good parent in my opinion is a person who is open to dealing with their own feelings and is honest about it." Adoptive parents responded by claiming imperfections, flaws, and confusions—though none expressed an inability to deal with feelings. "I remember telling very clearly that we've made some mistakes, that, why we felt our divorces had happened, why our marriages hadn't worked, my father had committed suicide," a woman reported her conversation with the social worker. "I told her that, how I had grown from that." And this woman concluded, "it's still not going to be perfect and we're not going to be perfect parents, but what we do promise is that we could keep growing."

They also likened themselves to their own not "chosen" parents. This had been part of the application process: "Please tell us about the people who parented you, your relationship with them, and how they parented you." But it was more than that. The comparison made the adoptive parent less special and emphasized the continuities of parenting from one generation to the next. "We don't pal around with those kids," a parent said, sternly. "We didn't pal around with *our* parents." They compared themselves with their own parents—and with each other, as in this adoptive mother's account: "Dave had a very easy-going, laid-back mom which is exactly the way he is, and a father at home up until he died when he was thirteen; he had a heart attack. And he was just very easy-going. And my mother, on the other hand, had divorced when I was four, had worked two jobs to raise three children, was a real stressed-out individual and a real screamer which is probably why I'm a reactor and I've been working on that forever."

And then it was traits of temperament rather than strategies of upbringing that were important: "to try to be somewhat stern but loving and compassionate," said an adoptive father. "And he can express his emotions a lot better than I can," a woman said about her husband. "I guess because growing up I had to keep mine all on the back burner. The way I was raised. Where his, they're always right there. And he's taught me a lot of emotions that I used to just keep in here and no one else seen or knew they were there but me, you know." There were a few specifics: one parent thought her parents should have been more "directive"; another man addressed his wife, "and I grew up, unlike you, in an atmosphere without a lot of books and verbal—," "stimulation," she interrupted. Mainly, being a good parent (as the courts had said) was a matter of character, compassion, and concern. And being able to act childlike: that too, it turned out, was an important part of being a parent.

"I've already spoken of being single. I haven't lost touch, especially as I see in some married people, toward what it was like when they were a child," said a father. "And adults seem to forget that after they become married and start having children." Another parent was more explicit. "I think one of the best tools a parent has in their hands is clear memory of their own childhood and I have that. I clearly remember what it was like to be a child, as clearly as I think a parent can." In another instance, this extended to an adoptive grandfather. "My father's still there [in childhood]," an adoptive mother said. "He never grew up with the rest of us." Her husband added: "If you go over there right now, he's probably got every piece of furniture upside down" playing with his grandson.

Being like one's own parents not only underlined continuities but also indicated that parenting "came naturally." There was an adoptive parent version of the Dr. Spock advice: trust yourself. "You just do it on faith," a mother told me. And a new adoptive father: "Actually, I don't have much self-confidence in myself but I guess I have more in being a parent than I do in just being me [laughing]. Kind of odd, huh? I don't know what else to say about that." Comments like this warded off the expectation that they ought to be perfect parents. As one adoptive mother put it: "I mean, I'm not saying I'm the best mother in the world. I'm not. I'm just an everyday person, but I try to be conscientious that my children are clean and they have stimulation in their—you know, I take care of them."

Dr. Spock (1985, 248) also pointed to a danger: spoiling the child. "But some parents are more easily drawn into spoiling than others—for instance . . . parents with too little confidence in their own worthiness who become willing slaves to a child and expect her or him to be all the things they felt they never could be; parents who have adopted a baby and feel that they have to do a superhuman job to justify themselves." The warning conflicted with advice given in adoption manuals. "As you grow to love this special little person, you give of yourself completely. You become almost a slave to your child—conscious of his every need, his every desire. You lovingly, willingly, devote your life to him" (Dywasuk 1973, 80). Parents experienced the dilemma between being devoted to and spoiling a child. "I mean, lots of people think I spoil the child. I'm sorry. I don't believe you could spoil a new baby, but lots of people think that." Thus an adoptive mother defended her position. Devotion, she and others had been told, sealed a bond with the child—especially an adopted child. Another parent voiced the distinction others left implicit: "I know some people that wouldn't even go to those extremes or those limbs with their own children."

This very distinction, of course, could cause tension. Caught between treating an adopted child like any other—remembering her own childhood—and acknowledging the difference in adoption, a mother admitted: "I started to say I was afraid I was too permissive because I, being able to remember my own childhood, I remember it being something of a painful time. You're real sensitive and you're easily hurt. You're so needy for love and attention all the time. So I smother him in that and so far it's been working like a charm in that he's very obedient and responsive and loving in return and all he wants to do is please me. I hardly ever have to get mad at him. Then you worry, well, am I being too permissive? Am I letting him have his own way too much?" Behind her sentiment may have been a thought that other adoptive parents articulated: the child had his own way, his own nature, which it was their job to "prune" but not to distort. An aspect of conventional childrearing theory, the view had special resonance when the adopted child's nature was not one's own.

The child was neither a bad seed nor a perfect specimen. "Here again, if he got into serious trouble, *then* we have a problem that needs to be addressed"—but not *before*, an adoptive father asserted. How to discipline a child was a big part of agency preparation, and adoptive parents found this a particularly constraining aspect of their self-conscious parenthood. Social worker emphasis on "talk" did not accord with their experience of real parent-child relationships. "But once in a while I do think they need spankings. I mean I used to get spanked and I don't think it hurt me. In fact, sometimes we used to put a pillow on our bottom when my father would come in at night when we were up half the night talking and playing, we'd put pillows underneath the blanket when he'd spank us so it wouldn't hurt." Another parent, too, came back to the problematic distinction between biological and adoptive children.[10] "When Ted [father] would discipline her, he'd walk over and he'd go, 'now Marsha don't . . .' You know, he didn't always do that kind—more than he did with our own kids. We were much tougher on our own."

"We'd scream and yell and carry on with our own kids." But, this woman continued, with an adopted child "we had to be some kind of professionals." For some parents, adoptive parenthood did seem a kind of "professionalized" parenthood. Others fell back onto the age-old, cultural formula: be "naturally" loving. The formula could provide reassurance, as another mother revealed: "And I know that what children need more than anything else is attention and love and that I have plenty of. There was no trick to that. Then the other stuff would come with time. So I wasn't insecure."

Finally too, as Dr. Spock implied, being naturally loving was a quality of motherhood more prominently than of fatherhood. Even if "you started off running in the same place" in adoption, as one father put it, the mother quickly outpaced the father. As one woman said: "And Ken was thinking that maybe he would like to be a father, but he says that he's not good enough to stay with it. It gets pretty hairy and he'd just as soon go to work." Exploring the difference, she came up with: "Well, frankly, I think it's in the genes. I just think women are more nurturing than men. There's something [pause]—I swear there's a switch that clicks in a woman. That switch just doesn't exist in a man. . . . And I thought they [infants] were kind of boring, too, but some kind of thing switched and all these chemicals started pouring into my body and it was like, ahh."[11]

Both adoptive mothers and adoptive fathers talked about how much closer a mother was to a child. "I think it's harder to men to sit down and talk to him about things. I would say, if Brian was having a problem it would be to myself that he would come to." Fathers had to learn. "Yeah, the first day she was worried," said a man who had been "put in charge" of the children. "She hurried up home, 'is everything fine?' 'Yeah, no problem.'" And what fathers mainly had to learn was how to express their love. "I don't think he knew his real dad but the love, the hug, the kiss is something that's very important to him," said a single adoptive father, proud of the lesson he had learned. "It still is. That need for nurturing—very, very important."

Not even mothers, however, expected raising an adoptive child to be without difficulty. "I know that there are gonna be special problems. Because kids can be cruel [about adoption]. But I think if we deal with it as it comes up and just let him know that he's loved and— Paul [father] keeps saying he's gonna be a basketball player."

"Having them develop to their potential"

Like any other parent, the adoptive parent raised the child with particular goals and expectations in mind. But they were not like other parents: adoptive parents distinguished themselves from foster parents, who learned they could "transform" a child, and from biological parents, who can expect a child to grow up in their image. Somewhere in between lay the task of raising the as-if-begotten child.

Publicity said adoption could work miracles. "To see the change in the child . . . to see dull, lifeless children begin to sparkle . . . , even their hair begins to shine" was a reward of adoption, according to some (*Pittsburgh Press*, 12/16/84: F4). Social workers transmitted the same message: "if you have certain kinds of people, it's those people that make the difference," one told me. "A miracle happens in those kids' lives." But a miraculous transformation was not natural— possibly the task of a foster parent, who had the child for a while, but not the real job of parenthood. This was one of the more persistent distinctions I heard: a foster parent *changed* the child; an adoptive parent provided the foundation for a productive and contented adulthood.[12]

The distinction was not firm. Adoption had always combined an idea of improving with an idea of incorporating the child. "I thought we could help a child become a useful member in society," an adoptive mother told me. "Parenting is giving; giving love, support, time, your good example, a sense of worth and all those skills needed to become a well-adjusted adult who is willing and able to contribute to society," wrote an applicant for adoptive parenthood. Childrearing, one adoptive couple told me, was a process of "civilizing" a child. The husband also said, "but you can't parent a stranger from 14 on, that's all there is to it." He, too, came at another difference between adoption and fostering, at least until recently: in the former you had a baby to mold and in the latter a child came with visible and definite traits. "You get a kid after 14, you can't parent them. You can give them a home but parenting stops at about 14." This was a strong conviction. "An infant, you know, you'd get to raise it up, rather than get someone who's like, say, 3 or 5. They already have a way about themselves and you'd be butting heads for a while to get them to get into your method or you'd have to adjust to their song."

"I don't have great expectations for him," another father began. "I don't expect him to, can't expect to erase thirteen years that went before and I think that's—. If you're going to adopt a kid that's old, you better have that feeling because if you expect him to suddenly become you, that's crazy. There are certain things that I couldn't accept from him, but I don't expect Raoul to change." Halfway through, he took a different tack. "If a kid's got a problem, he's going to have it the rest of his life; which I don't believe, because you and I change every day of our lives and it's never too late. Not that it will always be exactly the way you want it, but if both sides want to work at it—. There's certain things about him that are, that will carry through the rest of his life with him, but there's things that we can work out and change." And it might take years. "He just needs some time. You know, he needs a lot of work and a lot of love."

For all the adoptive parents I met, the issue was whether expectations went against those "certain things about him." "Yeah, one of the issues, I think, for both of us is we both have very high expectations for ourselves and also, as a result, of Joey. Which is, doesn't quite match him necessarily." This man's wife put it slightly differently. "But the one saving grace is I can always say to myself, you know, I can pull back and say he's got his history and he's got his own needs and stuff like that. I don't get so burned up in it. I can keep some distance and say, it's gotta, he's gotta do what he needs to do in his life, I can't. I don't know that I would be able to do that with a biological child. I mean, I might be so invested that I would really be a miserable person to be with [laughing]."

The problem of expectations not matching a child led parents to lean on generalities in talking about goals: a child should be good, conscientious, and responsible. As one woman explained: "And with that, I can remember him coming to the hospital to see me and sitting down and saying, 'Mom, you carry too much all the time, now it's time for everyone else to help.' And he helped in the responsibilities and I—that's one of the reasons that I can really see a change in Lyle." Another mother remarked: "I don't care about the little stuff, Judith, about food, shelter, clothing. That's easy. You know, the big stuff, the future, and the character, having them develop to their potential, to be good people, that was the big stuff we always worried about."

Such an equivalence between "developing character" and "letting their natures unfold" might not be so different for adoptive than for biological parents—except for the unknowns in the adoptive child's nature. "I mean, I don't sit my children and talk to them and say, 'this is very important to be yourself,' but I try to impart that message, 'be yourself,' no matter what," an adoptive mother said, explaining her theory of childrearing. "'Be yourself,' and what you are is what you are and if you're doing the best you can, it makes no difference whether you can trace your family tree back to 1680." As general as "conscientious" and "responsible" were and as vague as the idea of "be yourself" might be, these concepts explicitly linked the child with his or her adoptive parents. "But really showing a concern for others" is what we want from a child. "Because I guess we both tend to feel, not just me, we both tend to feel that that's where you derive a lot of happiness from, from love and giving to others," said a woman for herself and for her husband, who nodded his agreement.

And one mother, who tended to put things well, conveyed the complexity of acknowledging nature and hoping the adopted child would be "like us." "I really want him to grow up to like himself and to know that he's a worthwhile guy. And he's here for a reason. I just hope he's a nice guy. Paul's [husband] got a real sense of humor and I hope he can, he can pick up on that. I think he will. But I really just want him to be happy." A father laughed at his admission that he wanted the adopted children to be: "Oh, geez, just like us, I guess." The notion that resemblances indicated connectedness and bonding was as prevalent for adoptive parents as for the other two members of the triad. "And now she's got this awful 'uhhhh.' She does it just like me and I hate it. I listen to that and think 'oh, there you are.' You know? But she does so many things just like us, and Dave too."

The adopted child could be as-if-begotten. "But everyone says he couldn't be more ours and you know he is because when you look at Lyle, he and I have the same hair color and so much of the same thing. And like Larry says, he scares him a lot because he's so much like him. I don't think he could, you know, act or be more like ours if we had our own." Yet, as this mother implies, he was not "our own," and every adoptive parent had to say so.

"His right to know"

"I'm going to next, certainly by the time he's 2 years old, going to start telling him bedtime stories about how we got him, and how much we love him, that he's adopted, that sort of thing." As this mother recognized, telling a child he had other parents was a major part of adoptive parent childrearing and a task that absolutely separated adoptive from biological parents.[13]

Adoptive parents knew the dangers of secrecy. "I don't want him coming home from school saying, 'the kids tell me I'm adopted and you never told me that,'" a mother said. Another parent explained why she would tell. "I don't believe in hiding things from, these type of things anyhow. I know the old school was they didn't tell you that you were adopted and that's what you read and hear anyhow. You were older or sometimes you found out in horrible ways from some stranger . . . I don't believe in any of that. I think they need to know and know from you, whenever they're of an age when they can grasp that." Even those who had adopted infants who could be presumed to look exactly like the "new" family denied they contemplated hiding the adoption. "It never even entered our mind to try and pass him off as not being adopted." Enjoyment of a resemblance was not going to tempt a 1980s parent into keeping secrets.[14]

"We would certainly want him to know that he's adopted and so forth, age appropriately. And I mean, my family and everybody knows. I mean, we certainly don't make a deal of it to say, 'oh, he's adopted.' We, it's kind of interesting hearing people say he looks like my family and people don't know—everybody thinks he's a Bateman, that's my maiden name. And it's, you know we just take that with a grain of salt and get a chuckle out of it actually. But most people that know us fairly well know that he's adopted." The comment this mother made to me suggests the fine line adoptive parents walk between telling about and not stressing adoption, between incorporating the child into the family and reminding him of his difference. Telling epitomized the "uncomfortable double bind" of adoption: " 'Make the child your own but tell him he isn't' " (Sorosky 1979, 66). And what was "age appropriate"? Hard for the adoptee, the conversation could be even harder for the parent of the child who had once been given away.

The CWLA instructed its agencies to help, but with a qualification. "Social workers can give adoptive parents only general guides, not a formula" (CWLA 1978: 52). There were no formulas for explaining why one parent would surrender and another surely keep a child. Agencies had no answer to "age appropriate" either. According to the CWLA, "the explanation of adoption to the child has to be an ongoing process over a period of time related to the level of the child's ability to understand" (CWLA 1978: 51). But that did not ensure that others would understand or that the child would experience "telling" as an ongoing process. At McDonald's one day, a mother remembered, her son and his friend "were talking about babies being in bellies. And Brian says, 'Well, I was never in my mom's.' And the kid says, 'Uh huh.' And Brian says, 'No sir, cause I'm adopted.' And the boy turned around, and I'll never forget it, and says, 'You're one of *those* kids?' And from that time on, he [Brian] didn't want to talk about adoption."

Adoptive parents did not want to dwell on the issue either. According to Kirk (1988, 72), "by telling the child that they did not bear him the parents actually differentiate him out of their blood relationship." By telling, moreover, parents reminded themselves of another blood relationship and of a "conditional" attachment. And so, as adoptees remembered, adoptive parents emphasized their commitment and not someone else's surrender. "We want the kids to know that they weren't rejected because they were awful kids. They weren't rejected period." It helped when, like this father, adoptive parents *knew* the birthparent had had no choice: "from what we understand the maternal grandfather insisted that the mother give up the children and absolutely there could be no black children in their family blood line. That was all there was to it, and that she, if she ever wanted to be a part of the family again, those kids would go." But most knew little about the relinquishment and less about the person who had had to "give up."

"We tell him he's adopted and he knows he's adopted," a mother told me. "And, you know, I don't think he really understands what it means and if anything I think he—you know, I'm expecting that he's gonna have problems later on. . . . I think all children at some point question where they come from. Even children that aren't adopted . . . wonder, 'was I maybe adopted and they're not telling me something?' And what their heritage is."

And what their heritage is: in the end, that was the unique feature of adoptive parenthood. The child had a heritage of his or her own— and a parent to go with it. Some parents did begin to wish for more than the thumbnail sketch they had originally been given. "Back then, you know, we had that chosen baby story that was read [to] them," recalled an adoptive mother. "We filled it all in and we would read to them. But that's really in a way a lot of fantasy in it. I think it would have been so much better if, just, all along [they could have known more]. . . . I think that then that would have been so much better for the child. But we knew so little." Wanting to know more was often prompted by the child's development, and sometimes by awareness of the rising search movement. The phenomenon of searching clearly made a difference in how parents felt about "telling." An adoptive father guessed he would be sympathetic, when the time came: "By the same token, weighing the child's need to know from whence he came—everybody needs to know from where they came, you know, certainly the question's gonna come up." And an adoptive mother of an adolescent pronounced, "Because they still, as long as they've been told they're adopted, it's natural to be curious and anybody that says they're not curious about their background or their family history is not telling the truth." "And many children," she added, "say that they don't care about their natural parents because they don't want to hurt their adoptive parents. But I feel secure. Brian loves me for who I am and what I am. And I'll always be his mother. And I just feel that it is his right to know."

"Opening Pandora's box"

For most of the parents I interviewed, the possibility of searching lay in the future: their children were too young to think about "origins" and "natural parents." Their responses to the searches they saw on television and read about were both tolerant and abstract. "I don't know how I'll feel when I'm a mother of a teenager," said one woman, "but I think we're good enough parents that they'll love us and that they won't feel like they have to run away . . . to, that they need another parent, [or] we're not good enough." And adoptive parents borrowed the words of adoptees who had searched, talking about roots and identity.

Yet, as the following dialogue indicates, it took some effort to accommodate to the newest wrinkle in adoptive parenthood.

Luke: You know, but in the future he will probably, would maybe have, probably have a desire to maybe search them out or something.

Virginia: And that would be fine. . . . From what I've read and from what everybody's, they say that frequently they have that need to find where they came from and find their roots and then that's usually the end of it. So if they wanted to do that—. I mean, who knows how you're going to feel when they come and say, 'I want to go find out who my real mother is,' you know.

Luke: The way I look at it is that—

Virginia: That's a natural instinct almost.

Luke: If he wanted to do it, by the time he, I think, would reach that stage he'd probably be older and at that point we've done—.

Virginia: He's appreciated what we've done and gave him and loved him—.

Luke: You know, whatever we could. And probably by the time he would come to want to do that and be able to do that, then he would be old enough to make up his own mind and so forth.

Even when searching was put in terms of the child's right and choice, it awakened concerns about an attachment to the natural parent, despite years spent in the adoptive family. "It's more up to them to find their roots than it is up to us, I think," a father of two children said. "And we've heard that that becomes a priority in the child's life for a while but it fades. They find out things are pretty good where they are. It's another one of those, you-just-have-to-do-it-to-find-out kinds of thing. You can't make any presuppositions about the whole situation. It's cruel to hide it from them but it's also cruel to yourself to let them go off and be bowled over by some lady or ever want to know. But it's their choice. It really is their choice." Searching opened a "Pandora's box"; what might emerge was a bond stronger than the one formed by law.[15]

Parents expressed sympathy for a child's perhaps inevitable curiosity, but they were not at all certain the child ought actually to *know* the other parent.[16] "But at some age, maybe that's sixteen, maybe that's eighteen, if Jill wanted to know her birthmother and put her birthmother into her life, I don't know that you put her into a life as a mom, you put her into your life as someone you love without a title perhaps. I don't know that that takes away from our love." Then this mother of an infant admitted: "And it's going to be a little scary if that comes. I think it'd be a whole lot scary because I'm sure I'd feel a little bit like, 'oh, I'm being replaced.'"

One way of not being replaced was getting involved in the search. "I myself," said a social worker who was also an adoptive parent, "if my boys decide to, I know there's going to be a little aggression, but I want to get over that because I want to be in on it and I think it would be very neat to find out if you have other brothers and sisters and another mother. Because that birthmother cannot be a mother to them any more. She can be a friend."

I met one adoptive mother who herself initiated the search for her sons' parents. "And one day, about two years ago—for some reason, I always read the personals and the classifieds, and I noticed an ad that said, 'Adoptees: time is running out to find your natural birth—to get your birth certificate.' And I was so astounded because I never dreamed that they could have their certificates." She did the search, including making the initial contact. "The line was busy, busy, busy, and each time I dialed. And finally I dialed and it wasn't busy and you could tell this person, this man answered and was just so pleasant, and you could tell, you know yourself when you're on the phone with an-other person and you're still thinking about it when another call comes in. And so I sort of caught him unawares, and I said to him, 'Hello, I'm an old friend of Vivian's and I want to get in touch with her.'"

Vivian was the birthmother and she refused to meet her son. The other search was more successful. "And I said, 'our oldest two chil-dren are adopted and I'm calling about our son, that was born Oc-tober 11 in 1953.' I said, 'would you just like to talk?' And he [birth-father] said, 'no, please go on.' He said it with such a beautiful voice, he had such a beautiful voice. . . . And I said, 'my son really wants to meet you.' And he said, 'really wants to meet me?'. . . And also right in the beginning I said to him, 'is this something that you would want to block out of your mind?'—because of what Paul's [other son] mother said. And he said, 'Oh, no, there isn't a day that's gone by when I haven't thought about it.'" In this case, the two families had a reunion, and the adoptee found himself with two mothers, two fa-thers, and two brothers named Jim.

The adoptive mother told me the reunion "transformed" her son. "But it really was, it was just—it was like heaven on earth." The changes were visible. "Dick was very reserved. Ever since he's met them, he's a regular chatterbox. The whole family has noticed it. He's just not, you know, really he's just much more self-confident." She also recognized that the reunion was easier for her because she already had a big family. "And I think, too, because I have six children it's easier to share them—they drive you crazy [laughing]. When they're all, so that they're, I mean kids are just coming and going all the time." Moreover, her children were grown up. "And I think it's easier because I've had children married. I think once they're married, you know that they're still yours but you do share them at holidays and all. And it's—they're their own person, you know."

But it was not quite heaven on earth. "The only thing I have found a little difficult is that I—and he doesn't call them mother and dad in front of me. And I can't quite understand myself. I've told him to call them mother and dad and I know he does. . . . But for some reason I don't want to hear him call them mother and dad. Isn't that strange?" Just as adoptees and birthparents discovered, she found that kinship terms had definite meanings that were not totally negotiable—by anyone. "I just thought automatically this lady will be just like a sister," she said about the birthmother. "I really did think that we could be close." But they were not close. If the son struggled with having two mothers, the mothers had even less guidance for their relationship with each other. This was family and yet not family.

The reunion occurred when her son was in his 30s. She told me she was glad the adoption itself had been closed, with no chance of encountering the other mother while the child was still a baby.

Contact was different when the adoptee was an adult; at that point, the other mother could be a friend, maybe a distant relative, but not a "mom." From the adoptive mother's perspective, the birthmother's relationship with "their" son was her business, and in a sense not part of the "real" family at all. On the periphery, in her son's kin group, the birthmother did not have to be a full member of the adoptive mother's own family. Other people distinguished searching from open adoption in much the same way: searching went on between adults, free to "make" their relationships; open adoption involved equal participation in who the child was and what the child would become. An adoptive mother of a young baby recalled seeing a television program about open adoption. "Now I really just don't see how that can work. I don't think that would be good for the child. I just can't see how that works in the long run. I do feel they [children] need to know who they are and really I believe in that." Belief that a child should know his or her origins typically did not lead to support of open adoption; "biological ancestry" was not the same as "another mother." Adoptive parenthood depended, still, on entitlement and exclusivity.

Confirming this, one parent who *was* favorable thought open adoption would help the birthmother forget and move on with her life. "But if you want to be sure that, if you want to try to be sure that the mother will be happy to the extent that she can be with her decision and satisfied that she won't have this longing for the rest of her life to find them, then I think open adoption is the best way to try to accomplish that." She clarified her position. "And I don't mean having her visit the kids, or knowing who we are or where we are, but I sure wouldn't mind writing to her and sending her pictures once a year. My understanding is that with a lot of women, after you do that for a year or two, then they're ready to put it behind them and they don't need that any more."

Adoptive parents who had no trouble telling a child about adoption, and thus acknowledging difference, expected to be the only parents of that child, as if genealogical. But this was no longer a certainty: the search movement alters adoption and the experience of adoptive kinship. Increasingly, knowing two sets of real parents is seen as the child's "right"; however that right is enacted, it changes the parent-child relationship. "Shared parenthood" is less and less an agency phrase and more and more a possibility. These changes push at the limits of kinship terminology—up to now, the stable framework for child exchange in an American context. Reunions and, more so, open adoptions have the potential to release the concepts of mother (and father) from a link with the natural world, and reproduction from its link with biology. In the next, concluding chapter, I discuss the ramifications of these changes for American kinship.

PART FOUR

Conclusion

10

A New Kind of Kinship

The Implications of
Change in American Adoption

"Without the biological relationship"

My book began with change, with the reunions that are described in newspapers, on television, and in autobiographies. The book will also end with change: the move toward open adoptions, or openness in adoption, that is partly a response to reunions and partly a recognition of individual autonomy in the exchange of a child. Openness alters the relationships established by adoption; given the link between fictive and real, open adoption could also revise the role of biology in cultural interpretations of kinship.

The preceding chapters showed the significance of the as-if principle in American adoption. The adoptive family is "just like" a biological family, the child as-if-begotten and the parents as-if-genealogical; for her part, the birthmother is as-if-childless. Adoption makes absolutely no sense, David Schneider wrote, without the biological relationship. More than that, adoption makes sense of the biological relationship. The "made" relationship delineates the terms of the natural relationship: a child born of two parents, the product of their sexual relationship. Fictive kinship tells participants that real kinship means "blood ties." These determine the structure of a family and also the emotions of its members: the feelings of *being* a parent and a child.

For people whose kinship is fictive, however, blood also represents what is missing. It is this dimension of "non-reality" that makes an adoptive relationship different, paradoxical, and in need of work—a self-conscious kinship. It takes work to maintain the "fiction" of being a childless parent, a parent without having given birth, and a child who lacks a "genetic map." The spurt of consciousness-raising in the 1960s and 1970s altered the content of this work, bringing out the deceptions of an as-if axiom and prompting the changes in adoption with which my book concludes, but which themselves are only beginning.

The symbolism of blood dominates interpretations of kinship in American culture, subsuming references to sexual reproduction and to biological ancestry. In an as-if relationship, blood is the model for conduct and for emotion, representing the unconditional love and enduring solidarity of a parent-child relationship. As a model, too, blood transforms the contracted into a seemingly reproductive link; the child is as if a product of the parents' union, deserving the attention and care any such child would receive.[1] Furthermore, with blood as the model, adoptive parents are "re-gendered," after having started off "running in the same place." The adoptive family is as traditional as the stereotypical biological family: father, mother, and children—"the natural setting for a child," as the CWLA tells its member agencies.[2]

The symbolism of blood sustains the fiction of adoption, but it also lends the transaction a fatal flaw—an inevitable comparison with "real" blood ties. "Blood" is a reminder that adoption is a *paper* kinship. The application forms filled out by adoptive parents, the surrender papers signed by a birthparent, and the amended birth certificate all assert the fictive in this kind of kinship. And fictive here connotes "unreal" rather than "created." A paper parenthood cannot compare with the "physical realities" of conception, creation, gestation, and birth, not in American culture anyway. "I felt as if I had kidnapped a baby," an adoptive mother said to me, revealing a fear that the contract she had signed was not a true bond. Nor was she reassured by the birthparent's signature on a piece of paper. The same sense that "blood" had primacy, and nature had rights, led adoptive parents to reject information about the birthmother: "We didn't even know the date of birth," another parent said, only half in self-mockery. The facts of birth had vanished.

On their side, birthparents expressed astonishment at the presumption that signing a paper would erase the memory of having had a child. For them, blood was an enduring and unbreakable bond; a signature did not make it go away.[3] Thus, papers *did* and did *not* redo parenthood, creating the ambiguous status both parents in the triad experienced: one a childless mother and the other a "birthless" parent. For the adoptee, papers play a perhaps even more powerful role, producing a "juridical rebirth." The adoptee is granted a new birth certificate, his social parents listed as if they were his biological parents, in lawful wedlock.[4] The paradox embedded here is that the child is as-if-begotten but not *born*. In one sense, then, an adoptee's birth certificate is a profound lie. In another sense, however, it is true; with adoption, the legal parent completely (and absolutely) replaces a parent by birth. An amended birth certificate stands for the transformation adoption achieves and, simultaneously, asserts the significance of "blood" in the parent-child relationship. A social relationship makes no sense without the reference to a genealogical relationship.

In the mid-1960s, the inherent ambiguity of an as-if birth became oppressive at least to some adoptees and, supported by one another, they claimed the right to a real birth, represented by an unamended birth certificate. These adoptees initiated the critique of adoption I have described, a critique that spread through the triad and then into professional and legal circles. And "paper" can, as I have suggested, be taken as its propelling metaphor, directing attention to the claim that nature can be rewritten and a replica be indistinguishable from the original. That is the "perfect simulation" the nineteenth-century jurist Sir Henry Maine advocated and American adoption law enacts. It is the perfect simulation that also makes participants in (and observers of) adoption "uncomfortable"—not to say "frosty." Papers are not a mere matter of contracted parenthood and altered birth certificates; they represent a denial of the facts of life for all three members of the triad. The adoptee's call for an "unamended" certificate and the birthparent's for acknowledgment of the missing chapter, if different rhetorically, have the same impact on adoptive kinship. The adoptive parent, contemplating the end of confidential records, as thoroughly discards the fiction of his or her parenthood for the "reality" of shared parenthood. As-if collapses, and with it the elaborate system of judgment and evaluation that framed the experiences of everyone in my book.

One could say the adoptee demand for "facts" begins with growing up adopted and comparing two parents, one who gave away and one who took a child: an unknown and a known parent; a bad and a good mother. The comparison focuses on the mother and virtually excludes fatherhood from the equation. This is true for several reasons: not only are adoptees more likely to think about the mother who gave away and the mother who took a child but also, as adoption illustrates, "mother" comes to represent "parent" more generally in American culture.

Discussing the experience of growing up adopted, adoptees reversed the conventional contrast and portrayed the birthmother as good and generous, the adoptive mother as selfish and stingy—and said they had done so as children. The birthmother, then, not the adoptive mother, fits the cultural interpretation of motherhood: loving, emotionally giving, and sexual—*productively* sexual. By contrast for the adoptee (even those who grew up happily), the adoptive mother was rigid, materialistic, emotionally cold, and unsexual—or sexually *unproductive,* and not exactly a real parent. This reordering of the conventional dichotomies effectively uncovers the paradox in American adoption: the *natural* mother—the conventionally (and often legally) ideal parent—loses her child to a parent who meets criteria and is judged *worthy.* The interests of the child are translated into a calculation of advantage that contradicts the kinship basis of the exchange. This is the knot adoption law and policy have not successfully untangled in over a hundred years. Birthparents put it in their way: those who "love" lose to those who are "well-off."

The birthparent analysis adds another level to the critique of fictive kinship. If adoption is impossible in a genealogical culture without reversing the values attached to "parent," it is also impossible without commercializing the exchange—or so the birthparents' "storied" experiences indicated. Birthparents, like adoptees, drew the contrast between a selfish adoptive parent and a generous birthparent; one greedily took and kept another person's child, while the other lovingly and altruistically gave away her child. For birthparents, the intervention of experts truly distorted the exchange, by introducing "objective criteria" into the delegation of parenthood. In this view, the *selection* of a parent turned relations of kinship into relations of capital; calculation of comparative worth intruded upon a familial transaction.[5] Capability and performance, rather than the appropriate dimensions of nurturance and commitment, qualified a parent in this transaction. If somewhat self-serving, the birthparent critique is a cogent comment on child exchange in the United States—an exchange that cannot, it seems, be "right."

But it might be right, the implication is, if "blood" were acknowledged, not just as a model for the parent-child attachment or a symbolic reference to nature, but as an aspect of any kind of kinship. By this logic, if "blood" dominates cultural interpretations of kinship, then blood kin exist. By this logic, too, birth relatives exist, no longer a threatening presence in the child's past, but part of an ongoing family constellation—of some sort. Birthparents, then, are not the "kids" who "had babies right and left," or the natural mother with a natural right to the child: they are parents by birth to a child others have by law. Focused on opening documents and unsealing records, the effect of reform is to bring every part of the child's ancestry—the child's biological and social collectivity, in the Eriksonian phrase—forward. The slippery categories of fictive and real—"and when I say my real parents, I mean my adoptive parents, ok?"—are superseded by "birth" and "legal" parents. As one adoptee said about those who know both sets of parents, "If you say, 'who is your mother and father?,'" they know which is which.

Fictive can also take on another meaning. Rather than referring to "not real," as it currently does, fictive can connote made, created, and crafted. The problem with this, as my research shows, is the sharp discordancy between a crafted kinship and cultural notions of parenthood. The experiences of all three members of the triad argue for the awkwardness—the discomfort—of a made parent-child relationship.[6] When it comes to the parent-child relationship, in American culture nature prevails, not "contrivance" (Kirk 1981, 39). And so, by one strategy or another, adoption in the United States—an *opted-for* kinship—has simulated a destined parenthood. "Falling-in-love" and "meant-to-be" convey the inevitability of the adoptive relationship—as if natural. Birthparents present the "other" inevitability: "she still has my blood running through her."

But if the initiation of a parent-child relationship ought not be "crafted," its evolution can be *worked* through. "All relationships need work," the coordinator of ASG said, and detected no incompatibility between that and an "out-of-the-blue" notion of parenthood. Yet the emphasis on work implicitly recognizes the contrivance in this kind of kinship—the "made" aspect of fictive—without relinquishing the "rush" of feeling that cements the bond. Predictably, the significance of *work* in kinship will increase the more open adoption becomes. "I am perplexed about where we go now," Diana said about her relationship with her found daughter. But she fully intended to "make a new one," a relationship in which "mother" was not equivalent to "parent."

Particular actions like requesting a birth certificate, meeting a "lost" child, and reinterpreting the meanings of "Mom" and "Dad" forecast even more radical change.

"The winds of change"

Adoptive parents are most thoroughly caught in "the winds of change" that "are swaying the structure of adoption" (Schechter and Bertocci 1990, 62). The requests of their children for open records and the claims of parental status by the "vanished" birthparent alter the position of the adoptive parent in the adoption triad. No longer able to be as-if-genealogical, to forget the background of the child, or to be sure of having the child forever, adoptive parents stand at the edge of a new kind of kinship.

"Confidentiality cannot be guaranteed in any adoption, even the so-called closed or traditional adoption. Laws governing confidentiality are changing and may continue to change to permit greater openness; courts can issue orders to open adoption records, and members of the triad may establish contact even when existing laws support confidentiality," stated the Task Force report of the moderate CWLA (Watson and Strom 1987, 9), not without sympathy for this development. The end of confidentiality represents the opening of adoption—hard to accept, but not as hard as a completely open adoption, in which birth and adoptive parents know one another, arrange the transfer of the child, and continue to have contact after the transaction has been completed. Open adoption polarizes people who participate in, and think about, adoption more than has anything else in recent decades.

Why is it so disturbing? Open adoption ought to be appealing: the concern of parents about a child brings them together in love and in generosity. This is the way adoption is understood and practiced in other societies—and in some subcultures of our own society.[7] Nor are love and generosity inconsistent with the attitudes presumed to be part of any adoption in the contemporary United States. In addition, the dangers of secrecy in a closed adoption, of hiding his or her "facts of life" from a child, and of disguising the terms of a relationship are generally recognized. Still, the idea of open adoption strikes a chill—especially in adoptive parents, but in the public as well.[8] Open adoption is not greeted with the fascination and appreciation that a reunion between long-lost kin is, even when those kin were not supposed to know one another. Reunions are perceived as *re*-activating existing, natural bonds, whereas open adoptions are seen as permitting people to construct "unnatural" bonds, on purpose and from the very beginning. Above all, open adoption is disturbing because it does not allow adoptive kinship to be just like biological kinship.

Opposition to open adoption, then, represents more than selfishness on the part of adoptive parents who want a child "of their own" or desperation on the part of birthparents who want to "keep" the children they relinquish, or jealousy on the part of social workers who want to control the placement of children. These elements influence the arguments against open adoption, but what really is troublesome is that open adoption threatens deeply held assumptions about the American family. By dismantling the biological premise, open adoption exposes the entailments of that premise: biology represents permanence, stability, and exclusivity—the core of parenthood. "It is, therefore, the essence of human parenthood that through the building of strong emotional attitudes on biological foundations, it endures, it leads to the establishment of a lifelong social relationship of mutual obligations and services" (Malinowski 1930, 162).

A parenthood not just like the biological will be contingent, unreliable, and unloving. In an open adoption, say opponents, the adoptive parent cannot achieve the entitlement that substitutes for a blood connection. Shared parenthood dilutes "the process of parental entitlement," confuses the child's identifications, and risks the interference of a birthparent. "Open adoption violates the very essence of sound adoption practice since there is no unconditional severing of the earlier parental ties, the legal relinquishment notwithstanding" (Smith and Miroff 1987, 7). Under these conditions, the adoptive parent cannot feel like a real parent. Adoptive parents "have every right to have that child be their 'own,' without interference or undue worry" (Smith and Miroff 1987, 118). It is not that open adoption makes biology less significant. Rather, open adoption puts biology in the "wrong" place—not a model for the adoptive parent, but another presence in the adoptive family.

This leaves adoptive parents without a script and with a fear: the bond formed by biology will triumph, the mother by birth take preeminence, and genealogy supplant role in establishing a parent-child relationship. In this imagined scenario, "mother" assumes the conventional meaning of the person who cares for as well as gives birth to a child and the birthmother assumes the tasks that go along with her status as mother. From this point of view, contracted parenthood cannot compete: there is no equivalent aspect of parenthood the social parent can absorb that will have the strength of the "blood" tie. (The symbolism of "blood" may also explain why adoptive parents in open arrangements concentrate attention on the relationship with a birthparent rather than on an altered relationship with a child.)[9] Open adoption, then, exposes the weakness in an assumption that "papers" can make kinship equivalent to blood; it is just paper: that a contract is not as binding as birth in a parent-child relationship is a strong cultural convention. But it *is* a convention, and as a convention it can change. Paradoxically, open adoption also indicates the strength of "papers." In an open arrangement, a paper kinship can be as strong as a blood kinship for the very reason that it does not replace (or substitute for) the blood kinship; rather, the contract establishes a *parallel* legal kinship. Open adoption introduces not "alternative parenthood" but alternative parents, and the distinction is not trivial. One parent is not "real," the other "unreal"; one is not "natural" and the other "fictive."

Open adoption is radical enough to have disturbed almost everyone I met—even those who eagerly entered reunions. But open adoption does not call for a total revolution in notions of kinship or in the purposes and principles of adoption. Blood remains central; adoption is still in the best interests of the child. It is "well" for the child to know all his or her parents, even if the arrangement confuses the parents.[10] But advocates also argue that open adoption serves the interests of the parents. The exchange is conducted by the participants, a form of self-determination that disappeared from adoption in the twentieth century. "Consider the paradox," the executive director of the CWLA said in 1985, "that while we entrust adoptive parents with the lives of adopted children, we too often do not trust them with all the information we have on the child's family background." She added, "the same staff will not allow these 'superior' [adoptive] parents who wish it to have contact with bioparents." Rather than letting people make their own decisions, we "commit social work on them" (Cole 1985, 89–90).

In open adoption, people make their own decisions, whether

through an agency or independently. These decisions include designating a "good parent," and the criteria—probably personalized—may
well be utterly arbitrary. "What is important [here] is that an open
adoption permits, within its framework, whatever is necessary and
meaningful for the individuals involved" (Baran and Pannor 1990,
331). Such freedom of choice may be more threatening than the disappearance of an as-if principle or the acknowledgment of several real
parents. The discomfort arises, I think, not only from a sense that free
choice might *not* be "well" for the child, but because it violates notions of parenthood.

Choice violates the cultural assumption that a parent-child relationship is a *necessary* relationship. Adoptees implied this when they
complained about being told they were "picked out" to belong to
a family. So did adoptive parents when they complained about the
"laundry-list" of agency adoptions; selecting a baby introduced the
possibility of returning a child. A parent-child relationship should happen, without calculation of the conditions. This sounds like what
Ginsburg described in *Contested Lives* as a strand in the abortion debate. For its opponents, pro-choice denies the *imperative* of motherhood. "The links [between reproduction, sex, and marriage] are
exposed as social constructions—that is, not inevitable—and the imperative of motherhood as a condition beyond human control is dis-
mantled" (Ginsburg 1989, 215). What emerges from the debate over
open adoption is not an imperative of motherhood so much as the imperative of a relationship between parent and child. The bond is inevitable, however initiated. And so advocates of open adoption also
talk about fate, destiny, and God's will: the parent-child relationship
"had to happen."[11]

In this view, having and not having a child ought to be a matter beyond the whim or will of the interested parties—beyond human control. In this way as well, despite its revision of practice, open adoption
shows a conservative bent, acknowledging the "mysteries" of conception and birth quite as concertedly as does closed adoption. In both,
the imperative of parenthood serves as an antidote to the contrivance
of adoptive kinship.[12]

Open adoption is currently betwixt-and-between. The arrangement
offers its participants choice, yet the choice is constrained by the notion of an inevitable relationship. The differences in interpretations of
choice in adoption and choice in marriage underline the distinctiveness of the parent-child relationship in American culture. (Or, one

might say, because of the difference between these two contracted relationships, "choice" comes to mean different things in each.) If adoption were too much like marriage, there would be divorce—and in American culture, children and parents do not divorce one another.[13] Permanency is as strong a core of kinship as is the genealogical principle with which it is intertwined. But permanence, like genealogy, is a cultural convention, not a fact of nature. Divorce might even be good for parenthood, as Anthony Giddens suggests it is for marriage. "It needs no great insight to recognise that rising rates of divorce may indicate, not a deep dissatisfaction with the marital state or with the family as such, but an increased determination to make of these rewarding and satisfying relationships. If divorce rates have risen to previously unheard-of levels, they have been accompanied by very high rates of remarriage" (Giddens 1987, 129–130). Might it be possible to consider an institution of "re-parenthood"?

Probably not—or not soon. And certainly not by those who support open adoption, who do so with the hope of securing the placement unconditionally. But despite its shying away from choice in favor of fate, open adoption does create an alternative model for chosen parenthood. A direct exchange between participants is not the same as an exchange arranged by a social worker or a lawyer. Supporters of open adoption use the word *gift* to describe the transaction: a child, freely given and received, who creates a bond between the adults. Once more there is ambiguity: in one respect, this reaches back to traditional modes of child exchange; in another respect, a gift model radically restructures American adoption. In forming a bond, a gift eliminates the distance between giver and taker; they are united by the "item of value" they share.[14] Behind a vocabulary of love and generosity, then, the linchpin of American adoption is pulled out: if birthparent and adoptive parent are close to one another—even like (in both senses of the word) one another—why should an adoption occur at all?[15] In addition, the closer an adoptive parent and a birthparent are, the less can adoption serve its function of social control— redistributing children from an "unprepared" to a "prepared" parent. In open adoption, the exchange is just that: an agreement between individuals about the place of a child, unsupervised and free of external judgments of comparative worth.[16]

And so open adoption is more radical than it looks, or sounds, at the moment. It contains the seeds of a thorough upheaval in adoption.

"The counterhegemonies they construct"

Advocates of open adoption recognize the complications in practice, but not always the implications of such arrangements for cultural interpretations of kinship. The move toward open adoption is more subversive than even its opponents claim, constituting an "unselfconscious resistance" to ideologies of the family, parenthood, and gender that adoption has upheld for over a century. Eliminating the separation between giver and taker of a child, distributing the components of motherhood over several individuals, and attaching a child in different ways to different parents represent substantial revisions of familiar custom. Those who do so may "remain largely unselfconscious in any literal sense of the counterhegemonies they construct" (Comaroff 1985, 261). The "resistance" involves reorienting the values surrounding parenthood, and the parent-child relationship, in their context.

This is not the resistance only of mothers and women, though women tend to be the primary voices.[17] It *is* the resistance of those who view themselves as powerless in decisions about having—or not having—a child. Birthparents and adoptive parents, both male and female, assert that "others" control life-course decisions for them. Adoptees share the viewpoint when they claim they are lifelong victims of contracts made by others; they align themselves with the parents who signed these contracts by blaming a larger, oppressive system of law, policy, and "market forces." And like those in other situations who feel themselves to be vulnerable, members of the triad have developed subtle forms of resistance. These were apparent at support group meetings, but not only there. A birthmother refusing to sign surrender papers without seeing her baby, an adoptive applicant insisting her sexual behavior had nothing to do with being a parent, and an adoptee rejecting the chosen-child story in favor of a "real" birth story all displayed resistance to the conventions of American adoption practice.

At my first CUB and ASG meetings, I was surprised by the anger expressed in personal stories—even those told by people who liked their adoptive families, were pleased with a social worker, or had accepted the necessity of a relinquishment. I came to understand this anger as a response to the contradictory messages that frame the experiences of adoption described in chapters 4 through 9. By the 1980s, awareness of the ambiguities in a "just like" kinship turned to anger at a system that not only perpetuated contradictions but also made them the basis of a parent-child relationship. These feelings led in several directions: to the insistence on "unsealing" records, extending "freedom of information" to adoption, and recognizing that contracts do not have to last forever—a request for confidentiality need not apply for the lifetime of those who sign such papers. They also led to the reunions I have described, and to the move toward open adoption.

All of these mark substantial changes, a genuine open adoption most of all. For that arrangement has the potential not only to alter practice but also to undermine the structures and ideologies that have sustained a *fictive* kinship in American culture. The direct exchange of a child eliminates the sharp evaluative differentiation between a birth and an adoptive parent, between a person who "just has" a child (the stereotypical "kids in the mall") and a person who is "qualified" to be a parent. Moreover, the degree of choice offered by open adoption cuts at deep-rooted convictions about the inevitability, the *imperative*, of parenthood. Carried to a logical end, open adoption "opens" concepts of parenthood, of mother and father, and of family—thus of kinship altogether. If people who are unrelated, and not otherwise "bound" to one another, share a child, what does that do to the notion of being a parent? If "mother" includes the woman who bears but does not raise a child and, with equal significance, the woman who raises but has no birth tie to the child, then "mother" is no longer absolute—or absolutely linked with nature. A family composed of people with a common interest in a child, a *blended* family, is not the same as a family extended by genealogy and by marriage.

People now arranging open adoptions, like those who have had reunions, have no maps, a good deal of confusion, and a fair amount of distress. "I don't like to call them Mom and Dad in front of Mom and Dad." "In other words concepts such as mother, father, and family do not possess any form of absolute meaning but are problematic" (Haimes and Timms 1985, 99). Free-floating kinship terms erode the structures of more than kinship. And for most of its history in the United States, as I have suggested, adoption prevented these terms from floating. Substituting one mother for another, adoption fixed the meaning of "mother" and perpetuated "motherhood" as the model for parenthood. The concept of father also had a fixed, if less prominent, meaning: the person who stabilized and legitimized (rendered "fit") the adopting family—completing its "moral character"— as the twentieth century carried forward the gender stereotypes of the nineteenth century. Thus, problematic kinship terms render problematic the link of "mother" and "father" with gender ideologies, with a particular mode of childbearing, and with a type of affectionate and enduring bond to the "product" of a sexual union. Freed from sex, gender, genealogy, and nature, "parent" becomes a category into which many (or few) can fit, by choice and contingently.

By making kin terms problematic, open adoption is more subversive than its rhetoric implies. For those who support it, openness is not a breakdown but a restoration of values—putting adoption back on course, away from the commerce and calculation that have come to characterize this transaction in kinship. Inserting love and generosity into the exchange of a child, however, has the effect of making the transaction seem anarchic—if *sentimentally*, then not *sensibly* appropriate to the "extreme act" a legal adoption (still) represents in American culture. Opponents of open adoption do not trust parents any more than did charity societies in the late nineteenth century or social workers in the early twentieth century.

"A new kind of kinship"

I am not sure that open adoption is the ideal adoption. It is not easy to contemplate sharing parenthood with someone who is in other ways a stranger or releasing the transfer of a child from experts and noninterested criteria for parenthood. But it is clear that openness is "swaying" adoption policy and practice—and not because laws make it necessary, but because people choose to transact parenthood that way.[18] Resistant to being judged by experts and held to standards of parenthood no one else has to meet, adoptive parents and birthparents are taking action to alter the existing modes of child exchange. Both agency and independent adoptions have changed accordingly. Most agencies support some form of openness: a meeting between parents without identifying information; an ongoing exchange of letters; visits by a birthparent; a complete file for the adoptee.[19] Independent adoptions also involve more communication and contact between birth and adoptive parent.

This mode of change has characterized adoption history all along. The accumulation of individual behaviors leads to the passage of a law or the alteration of a policy—a response to the "felt necessities" that are first evident in the way people take action. The new development, in the late twentieth century, is the self-consciousness that emerges out of support groups; individual behaviors occur in a context of critical examination of the terms of adoptive kinship. Just as adopting never just happens, so it seems that future changes in adoption will not occur unselfconsciously. And they will not occur easily either. The tension is apparent in the debate about opening adoption: changes in adoptive arrangements press against the traditional meanings of mother, father, and family.

Adoption has been curiously left out of discussions of the American family, whether these discussions lament the collapse of the family, support its flexibility, or analyze its rules and roles. This is partly because adoption has been considered a version of the normal family, forgotten after the transaction is completed. Alternatively, and simultaneously, adoption is seen as too marginal to merit attention; it is not central to the evolution of the American family or to interpretations of kinship. My argument, of course, is that it *is* central: as a mirror of the "real" parent-child relationship and as a statement of how people should be related. Every time a child is severed from blood kin, given to strangers, and accorded a new birth certificate, the lineaments of kinship are drawn. Adoption "shows" what kinship is supposed to do. And adoption has been ignored partly for this reason: inscribing the conventional kinship arrangements of an era, adoption seems a stable—conservative—backdrop to the "real" shifts in family, marriage, and modes of childbearing. Adoption is not dramatic, unless it is treated as a powerful interpretive tool, not only for observers but also for participants in this kind of kinship. In both capacities, I have tried to show how adoption interprets American kinship.

And up to now, it has interpreted kinship as "genealogical." In the conventional form I have described, adoption upholds the biological basis for parenthood and the gender assumptions that go with that model. As long as artificial kinship inscribes the natural relationship, "blood" remains the central symbol of being related. But, as I have also shown throughout this book, individual actors in adoption are currently redesigning the *fiction* of their kinship. Reunions, openness, and blended families form the basis of a new kind of kinship, in which genealogy is only one way of constructing parenthood. If genealogy is no longer the core of kinship, American culture itself will be different.

Notes

Notes to Chapter 1

1. In his critique of anthropological studies of kinship, David Schneider (1984) points out how fully taken for granted this assumption is. "Genealogy is at the core of kinship" is treated as an absolute, not a cultural, principle, framing the approaches anthropologists take in the field. According to Schneider, the centrality of "birth" is viewed as natural rather than as a social construct by anthropologists who should know better—trained as they are to examine diverse folk models. Kinship everywhere, he claims, has been mapped onto the particular interpretation favored in Western cultures.

2. Said to have been instituted in order to disguise the "stain" of illegitimacy, the amended birth certificate in effect makes adoption a "juridical parthenogenesis," as one commentator put it (C. W. Anderson 1977, 152).

3. This is a peculiarity of American adoption; in other societies, exchanging a child establishes a relationship between the adults who make the exchange (see Goody 1969; Carroll 1970; Brady 1976, among others). There are in-family adoptions in the United States, and the number of these is rising as the rate of divorce and stepparenthood rises. My book deals only with stranger adoption; in these, the as-if principle of American adoption has its purest form: blood is replaced by contract.

4. The phrase *child exchange* is more often used to describe adoption in other societies than in American society. Inasmuch as "exchange" suggests market not gift (the latter is the appropriate word for many non-Western understandings of adoption), reluctance to use the phrase reflects an effort to minimize the commercial aspects of transferring a child.

5. Both H. David Kirk (1981, 1984) and David Schneider (1984), from somewhat different vantage points, note the extreme discomfort adoption causes in American culture.

6. In *The Woman in the Body* (1987), Emily Martin points out that "particularistic, concrete stories" often contain an "analysis of society."

7. Working in two areas was the result of my own career, not a deliberate research strategy. I also did some interviewing in a small town in New England.

8. In *The Woman in the Body* (1987), Martin suggests that it is a form of activism to volunteer to be interviewed, and that may be true for at least some of my informants. On the other hand, many of them said that talking about adoption was just "fun" and assumed I was enjoying it as much as they were.

9. "Some experiences are inchoate, in that we simply do not understand what we are experiencing, either because the experiences are not storyable, or because we lack the performative and narrative resources, or because the vocabulary is lacking" (Bruner 1986, 6–7).

10. In 1964, in the first edition of a book called *Shared Fate*, H. David Kirk argued for the "acknowledgment" rather than the "rejection" of difference in an adoptive family. His conclusion was based on data collected from a number of adoptive families, intertwined with references to his own experience as an adoptive father. He makes a persuasive case for the necessity on the part of adoptive parents to acknowledge how different they are from biological parents. He further suggests that adoptive parents in fact share the fate of being different with their adopted children—all the more reason for "difference" to be part of family life. Though most practitioners accept Kirk's theory, and probably many adoptive parents do, it may not be easy advice to follow—as the accounts of adoptive parents and adoptees in the following chapters indicate.

11. In 1980, Congress passed an Adoption Assistance and Child Welfare Act (P.L. 96-272) without much fanfare or publicity; so lackadaisical has been the response that many of its provisions sit unimplemented and unnoticed. Yet several of the provisions, like granting subsidies to adoptive parents, suggest a profound revision of notions of parenthood.

12. Influenced by Joseph Gusfield's 1981 analysis of "drinking-driving" as a public problem, Joel Best (1990) shows the importance of rhetoric for creating various public problems in the history of child-welfare practice in the United States.

13. Recent studies on adoption tend to use the figure of 5 million adoptees, probably borrowed from a summary of the "facts" collected by the NCFA.

14. These surveys, conducted in 1973, 1976, 1982, and 1987, have been analyzed by Christine Bachrach for their information on adoption—including data on relinquishing and adopting mothers; see bibliography.

15. Data for the *Factbook* were elicited by the group from its member agencies.

16. Individual states, private and public agencies, and adoption groups keep records, but these have not been compiled on a national basis in the past 20 years. The 1980 Adoption Assistance and Child Welfare Act (P.L. 96-272) argued forcefully for systematic data collection *on a national level*, but this

has not yet been implemented. The 1987 CWLA Task Force also argued for better data collection. "The goals of the newly-appointed National Adoption Task Force include revising adoption standards and developing, publishing, and disseminating critical adoption information" (Watson and Strom 1987, 2).

17. A failure to distinguish between number of adoptions in a year and number of adoptees in a (child) population per year is apparently not uncommon (Jonassohn 1965; Maza 1984). A further difficulty lies in the definition of an adoption "transaction" altogether. Are they only arrangements that have been through court? Or all instances in which a child has been permanently placed in another home?

18. Exceptions include Bachrach's analyses of the NSFG surveys, and a 1977 article by Gordon Bonham.

19. The books and articles on adoption by the sociologist H. David Kirk stand out here. Kirk has discussed and analyzed adoptive kinship not only as a personal event and a social institution but also as a reflection of dominant ideologies of family and parenthood. Adoption also appears in work by historians of the family and of childhood, as well as in those of anthropologists who have examined adoption in terms of kinship, exchange, and social mobility or, in a few instances, from a comparative perspective. My bibliography gives a fair sampling of this literature.

20. Two earlier books also had a hand in raising adoptee consciousness. In 1968, Jean Paton published *Orphan Voyage,* arguing against the secrecy and anonymity characteristic of American adoption. In 1973, Florence Fisher published *The Search for Anna Fisher,* an account of her search for her birthparents. As far as I could tell, neither of these made the impact that Lifton's books did, though Paton's *Orphan Voyage* serves as an important model for search groups, and Fisher's Adoptees' Liberty Movement Association (ALMA) is a successful national search group.

21. Talking about her difficulty in finding anything but the obvious in what the women she interviewed were saying, Martin quotes Marx: "People feel as much at home as a fish in water among manifestations which are separated from their internal connections and absurd when isolated by themselves" (1987, 11). Early in my fieldwork, I was struck by the sophistication with which the people I met analyzed a familiar kinship system. As they talked about relationships, they framed their feelings and their behaviors in terms of the dichotomies of blood and law, nature and culture, that are central to classic anthropological studies of kinship.

Notes to Chapter 2

1. Explanations appear in Presser (1971–1972), Benet (1976), Zainaldin (1979), Howe (1983), and Grossberg (1985), among others.

2. Adoption has a long history in Western and non-Western societies. Not

only was it a feature of the Greek and Roman landscape, but it persisted in one form or another into modern times (Goody 1969; Benet 1976; Cole and Donley 1990; cf. Boswell 1988). Moreover, any cross-cultural comparison reveals how common adoption is when the focus leaves the United States (e.g., Goody 1969; Carroll 1970; Brady 1976; Goody, Thirsk, and Thompson 1976; Waltner 1990).

3. Discussions of ideologies of the family, of gender, and of childhood are somewhat beyond the scope of my book; Grossberg (1985) has done an excellent job in relating such changes to the development of domestic law in nineteenth-century America.

4. In Massachusetts, for instance, between 1781 and 1851, over a hundred bills were passed altering the domestic status of children—what we would call adoption (Grossberg 1985, 269).

5. See below on the "troublesome question" of inheritance in American adoption laws.

6. The inclination of lawyers and judges to be lenient about "in-family" placements is a persistent theme in adoption history (e.g., Huard 1956; Fraser and Kirk 1983).

7. The reference is to Howe's suggestion that "the first known case of adoption in a common law state was in the colony of Massachusetts in 1693, when Governor Sir William Phips of Massachusetts mentioned his adopted son in his will" (Howe 1983, 175).

8. Standard discussions of adoption law see it as mainly directed toward children (e.g., Benet 1976; Howe 1983; Cole and Donley 1990). But with equal validity, such laws can be read as directed to parents—one who gives, the other who receives a child.

9. At least that was true in Massachusetts, as well as in the second state to pass an adoption law, Pennsylvania (1855). And though other states generally followed Massachusetts and Pennsylvania, not all included the provision of inheritance in adoption law.

10. One could write a longer history than has yet been done of the connections between child-saving efforts, apprenticeship and indenture arrangements, and the development of a policy and law of adoption. These issues are briefly mentioned in, for example, Demos (1970) and Farber (1972).

11. Greater tolerance of illegitimacy—bastardy—in the United States is said to explain the earlier passage of adoption law here than in England, which did not pass an adoption law until 1926 (e.g., Benet 1976; McCauliff 1986).

12. Adoption, implied a California judge in 1903, combines the doing of good deeds with the establishment of emotional solidarity. "Under the beneficent provisions of these statutes, such children are accorded advantages and opportunities for better moral, intellectual and material advancement; a measure of happiness is secured to the adoptive parents and the children adopted" (quoted in Witmer 1963, 32).

13. Obviously, any parent can leave a will; these provisions apply to cases in which a parent dies intestate.

14. Benet (1976) and Goody (1969), among others, point out the distinctiveness of this approach to adoption; in many societies, adoption was designed specifically to carry on the family property, name, and status.

15. "The focus of legislative intent in drafting consent provisions has been primarily upon the safeguarding of natural parents' rights by preventing parental surrender of children under duress or in any ill-considered manner" ("Natural Versus Adoptive Parents," 1971, 182).

16. Bruce Bellingham (1986) suggests that confusion about the temporary or permanent nature of "putting out" could result in a birthparent losing rights to a child without intending to consent to a termination. A few birthparents I interviewed were uncertain about whether foster care—a kind of "putting out"—meant a permanent relinquishment or could be a temporary resource for an unprepared parent.

17. State of Pennsylvania (1887), *Laws of the General Assembly*, Act 66. A century later, in 1980, the Pennsylvania Adoption Act mandated that parental rights be terminated for (among others) the following reason: "The repeated and continued incapacity, abuse, neglect or refusal of the parent has caused the child to be without essential parental care, control or subsistence necessary for his physical or mental well-being" (State of Pennsylvania [1980], *Laws of Pennsylvania*, Act 1980-163).

18. This is a central argument in the 1986 "best interests" volume, *In the Best Interests of the Child* (Goldstein, Freud, Solnit, and Goldstein).

19. Attempts to guard against an unreasonable and unjustified termination now include ensuring that the parent will not be deprived of the child on the basis of "environmental and financial considerations" beyond her or his control (cf. State of Pennsylvania [1980], *Laws of Pennsylvania*, Act 1980-163). Determining this is, however, a matter of judicial discretion.

20. Grossberg quotes the debate in the New York State legislature: there are "many childless parents who would gladly adopt children, but for their well-founded fears that they could never hold them securely" (Grossberg 1985, 272).

21. This is especially but not exclusively true when a child has been placed in a family of different racial, ethnic, or religious background from his birth family.

22. As Grossberg (1985) suggests, throughout the nineteenth century courts veered between honoring social parenthood and falling back on the inalienability of natural ties. This oscillation persists into the twentieth century, in adoption, foster care, and custody cases. The 1978 CWLA *Standards for Adoption Service* takes care to remind its readers that the "natural" family is the best place for a child.

23. "For the parent-child relationship was no longer defined in law exclusively in terms of kinship, but now also by a pattern of conduct, a state of mind defined in part by the mutuality of emotional bonds" (Zainaldin 1979, 1085). By the end of the century, too, the child who was at an "age of discretion" also had a say in placement, becoming another "judge" of care and love (cf. Witmer 1963).

24. A reference to material conditions also had precedent in *Chapsky v. Wood*: "Involved in the question as to what will promote the welfare of the child, are questions of wealth, questions of social position, of health, questions of educational advantages, moral training—of all things, in short, which will tend to develop a little girl into a perfect woman" (26 Kansas 650).

25. Commentators also warned about the racial and class biases built into such criteria (e.g., Chemerinsky 1979–1980, 105).

26. In a well-known 1960s case, a boy was removed from his father's "Bohemian" home in San Francisco and placed with his grandparents on their farm in Iowa, a case that reveals the persistence of assumptions about the "goodness" of farm life (Foster and Freed 1968). This has an odd resonance to the nineteenth-century child placement practices established by Charles Loring Brace. Head of the New York Children's Aid Society, Brace was convinced that children abandoned or on their own in cities ought to be housed on farms and in the country; he sent these "waifs" west, often without regard for the birthparent's situation. The presumed benefits of rural living apparently still affect custody and foster-care decisions.

27. "Moreover, it is usually held that, at least in the case of children of 'tender years' the mother prevails over the father, even though the 'best interests' test theoretically affords each parent an equal claim to custody" (Foster and Freed 1968, 41).

28. Some writers sympathize with the impulse to ignore *Stanley v. Illinois,* partly, at least, because searching for a father can delay placement; others see ignoring the ruling as denying a man his fundamental rights (Brown and Brieland 1975; Howe 1983; Cole and Donley 1990).

29. In 1980, Congressional hearings on adoption critically noted the spreading tendency to deny fathers the rights to their children in cases of illegitimacy or dispute. In response, the advisory panel took an "approach which permits a putative father to assert or to terminate his parental rights, or to disclaim paternity. If he fails to take any action within a reasonable time, that is grounds under the Act to terminate his rights and to free the child for adoption" (United States Congress, 1980b, 73).

Notes to Chapter 3

1. "Contrived" is Kirk's (1984, 39) word for the arranged family of an adoption.

2. "The first evidence of the professional practice of child-placement for adoption appeared in 1921 with the preparation and use of a manual of instruction by Sophie Van Senden Theis for students of the New York School of Philanthropy of the Charity Organization Society of New York" (Schapiro 1956, 19). Fifty years later, social workers were still reminding colleagues about the importance of expertise: the protection of children's rights "entails the screening of applicants to identify those most suited for the role of adoptive parents" (Brown and Brieland 1975, 291). See also H. David Kirk (1988, 89) who asks "By what means did social work come to establish its claim to special competence in the adoption of children?" in an article discussing social work criteria for selecting adoptive parents.

3. Lawyers as well as social workers have worried about the validity and "testability" of criteria like a good marriage and emotional stability. See, for

instance, the comment in the *Rutgers University Law Review* which refers to the lack of consensus on the part of member agencies of the CWLA concerning qualifications for adoptive parenthood ("Adoption . . . ," 1972, 704).

4. Thayer criticized this unstated aspect of child placement practice in 1963, and anecdotal evidence suggests the criticism can still be made.

5. One interesting recent proposal is to have adoptive parents help select other adoptive parents, though what criteria they would use, beyond empathy, is not stated (Cole and Donley 1990, 289).

6. A variety of explanations are offered for the shift from older child to infant adoptions during this period, including a decline in infant mortality and the lessening of fear about the inheritance of bad traits (Zelizer 1985; Cole and Donley 1990).

7. E.g., Burgess (1981, 20).

8. Babies might be left in an agency or placed into a foster home while they were being tested. Tests could take anywhere from 6 months to a year, and leaned heavily on contemporaneous theories of child development.

9. Social workers "matched children with parents of similar backgrounds, anticipating that the adoption would develop smoothly if the biological background was like the adoptive one" (Burgess 1981, 14; cf. Feigelman and Silverman 1983, 18).

10. "Special needs" is loosely defined, but generally refers to children with physical or mental handicaps, older children, and siblings who ought not be separated (CWLA 1978; cf. Feigelman and Silverman 1983). In 1986, special needs made up about one-quarter of all adoptions (Adamec and Pierce 1991, 320).

11. Currently, an effort is being made to give foster parents the right to protest an unanticipated removal of the child; foster parents now can request a hearing and petition for the child's continued stay (Derdeyn 1990). There is still a feeling among foster parents that they can "lose" a child without any warning or recourse.

12. Triseliotis and Hill (1990, 214) mention that some foster parents give the child their last name, in the hopes that he will feel more at home.

13. "The role of the foster parent is shaped by the child welfare profession" (Rein, Nutt, and Weiss 1974, 31). "Foster homes are a mainstay of the adoption agencies" (Burgess 1981, 60).

14. In his still influential study of foster care, Weinstein (1960, 17) states: "Our data strongly suggest that continuing contact with the natural parents had an ameliorative effect on the otherwise detrimental consequences of long-term foster care."

15. The problem of arranging visits, and of recognizing the child's interest in the matter, is thoroughly discussed in social work literature (e.g., Holman 1973; Hubbell 1983; Humphrey and Humphrey 1988; Triseliotis and Hill 1990).

16. For a combination of reasons, too, foster parents tend to be older and less well-off than adopting parents—not exactly the "average members of the community." Some critics have claimed a distinction is deliberately maintained, so that agencies have one kind of parent to draw on for temporary care

and another for the "permanent" placement of a child (see, e.g., Rein, Nutt, and Weiss 1974; Bush 1988).

17. The Act responded to, among other things, the phenomenon of "foster care drift," in which children were moved from family to family and occasionally lost in the "cracks" of the system. The "drift" phenomenon was well-documented by then. "Most foster children grow up without a permanent and secure home" (Mnookin 1973, 201).

18. In their 1983 book, *Chosen Children*, Feigelman and Silverman distinguish between those who adopt for "social and humanitarian reasons" and those who adopt for "personal" reasons.

19. "It is natural for a childless couple to care for parentless children who need care and for infants whose biologic mothers sign releases for them" (Schechter 1970, 355).

20. This has not changed in the forty years since Brenner's book (Ehrenreich 1985). Recently, some agencies have considered "infertility" the client's problem so there is a condition to treat (personal communication).

21. Some combination of the personal and the professional is generally held to be the best qualification for adoption work. "The examination and appraisal of adoptive applicants is a demanding task and requires rapid assessment by the adoption worker. Only with long experience and a clear sense of her own values can she handle this sensitive and vital area well" (Burgess 1981, 7). "Being a parent was my best training," a social worker told me. One adoptive parent, in turn, asked me how a "nun could think she could place babies."

22. H. David Kirk uses the term "sacred" in connection with the change in the child's life, but his point applies to all three members of the triad. "In shifting human beings by social and legal contrivances from one set of forebears to a new kinship system, they were in fact manipulating one of the last strongholds of ascribed and thus sacred relationship left in an otherwise achievement-oriented and secularized society" (Kirk 1988, 89). For a similar point about the social worker's "awesome" task, see Burgess (1981) and Cole and Donley (1990).

23. Feigelman and Silverman (1983, 18–19) see the redirection beginning earlier, in the late 1950s. Other evidence, however, suggests that adoptive parents continued to be primary clients into the 1970s.

24. Adamec and Pierce (1991, xxx).

25. "Clearly, the primary factor encouraging prospective adoptive couples to seek children independently is the shortage of white, healthy infants available through agencies" (Meezan, Katz, and Russo 1978, 228).

26. Independent adoptions are often called "private" adoptions, suggesting an equivalence between the two concepts. This is misleading, however, since agencies can be private, adoptions within any agency can be a private matter, and, on the other side, legalizing an independent adoption brings it into the public arena.

27. In order to avoid being called "baby markets" themselves, agencies for years avoided charging fees. Eventually, finding it impossible to survive on donations and good will, agencies began to charge for "professional services"—

still keeping at bay any suggestion of a commerce in children (Tiffin 1982; Zelizer 1985).

28. This is from her statement in the *Proceedings of the New York State Conference of Charities and Corrections* (in Bremner 1971, II, 149).

29. Hearings before the Subcommittee to Investigate Juvenile Delinquency of the Committee on the Judiciary, U.S. Senate, 84th Congress, 1955. The juvenile delinquents included unwed mothers who might compound their error by marketing their children, and those children who would, presumably, grow up to be delinquents themselves.

30. Payment here refers to gray market adoptions, in which expenses and fees for legal and medical services are paid; there is "no thought of profit," unlike a black market adoption. Gray market arrangements are legal in many but not all states (Zelizer 1985).

31. Follow-up studies are no more abundant for independent than they are for agency adoptions, but those that exist suggest the outcome is as successful as in any other form of placement.

32. National Committee for Adoption 1985; Bachrach 1990.

33. Social workers who support open adoption recognize the risks and the lack of information on how such arrangements work out for individuals; they advise continuing caution and, frequently, counseling (e.g., McRoy, Grotevant, and White 1988).

34. "Semi-open" is the recommended form: parents have information about each other, but not an ongoing relationship (McRoy, Grotevant, and White 1988).

Notes to Chapter 4

1. Literature about pregnant teens and unwed mothers is not about the individual who claims an identity as the parent of a child given away. A separate literature on birthparenthood has begun to emerge over the past two decades (e.g., Sorosky, Baran, and Pannor 1979; Silber and Speedlin 1982; Inglis 1984; Winkler and van Keppel 1984; Gediman and Brown 1989).

2. "Whatever else the story is about, it is also a form of self-presentation, that is, a particular personal-social identity is being claimed; second, everything said functions to express, confirm, and validate this claimed identity" (Mishler 1986, 243).

3. With two exceptions, the people I interviewed had not planned to have a child. The exceptions included a woman who relinquished a child after a divorce and a man who said his wife just decided she did not want to raise their child.

4. One birthparent who was also an adoptee had a distinct perspective on being pregnant. "I was just devastated. But in a way secretly happy because this would be my first flesh and blood."

5. Pregnant in the late 1960s, this woman had considered an abortion and decided it was too dangerous. She was unusual in talking about abortion as an

option, apparently not embarrassed to admit she thought about a then-illegal alternative. She was also the birthmother who repeatedly minimized her "maternal" feelings.

6. The memories of the birthparents I interviewed are supported by a literature that attributes irresponsibility to the unwed mother who keeps her child and maturity to the one who decides to surrender (e.g., Vincent 1961). In the past two decades this view has changed in letter but not in spirit: adoption is still regarded by many experts as the mature decision for an unprepared parent. The implications of this view are discussed in, for example, A. Brodzinsky (1990) and Else (1991).

7. Rillera's book is a collection of search stories, based on interviews with birthparents. It was published by Triadoption Publications, a clearing-house for literature on adoption.

8. Virtually all literature on birthparents now agrees on the importance of seeing and holding the baby before relinquishment (e.g., Inglis 1984).

9. Over the past ten years the assumption that not seeing the baby will help the birthparent forget has been replaced by a theory that the birthparent should see the child and validate her or his experience; then, too, the parent can mourn the loss (A. Brodzinsky 1990; Else 1991).

10. The hostility of nurses and doctors was a common theme in my interviews, upholding the birthparent's self-image of being alone, stigmatized, pressured by "everyone" around her. A similar theme appears in most studies of birthparents (Inglis 1984; Else 1991).

11. Some social workers will provide the birthparent with the name the child was given, as long as that information is not identifying.

12. The perception was by no means unique to the birthparents I interviewed (see, e.g., Else 1991 on the same point).

13. She was 14 years old when she gave birth and did not know whether her mother had also had to sign the papers to make the relinquishment legal.

14. States have different laws about when a parent signs surrender papers and about the length of time during which an individual can change her mind. "There is considerable diversity among the jurisdictions as to the form of a consent"—including where, when, and how it is recorded (Leavy and Weinberg 1979, 40–41).

15. The memories these birthparents have reflect adoption policy of the 1960s and early 1970s, when the majority of them relinquished. "In the recent past, illegitimacy was less of a problem because, in addition to its dysfunctional aspects, it also served two valid social functions. The first was a supply of children for economically secure, but infertile families who constituted a sizable adoption market," wrote a social worker in the mid-1960s (Roberts 1966, 5). There is no clear "second" in the following paragraphs.

16. The assurance that a relinquished child will be placed with a married couple has long been part of adoption policy. Transferring a child from an unprepared, single woman to a stable, two-parent family is an underlying element of placement practice, and a policy that the birthparents I interviewed generally supported (cf. Brenner 1951; Witmer 1963; CWLA 1978; Burgess 1981).

17. Here again the self-selection of my informants is important. There may well be birthparents who forget; there are certainly birthparents who do not want to talk about the past. Obviously, I could not interview such people.

18. Experts on adoption are coming to recognize the importance of mourning. The current theory is that grieving will better resolve the feelings surrounding relinquishment than the silence and suppression of earlier decades (e.g., Winkler and van Keppel 1984; A. Brodzinsky 1990). Agencies in my area give birthparents Judith Viorst's book, *Necessary Losses,* to read, which helps them to grieve.

19. Not all birthparents know whether the child *is* alive. One of the arguments for modifying the traditional secrecy of adoption is that it is "a torture" to wonder whether your child is alive or dead: at least a birthparent should be told that.

20. The founder of CUB, Lee Campbell, offered another explanation for lack of sympathy on the part of an adoptive parent. "So while birthparents, by virtue of their subsequent parenthood, can empathize with adoptive parents, adoptive parents seem unable to empathize with birthparents, perhaps because they themselves have never had to surrender a child" (Campbell 1979, 25).

21. This was a theme in birthparent autobiographies. For instance: "Just because it's growing in me doesn't mean it belongs to me. I know that. It would be like saying that a flower belongs to the soil" (Thompson 1967, 58).

22. She had been given the information by the physician who had arranged the adoption.

23. "Your legal relationship to your child would be severed by adoption, but not your genetic or emotional relationships," said a CUB pamphlet (1981, 21). This seemed to be true as well for birthparents who had children at home. Slightly less than half the birthparents I interviewed had other children. Studies of subsequent infertility in parents who once relinquished a child have not been conclusive, though popular birthparent literature argues that infertility is especially high among birthparents.

Notes to Chapter 5

1. Studies of the reasons for adopting have increased in the past quarter century or so. Many of these are qualitative, involving case studies of adoptive families; Feigelman and Silverman (1983) is one example, but see also Jaffee and Fanshel (1970), Kirk (1984), Daly (1988), and Brodzinsky and Schechter (1990).

2. This profile has been changing in recent years, as more lower-income families are accepted as adoptive families (sometimes after having been foster parents) and as agencies become alert to the need to accept non-white families altogether. By and large, though, one can still say adoption is a white, middle-class phenomenon. As Bachrach (1990) claimed: "The overwhelming majority (93 percent) of unrelated adoptions by women 20–54 years of age in 1987 involved white adoptive mothers [most of whom were married]."

250 NOTES TO PAGES 93–102

3. Findings from the National Survey of Family Growth combined with those from a National Health Interview Survey show that better-educated and middle-class couples are more likely to adopt than less well-educated and poorer members of the population. One has to remember that adoption involves a court finalization; informal adoptions exist throughout the population, unreported and untabulated (Bachrach 1990).

4. Generally, my sense was that, despite having talked a good deal about adoptive parenthood, they did not simply repeat what they had told social workers.

5. In their 1983 book, *Chosen Children*, Feigelman and Silverman distinguish between people who adopt for themselves and people who adopt out of altruistic motives; the former are "personal" adopters and the latter "preferential" adopters. The authors admit that the distinction is not hard and fast.

6. The people I met were not unusual in complaining about the intrusive questions. The "investigatory" nature of in-take interviews has become a subject of discussion in adoption literature (cf. Kirk 1984; Miall 1987; Daly 1988).

7. "Becoming an adoptive parent as a consequence of being blocked from biological parenthood can be viewed as a transformation of identity" (Daly 1988, 43). My study suggests that all adoptive parents, even those with biological children, experience a transformation in their sense of themselves as parents as a result of the adoption process.

8. Another parent's slip of the tongue was revealing. "As a matter of fact I think you have to ask some of that stuff because, you know, you got to find out what kind of child you place in these, you know, what type of parents the child's getting. So they have to know all this stuff." She may well have felt that it was really the child who ought to be investigated.

9. It is true that single adoptive fathers probably are the most rigorously investigated; such placements occurred in my area, but are not available in every state.

10. "Most adoptive applicants, regardless of their own ages, have a consuming desire to experience normal parenthood to the fullest" (Hallinan 1952, 22). This conventional social work perspective would not have surprised, or pleased, the people I interviewed.

11. "Alternative parenting" covered three types of nonbiological parenthood: foster parent, adoptive parent, and fostadopt parent. The third category referred to people who fostered a child in the hopes that the child would eventually be freed for adoption. In our group, one person wanted to be a foster parent, several were willing to be fostadopt parents, but most wanted to be adoptive parents. The likelihood of anyone getting an infant was small.

12. Some of us already had the experience. Aside from myself, there was a couple receiving training for children who had been placed but not yet legally adopted, a man with one adopted child who wanted another, and a woman who had had several foster children.

13. None of the parents in the group had been fostered or adopted.

14. I interviewed five of the participants several weeks after the training sessions.

15. Though she may not have outlined all her criteria, Mrs. Granger did have requirements. She asked that "her" parents be church-goers and pro-lifers. But since contact with her was relatively short, most people found it possible to bow to these demands.

16. In 1970, in a *Redbook* column, Margaret Mead reminded adoptive parents that rather than be so "demanding," they should accept the "hazards and joys and uncertainties of the natural parenthood that was denied to them."

17. I am talking about the ideal for an adoptive parent-child relationship. That these are contracted means there is a possibility of severing the relationship—a possibility that perhaps made the ideal even more powerful. Barth and Berry (1988) is a thorough study of broken or "disrupted" adoptions.

Notes to Chapter 6

1. Some writers argue that all adoptees think about their genealogical parents but that a number of them are afraid to admit it. Others claim that for most adoptees the adoptive parents are their real parents and, if they are passingly curious, they do not need to know more about a birthparent than they have been told. My interviews suggest that most adoptees do wonder about the parents who relinquished them, and the efforts of professionals to provide more information to adoptees suggest this has grown increasingly true.

2. Clearly it is hard to study those adoptees for whom adoption means nothing. They tend not to volunteer for studies or interviews; they are a silent member of the triad—if not for the same reason as the birthparent (see McWhinnie 1967; Triseliotis 1980; Stein and Hoopes 1985, among others).

3. One adoptee who did a search when she was in her 30s discovered that her birthmother was her adoptive mother's sister. This was not part of her growing-up experience, however.

4. "The how and when of 'telling' are still very controversial questions for which adoptive practice and research offer no clear guidelines" (Triseliotis 1973, 3). "[T]here is no unanimity, however, on the old question of 'when and how to tell.'. . . Useful guidelines for adoptive parents are in short supply" (Nickman 1986, 366, 370; cf. Schechter 1970; D. Brodzinsky, Singer, and Braff 1984; Brodzinsky, Schechter, and Brodzinsky 1986; Brodzinsky 1987).

5. David Brodzinsky points out that children may hear the word *adoption* at a very early age but not understand what it means. Understanding probably occurs around age 6, and some writers advise waiting and telling the child then (e.g., Schechter, Carlson, Simmons, and Work 1964; Brodzinsky, Singer, and Braff 1984). Brodzinsky has done a number of studies on the significance of "comprehension" for adoptees.

6. "What I am dwelling on—the pain, the feeling of emptiness, of being outsiders—is the neglected dimension of the adoption experience" (Lifton 1979, 7).

7. "Frequent discussion of the adoption situation was a rather unusual phenomenon. . . . The total picture that emerged was one of silence and evasiveness and often of deliberate distortion, sometimes with well-meaning but misguided motives" (Triseliotis 1973, 42).

8. Follow-up studies reveal that adoptive parents and adoptees significantly disagree about the amount of discussion there was and whether the initiative was taken by parent or by child (Jaffee 1974, 218–219; Nickman 1986, 396).

9. Adoptee reluctance to talk is not at all uncommon. "Even when and if the subject were introduced by their adoptive parents, although the child might be curious and waiting, and even eager to be told, they would not ask and in some cases feigned indifference . . ." (McWhinnie 1967, 248).

10. "One of the major characteristics of many adoptees in this group [in the study] was the way in which they often split the adoptive parents into wholly good or wholly bad ones. Frequently it was the mother who was seen as the wholly bad figure whilst the father was kept as a 'good' figure" (Triseliotis 1973, 70).

11. "From the adopted child's point of view, however, there was no doubt that the majority of those in this study wanted to have information which would have given them a clear picture of their biological parents, particularly of their mother" (McWhinnie 1967, 243; see also Triseliotis 1980).

12. The importance of the adoptee's fantasizing is disputed, partly because all children do fantasize about a perfect parent, another family. Yet some writers insist that the fact that the adoptee actually has another parent makes his or her fantasizing different from that of the biological child. The controversy has been somewhat resolved by the general agreement that adoptees should have as much information as possible about their other parents (Schwartz 1970; Stein and Hoopes 1985; Nickman 1986; Smith and Miroff 1987).

13. Adoptive parents "may be aware of the circumstances that led to placement and must be tactful in dealing with those, placing their emphasis instead on their delight in being able to care for and love the child as his/her parent(s) would have wanted" (Schwartz 1984, 54–55; see Jaffee and Fanshel 1970, who make a similar point).

14. Adoptive parents, of course, did not always have any information to give and had to do their best when a child asked. This was true of the adoptive parents I interviewed and also seems to be quite generally true (McWhinnie 1967; Jaffee and Fanshel 1970). It is hard to get information later on, if an adoptive parent has a change of heart about what to tell, since birthparents lose contact with the agency or person who made the placement.

15. There were explanations for every decade: a war in the 1940s, a fatal car accident in the 1950s, lack of social and economic support for a single mother in the 1960s, a mother's love and concern for her child in adoptive parent explanations of the 1970s and 1980s (cf. Lifton 1979; Triseliotis 1979; Powledge 1985).

16. Cf. Rondell and Michaels 1951; Dywasuk 1973; Krementz 1982.

17. "With regard to the self-esteem dimension, some adoptees reported that the fact of adoption actually enhanced their feelings of self-worth by cre-

ating a feeling of 'specialness' because of their 'chosen' status" (Stein and Hoopes 1985, 37).

18. See Priel (1986) and Winnicott (1967) on the importance of a mirror image to a child's sense of identity.

19. "Genealogical bewilderment" refers to "a state of confusion and uncertainty in a child who either has no knowledge of his biological parents or only uncertain knowledge of them" (Stein and Hoopes 1985, 16). "The resulting confusion undermines the child's security" (Lifton 1979, 49).

20. Lifton's work is influenced by that of Erik Erikson, and her views of identity are not unlike his, though they may be more fraught with meaning in the adoptee's case. "The sense of identity, then, becomes more necessary (and more problematical) wherever a wide range of possible identities is envisaged" (Erikson 1968, 245).

21. "Related to the task of differentiating between birth and adoption is the child's task of integrating two sets of parents into his or her mental and emotional life" (Brodzinsky, Schechter, and Brodzinsky 1986, 218).

Notes to Chapter 7

1. Tales of a child searching for an unknown parent are not uncommon in Western literature. That these have reemerged in the late twentieth century has to do with changes in notions of parenthood, family, and kinship that adoption reflects as much as causes. Lifton (1977, 1979) draws heavily on myths in her accounts of adoption, but references to Oedipus and Moses appear in virtually every account of the arrangement.

2. No one knows how many adoptees are searching for biological kin. Given the general lack of data on adoptees, the secrecy surrounding adoption, and the taboo against altering the adoptive arrangement, this is not surprising (Sorosky, Baran, and Pannor 1979, 126–127; Sobol and Cardiff 1983, 477; Schechter and Bertocci 1990).

3. But most adoptees would say that finding blood kin was a way of resolving a normal identity crisis (cf. Sorosky, Baran, and Pannor 1979). "My own research with adopted people seeking access to their birth records in Scotland has convinced me of how important and necessary it is for adopted people to know about their heritage and to have as much meaningful information as possible about their genealogical background. All adopted people have a deep psychological need to know about their families of origin" (Triseliotis 1980, 227).

4. Cf. Triseliotis 1973; Simpson, Timm, and McCubbin 1981.

5. The rather large number stems from the fact that I met adoptees through a support group that encouraged searching.

6. "It was not until the late sixties and early seventies that the first generation of adoptees affected by sealed records came of age in large numbers and, with mutual support, sought ways to learn about their natural origins" (Harrington 1980, 31).

7. Paton's book, *Orphan Voyage* (1968), was an early statement of the adoptee's need to know. Her reunion registry, "Soundex," is now one of the largest in the country.

8. Unlike Concerned United Birthparents, adoptee groups did not have an overwhelming majority of female members. At ASG meetings, however, women tended to be more outspoken than men.

9. In most states, a judge can grant a court order to open records "for good cause." What good cause is, is subject to judicial discretion. Perhaps the most common "cause" to date has been the need for medical information. In addition, twelve states have search and consent laws that allow an adoptee to contact an agency and request a search for a birthparent; twenty-four states have "mutual consent registries" (Adamec and Pierce 1991, 255). From the point of view of the people I interviewed, mutual consent registries did little good, since the chance of both parent and child signing was small.

10. Researchers have not found reliable correlations between experiences of adoption and decisions to search (Triseliotis 1973; Simpson 1981; McRoy, Grotevant, and White 1988; Schechter and Bertocci 1990). Different studies present different findings, agreeing only on the fact that "ever increasing numbers of adult adoptees" currently search for a birthparent (Sobol and Cardiff 1983, 477).

11. Just before Mother's Day, in 1984, Dear Abby ran a series of letters from birthparents about being found by a child. Some were "thrilled" while others were truly horrified. "I had to tell my daughter that I wanted her out of my life forever!" (*Morning Sentinel,* 4/30 and 5/1: 22 and 24).

12. "The desire for genealogical background information is probably shared by all adoptees, but interest in the birthparents can become a burning desire for some, simply because they have curious minds and approach all life's mysteries in an inquisitive manner" (Sorosky, Baran, and Pannor 1979, 200).

13. Her self-designation may have been borrowed from Betty Jean Lifton's *Lost and Found* (1979). A chapter called "Good Adoptee-Bad Adoptee" suggests that the contradiction between being unworthy and being "picked out" drives the adoptee into sometimes acting bad and sometimes acting "perfect."

14. In turn, in 1980 a suspense writer published a book about an adoptee's search for her birthparent (see P. D. James, *Innocent Blood*).

15. Search manuals encouraged a detective-story model. "When you begin your search, you may be convinced that you face an impossible task. Tracking down one person out of millions may seem like trying to find a needle in a haystack. But each existent record serves as a thread leading back to that figurative needle, and dozens of threads radiate out through the haystack, some extended out beyond the haystack's perimeter. If you can locate one or another of these through sharp-eyed research, that can eventually lead you to your needle" (Askin 1982, 58).

16. A range of people call themselves "searchers," including professional consultants, adoptees who have completed their own searches, genealogists, and miscellaneous interested individuals. There are national groups that oversee search consultants, but many others who help search fall outside any supervision and may become involved in illegal activities in order to get in-

formation. The adoptees I interviewed were sometimes not sure how illegal certain strategies were, but they tried not to get involved in anything that was blatantly against the law.

17. How readily this would be granted depended on state policies; a good deal of the discussion at ASG compared "good" states with "bad" states.

18. "In recent years we have seen an upsurge of minority groups insisting on greater equality of rights with majority groups. In the USA there are at least two strong activist groups demanding right of access to their birth records" (Triseliotis 1980, 226). The groups are not named.

19. Legal scholars also support the search movement's position that biological ancestry is crucial to one's identity. "The biological family is the source of identity for a child" is the central point of an article advocating legal measures for ensuring contact between an adoptee and his or her birthparents (Beyer and Mylniec 1986, 237).

20. Triseliotis's (1973) study of British adoptees in the early 1970s indicates that some number of adoptees do remain content with a name and some information about the reasons for relinquishment.

21. ASG recognized the importance of the first phone call and provided detailed instructions to its members on how to conduct themselves—what to say and not to say, how to be cautious while letting the parent know who they were, how to respond if a parent did not want to acknowledge parenthood.

22. I did interview the birthmother in this case, and her version of the reunion is presented in Chapter 8. I was not able to interview the adoptive mother.

23. He probably would have envied the adoptee who said to me: "And when I say my mother and my father I mean my adoptive parents, ok? I want to have that terminology straight." On the other hand, this woman had not yet met either of her birthparents and thus did not have to find appropriate terms of address.

Notes to Chapter 8

1. Henceforth BSG *Newsletter*. Reference is to the 1988 killing of kindergarten children in a school in California. The Joel Steinberg case also contributed to the arguments made by birthparents against lack of information, placements that were too facile, and the general—often mistaken—assumption that an adoptive parent was bound to be a better parent than a birthparent. In this instance, the adoptive father abused the child so badly it led to her death; upon investigation it also turned out that the girl had not been legally adopted.

2. The majority of birthparents I interviewed waited until the child was an adult, thus elapsed time was generally at least eighteen years; three had searched for minor children and had contacted the adoptive family first.

3. At the time of my research, records of membership were not kept. I have not been able to get access to recent records and do not know how systematic the collection of data currently is.

4. CUB's registry, like the majority of state-sponsored registries, is what is known as "passive": both parties must register before a contact is made. There is a good deal of complaint about this approach among birthparents.

5. In the mid-1980s, CUB leadership divided over this issue. Factions developed and new leaders were elected; the former leaders left the organization entirely and one, a man, started a group for birthfathers.

6. The claim that one signed papers planning to search came up in other birthparent interviews (cf. Rillera 1982).

7. Before BSG was established, birthparents in the area joined the adoptee support group.

8. Coincidences run through the search stories Rillera collected, and such chance occurrences provide the kind of momentum for searching that the people I interviewed also described (cf. Rillera 1982).

9. In March 1992, at a meeting on "search" in my area, social workers expressed sympathy for a birthparent's need to know, but emphasized that the child's best interests and the principle of preserving adoptive parent privacy hindered their ability to help people conduct a search.

10. "It is difficult because we don't know the taboo of mother and child because we met on an adult level. He calls me by name and we do not touch. So my needs to be intimate remain. I feel that if I had physical (non-sexual) touching it would help. If he could call me 'mom' as a constant reminder of who we are instead of us being on an equal adult level that could help" (CUB *Communicator,* 4/87: 11).

11. The July 1990 CUB *Communicator* ran a long article on twin studies, encouraging the notion that different experiences did not erode fundamental, and by implication genetic, similarities between parent and child.

12. Ten years later the woman who wrote this pamphlet reported in the CUB *Communicator* that her birthdaughter, and her grandchildren, had all moved in with her.

13. None of the birthparents I interviewed had married the other parent after the relinquishment, though this certainly happens (cf. Rillera 1982; CUB *Communicator,* passim).

14. Having contact with the other parent after a reunion was not unusual, and was often problematic. Letters to the CUB *Communicator* describe, as this birthparent did, "feelings" and old stirrings.

15. That was the advice CUB gave. "You are related by the fact of birth and you will always have a relationship. But relationships are more than facts; they are also processes. Relationships are neither static nor pure; they are complicated and ever evolving" (CUB *Communicator,* 3/90: 2).

Notes to Chapter 9

1. "If true parenthood, whether intuitive or learned, implies an emotional link-up at the deepest level between the parent and the child, adoptive parents who feel guilty or uncertain about their 'entitlement' to the child may find it difficult to form this link" (Triseliotis 1973, 76).

2. There are "two major tasks facing the adoptive family: the first is the development of a sense of entitlement, that is, the sense that the couple has a right psychologically and morally to be parents of their child. The second is the development of appropriate family relationships" (Ward 1979, 96).

3. Such comparisons have also become part of popular journalism. "From the start, the baby was ours, to love and to nourish, as much as if Trish had carried her from the moment of conception" (Schaap 1985, 4).

4. One or two adoptive parents said, echoing adoptees, that a crisis convinced them of their total commitment. For instance, after hearing that the biological grandparents might petition for the children, an adoptive father realized "we're not making it contingent, we're not holding off attachments or anything like that." And his wife told me: "But I think of it [the "crisis"] now fondly, that he so quickly took a liking to the children and became more attached to them, I think, than he even knew until that very important moment when he was faced with it."

5. Meetings were often arranged at a restaurant or other public place so as not to put pressure on the child to perform or be pleasing. Sometimes the prospective parents were introduced to the child and sometimes they just observed from a distance.

6. Sentiments like these appear in adoption manuals; for example: "I've been told by many other adoptive parents that they, too, feel their adopted child was predestined to be theirs" (Dywasuk 1973, x).

7. Adoptive parents were not without warning that trouble might follow the bliss of the honeymood period. "You don't love him yet for what he is; now there he stands by the kitchen table: hostile, remote, immovably implanted in his imperious determination not to budge ever, not ever," wrote an adoptive father about his experiences (de Hartog 1969, 50–51).

8. Not even this sentiment was free of an implicit reference to marriage. "And as you get more used to each other, share those ups and downs together, and grow more closely in tune, you begin to know with certainty that this is 'your own' child, to love and to cherish for all your days" (Jewett, n.d., 26).

9. Few recent adoption books would go so far as one published in 1947. "In general, it is probably true that men and women who seriously consider the adoption of a child are people of more than ordinary emotional depth, greater than common seriousness in their relation to life and to each other, more than usual conscientiousness. . . . They are able, consciously, to examine their own feelings and to seek the full expression of those which are deepest, perhaps finest" (Lockridge 1947, 32–33). But even the careful language of the CWLA guide to adoption services makes the adoptive parent sound "special." Adoptive parents are individuals who "can meet the needs of an adopted child, and who can provide the conditions and opportunities favorable to healthy personality growth and the development of individual potentialities. They should be able to carry responsibility for the child's care, support, education, and character development, and to offer the child a reasonably happy and secure family life with love, understanding, guidance and companionship" (1978, 59–60).

10. Self-consciousness about discipline was evident in the amount of time adoptive parents spent talking to me about this aspect of their childrearing.

Several repeated agency policy, claiming they always had a "group discussion" when something went wrong; a few used elaborate punishment and reward systems, and some did spank if talking failed.

11. Several mothers who could not afford to said they wished they could stay home and be a "full-time mommy." Though agencies no longer asked it of them, traditional role segregation remained appealing to a number of people.

12. The fact that foster parenthood was more closely supervised also made a difference. Adoptive parents felt they could do more of what they wanted with an adopted child. As one parent explained, "Where with foster children you wouldn't dare do that [admit mistakes], because they would immediately bring it to the caseworker and the caseworker would reprimand you for admitting to a child that you messed up."

13. Everyone I interviewed had told or said they would tell. The insistence on telling is pervasive these days, and it is unlikely anyone would have admitted they were thinking of keeping the adoption a secret. Moreover, those who decide not to tell probably do not volunteer to be subjects in a study of adoption. One couple refused to be interviewed, and when I told the social worker who had made the contact for me, she said, "Uh oh, I suspected they weren't going to tell the children they were adopted."

14. The importance of telling was probably the most forceful message that came out of the application process; it certainly had the most lasting impact on adoptive parents (cf. Kirk 1988).

15. "The majority of adopters felt that the search would be like opening Pandora's box but none of them denied the *right* of the grown adoptees to search" (Burgess 1981, 132).

16. Most did not like the idea of a birthparent searching. "Where adoptive parents seemed to waiver in their enthusiasm for the search was in their willingness to extend similar rights of information and contact to birth parents" (Feigelman and Silverman 1983, 198).

Notes to Chapter 10

1. "The fact of nature on which the cultural construct of the family is based is, as I have already suggested, that of sexual intercourse. This figure provides all of the central symbols of American kinship" (Schneider 1980, 37).

2. The intertwining of an interpretation of biological reproduction with gender ideologies makes a particular impact on the adoptive family in an American context. The assumption that they are "just like" can mean that gender roles are delegated in a particularly conservative fashion: mothers are "moms" and fathers "dads." I was often surprised by the conservative gender role division in families that otherwise seemed quite liberal.

3. At least that was true for birthparents who talked about adoption. I sus-

pect that few birthparents do forget the birth, but that some insert the chapter differently into their life stories than did the women and men who participated in my study.

4. The original document is usually sealed, stored away, and secured from "prying eyes" in a state bureau of vital statistics.

5. The opposition between "commerce" and "nurturance" is an important theme in Ginsburg's *Contested Lives* (1989; cf. Collier, Rosaldo, and Yanagisako 1982). The dichotomy carries even more of a burden in discussions of adoption, which involves the "distribution" of children and the calculation of comparative worth of parents.

6. This came up in an interesting way in my study of an in vitro fertilization clinic. Patients there considered this high-tech birth more natural than adoption, inasmuch as it involved the "mysterious" joining of sperm and egg and, too, perpetuated the "biological" substance of the "social" parents of the child (Modell 1989).

7. African-American customs are cited in the adoption literature (cf. Stack 1974).

8. Lincoln Caplan's account of an open adoption, in the *New Yorker,* suggests why the arrangement may be appealing and also its potential for causing pain to both sets of parents (Caplan 1990).

9. That, at least, is what books like Lindsay's *Open Adoption* (1987) suggest.

10. A persuasive argument for open adoption has been made by Baran and Pannor (1990) in terms of the child's best interests.

11. After making a careful and presumably rational choice, the birthmother in Caplan's account of open adoption insisted that she "just knew" the adoptive parents were "meant to be" her baby's parents (Caplan 1990).

12. Virtually no birth or adoptive parent I met liked the agency phrase, "making a plan for the child," another rejection of too much deliberation in parenthood.

13. While I was drafting the conclusion, an 11-year-old boy sued for the right to live with his foster parents rather than his biological mother. Reports on his action in newspapers and on television revealed how distressing the possibility of a child "divorcing" his or her parents is.

14. Titmuss's (1971) discussion of the mechanisms for "exchanging" blood, and the ramifications of a gift and a market model, is relevant; like blood, a shared child suggests a shared "substance" between the adults—with the same sense of discomfort about a relationship that ought not to exist.

15. The importance of differentiating a birth from an adoptive parent is also evident in the lack of attention paid to middle- and upper-class birthparents in the literature, though they make up a substantial percentage of those who relinquish children (Bachrach 1990).

16. William Pierce, of the NCFA, has been a vocal opponent of open adoption. He claims that, beyond confusing the child, such arrangements do not allow the birthparent to "move past" relinquishment or the adoptive parent to gain a sense of entitlement and of real parenthood. His dire prediction is that open adoption will do away with adoption altogether.

17. This is true not because men experience adoptive arrangements differently from women but because women "handle" kinship and parenthood, and I might add love, in our society (cf. Stacey 1991).

18. Baran and Pannor make this claim in their 1990 article. In the forefront of support of openness, these authors are not alone in their prediction. The CWLA statement that confidentiality cannot be guaranteed is a sign of how far the move toward openness has spread. The CWLA advises member agencies to let clients make their own decisions about the relationship between a birth and an adoptive family.

19. There are agencies that maintain traditional closed policies; this is becoming harder to do in the face of increased demands for some kind of openness by birthparents, adoptees, and (some) adoptive parents. The cynical view is that such agencies will have to "open up" or they will lose their business. Independent adoptions can be arranged to suit the participants' wishes.

Bibliography

Among my primary sources are newsletters, handouts, and brochures distributed by groups and agencies whose confidentiality I have maintained; therefore, the materials are not listed separately here. These sources include the newsletters put out by the two local support groups I joined: The Adoptee Search Group (ASG) *Newsletter* and the Birthparent Search Group (BSG) *Newsletter*. I also draw upon materials distributed by the child welfare agency I worked with, which I call County Youth Agency (CYA), as well as those distributed by several other adoption agencies.

Adamec, Christine, and W. Pierce. *The Encyclopedia of Adoption.* New York: Facts on File, 1991.

Adoptees' Liberty Movement Association (ALMA). Miscellaneous publications. New York: ALMA, n.d.

"Adoption: Psychological Parenthood as the Controlling Factor in Determining the Best Interests of the Child." *Rutgers University Law Review* 26 (1972): 693–713.

"Adoption: Psychological Versus Biological Parenthood in Determining the Best Interests of the Child." *Seton Hall Law Review* 3 (1971): 130–142.

"The Adult Adoptee's Constitutional Right to Know His Origins." *Southern California Law Review* 48 (1975): 1196–1220.

Agar, Michael. "Political Talk: Thematic Analysis of a Policy Argument." In *Power Through Discourse*, edited by L. Kedar, pp. 113–126. Norwood, N.J.: Ablex, 1987.

Allen, Elizabeth Cooper. *Mother, Can You Hear Me?* New York: Dodd, Mead, 1983.

Amadio, Carol, and S. Z. Deutsch. "Open Adoption: Allowing Adopted Children to 'Stay in Touch' with Blood Relatives." *Journal of Family Law* 22 (1983–1984): 59–93.

Anderson, C. Wilson. "The Sealed Record in Adoption Controversy." *Social Service Review* 51 (March 1977): 141–154.

Anderson, Carole. *Are Adoptees Cutting Their Own Throats?* Dover, N.H.: CUB Headquarters, n.d.

———. *The Social Worker's Role in Adoption.* Dover, N.H.: CUB Headquarters, 1980.

Anderson, Carole, L. Campbell, and M. Cohen. *Adoption Abuse.* Dover, N.H.: CUB Headquarters, 1982.

Anderson, Judith. "Changing Needs, Challenging Children." In *The Adoption Assistance and Child Welfare Act of 1980 (PL 96–272): The First Ten Years,* pp. 41–49. St. Paul, Minn.: North American Council on Adoptable Children, 1990.

Arms, Suzanne. *To Love and Let Go.* New York: Alfred A. Knopf, 1983.

Askin, Jayne, with B. Oskam. *Search: A Handbook for Adoptees and Birthparents.* New York: Harper and Row, 1982.

Bachrach, Christine. "Adoption as a Means of Family Formation." *Journal of Marriage and the Family* 45 (1983a): 859–865.

———. *Adoption in the 1980's.* Hyattsville, Md.: U.S. Department of Health & Human Services, National Center for Health Statistics, 1990.

———. "Adoption Plans, Adopted Children, and Adoptive Mothers." Working Paper #22. U.S. Department of Health & Human Services, National Center for Health Statistics, Hyattsville, Md., 1985.

———. "Children in Families: Characteristics of Biological, Step, and Adopted Children." *Journal of Marriage and the Family* 45 (1983b): 171–179.

Badinter, Elizabeth. *Mother Love: Myth and Reality.* New York: Macmillan, 1980.

Baran, Annette, and R. Pannor. "Open Adoption." In *The Psychology of Adoption,* edited by D. Brodzinsky and M. Schechter, pp. 316–331. New York: Oxford University Press, 1990.

Baran, Annette, R. Pannor, and A. D. Sorosky. "Adoptive Parents and the Sealed Record Controversy." *Social Casework* 55 (November 1974): 531–536.

Barnes, J. A. "Genetrix: Genitor: Nature: Culture?" In *The Character of Kinship,* edited by J. Goody, pp. 61–73. New York: Cambridge University Press, 1973.

Barth, Richard P., and M. Berry. *Adoption and Disruption.* New York: Aldine DeGruyter, 1988.

Bean, Philip, ed. *Adoption: Essays in Social Policy, Law, and Sociology.* London and New York: Tavistock, 1984.

Bellingham, Bruce. "Childhood, Victorian Child Saving and the Hidden Economy of Child Abandonment to the New York Children's Aid Society at Mid-Century." Unpublished ms., 1989.

———. "Institution and Family: An Alternative View of Nineteenth-Century Child Saving." *Social Problems* 33 (1986): 33–57.

Benet, Mary Kathleen. *The Politics of Adoption.* New York: Free Press, 1976.

Berman, Claire. *We Take This Child: A Candid Look at Modern Adoption.* New York: Doubleday, 1974.

Bernstein, Rose. "Are We Still Stereotyping the Unmarried Mother?" In *The Unwed Mother*, edited by R. Roberts, pp. 105–117. Westport, Ct.: Greenwood, 1966.

Best, Joel. *Threatened Children: Rhetoric of Concern about Child Victims.* Chicago: University of Chicago Press, 1990.

Beyer, Margaret, and W. J. Mlyniec. "Lifelines to Biological Parents: Their Effect on Termination of Parental Rights." *Family Law Quarterly* 20 (1986): 233–254.

Bloom, Lynn Z. *Dr. Spock: Biography of a Conservative Radical.* New York: Bobbs-Merrill, 1977.

Blustein, Jeffrey. "On the Duties of Parents and Children." *Southern Journal of Philosophy* 15 (Winter 1977): 427–441.

———. *Parents and Children: The Ethics of the Family.* New York: Oxford University Press, 1982.

Bolles, Edmund Blair. *The Penguin Adoption Handbook.* New York: Viking, 1984.

Bonham, Gordon S. "Who Adopts: The Relationship of Adoption and Social Demographic Characteristics of Women." *Journal of Marriage and the Family* 39 (May 1977): 295–306.

Borgatta, Edgar, D. Fanshel, and H. J. Meyer. *Social Workers' Perceptions of Clients.* New York: Russell Sage Foundation, 1960.

Boswell, John. *The Kindness of Strangers.* New York: Pantheon, 1988.

Bowlby, John. *Maternal Care and Mental Health* [1951]. New York: Schocken, 1966.

———. "Substitute Families. Adoption" [1951]. In *Readings in Adoption*, edited by I. Evelyn Smith, pp. 434–442. New York: Philosophical Library, 1963.

Brady, Ivan, ed. *Transactions in Kinship.* Honolulu: University of Hawaii Press, 1976.

Bremner, Robert, ed. *Children and Youth in America.* Vol. 2 (1866–1932). Cambridge: Harvard University Press, 1971.

———. *Children and Youth in America.* Vol. 3 (1933–1973). Cambridge: Harvard University Press, 1974.

Brenner, Ruth. *A Follow-Up Study of Adoptive Families.* New York: Child Adoption Research Committee, Inc., 1951.

Brodzinsky, Anne B. "Surrendering an Infant for Adoption." In *The Psychology of Adoption*, edited by D. Brodzinsky and M. Schechter, pp. 295–331. New York: Oxford University Press, 1990.

Brodzinsky, David M. "Looking at Adoption Through Rose-Colored Glasses." *Journal of Personality and Social Psychology* 52 (1987): 394–398.

Brodzinsky, David M., and M. D. Schechter, eds. *The Psychology of Adoption.* New York: Oxford University Press, 1990.

Brodzinsky, David M., M. D. Schechter, and A. B. Brodzinsky. "Children's Knowledge of Adoption: Developmental Changes and Implications for Adjustment." In *Thinking About the Family*, edited by R. D. Ashmore and D. M. Brodzinsky, pp. 205–232. Hillsdale, N.J.: Lawrence Erlbaum, 1986.

Brodzinsky, David M., L. M. Singer, and A. M. Braff. "Children's Understanding of Adoption." *Child Development* 55 (1984): 869–878.

Brown, Edwin G., and Donald Brieland. "Adoptive Screening: New Data, New Dilemmas." *Social Work* 20 (1975): 291–295.

Bruner, Edward. "Experience and Its Expressions." In *The Anthropology of Experience*, edited by V. W. Turner and E. M. Bruner, pp. 3–30. Urbana and Chicago: University of Illinois Press, 1986.

Burgess, Linda Cannon. *The Art of Adoption*. New York: W. W. Norton, 1981.

Bush, Malcolm. *Families in Distress: Public, Private, and Civic Responses*. Berkeley: University of California Press, 1988.

Campbell, Lee H. *Beyond the Shadows: A Study of Birthparenthood*. Dover, N.H.: CUB Headquarters, 1982.

———. "The Birthparent's Right to Know." *Public Welfare* 37 (1979): 22–27.

Caplan, Lincoln. "Open Adoption." *The New Yorker*, May 21, 1990, 40–68, and May 28, 1990, 73–95.

Carroll, Vern, ed. *Adoption in Eastern Oceania*. Honolulu: University of Hawaii Press, 1970.

Chemerinsky, Edwin. "Constitutional Protections in Involuntary Adoptions." *Journal of Family Law* 18 (1979–1980): 79–113.

Chesler, Phyllis. *Sacred Bond: The Legacy of Baby M*. New York: Times Books, 1988.

Child Welfare League of America (CWLA). *Standards for Adoption Service*. New York: CWLA, 1978.

Cohen, Julius, R. A. H. Robson, and A. Bates. *Parental Authority: The Community and the Law*. New Brunswick, N.J.: Rutgers University Press, 1958.

Cole, Elizabeth S. "The Future of Adoption." In *Testimony and Speeches 1985*. New York: CWLA, 1985.

Cole, Elizabeth S., and K. S. Donley. "History, Values, and Placement Policy Issues." In *The Psychology of Adoption*, edited by D. Brodzinsky and M. Schechter, pp. 273–294. New York: Oxford University Press, 1990.

Collier, Jane, M. Rosaldo, and S. Yanigisako. "Is There a Family? New Anthropological Views." In *Rethinking the Family*, edited by B. Thorne with M. Yalom, pp. 25–39. New York: Longman, 1982.

Comaroff, Jean. *Body of Power, Spirit of Resistance*. Chicago: University of Chicago Press, 1985.

Cominos, Helen. "Minimizing the Risks of Adoption Through Knowledge." *Social Work* 16 (January 1971): 73–79.

Concerned United Birthparents, Inc. (CUB). *The Birthparent's Perspective*. Dover, N.H.: CUB Headquarters, n.d.

———. *Choices, Chances, Changes: A Guide to Making an Informed Choice About Your Untimely Pregnancy*. Dover, N.H.: CUB Headquarters, 1981.

———. *Growing Strong with CUB: Biennial Report of CUB Activities on Behalf of Families and Adoption-Separated Families, July 1981–July 1983*. Dover, N.H.: CUB Headquarters, 1983.

———. *Hosting a Search Workshop*. Dover, N.H.: CUB Headquarters, n.d.

———. *New Member Information*. Dover, N.H.: CUB Headquarters, 1980.

Cox, John Freemont. "An Analysis of the Functioning of the Adoption

Process in Allegheny County, Pennsylvania." Ph.D. diss., University of Pittsburgh, 1949.

Crapanzano, Vincent. *Waiting: The Whites of South Africa.* New York: Random House, 1985.

CUB *Communicator.* Newsletter, CUB Headquarters, 1979–1986 (Dover, N.H.) and 1986–1990 (Des Moines, Iowa).

Dally, Ann. *Inventing Motherhood: The Consequences of an Ideal.* New York: Schocken, 1983.

Daly, Kerry. "Reshaped Parenthood Identity: The Transition to Adoptive Parenthood." *Journal of Contemporary Ethnography* 17 (1988): 40–66.

de Hartog, Jan. *The Children: A Personal Record for the Use of Adoptive Parents.* New York: Atheneum, 1969.

Demos, John. *A Little Commonwealth.* New York: Oxford University Press, 1970.

Derdeyn, Andre P. "Foster Parent Adoption: The Legal Framework." In *The Psychology of Adoption*, edited by D. Brodzinsky and M. Schechter, pp. 332–347. New York: Oxford University Press, 1990.

Deykin, Eva Y., L. Campbell, and P. Patti. "The Postadoption Experience of Surrendering Parents." *American Journal of Orthopsychiatry* 54 (1984): 271–280.

Doty, Rosemarie, and R. K. Merwin. "Parents Relinquishing Rights to First-Born Legitimate Children." *Child Welfare* 48 (1969): 100–103, 110–111.

Dusky, Lorraine. *Birthmark.* New York: M. Evans, 1979.

Dywasuk, Colette Taube. *Adoption—Is It for You?* New York: Harper and Row, 1973.

Ehrenreich, John H. *The Altruistic Imagination: A History of Social Work and Social Policy in the United States.* Ithaca: Cornell University Press, 1985.

Else, Anne. *A Question of Adoption.* Wellington, New Zealand: Bridget Williams Books, 1991.

Erikson, Erik. *Identity, Youth and Crisis.* New York: W. W. Norton, 1968.

Family Service Association of America. *Adoption Principles and Services.* New York: Family Service Association of America, 1952.

Fanshel, David. *Foster Parenthood: A Role Analysis.* Minneapolis: University of Minnesota Press, 1966.

Farber, Bernard. *Conceptions of Kinship.* New York: Elsevier, 1981.

———. *Guardians of Virtue: Salem Families in 1800.* New York: Basic Books, 1972.

Feigelman, William, and A. R. Silverman. *Chosen Children.* New York: Praeger, 1983.

———. "Preferential Adoption: A New Mode of Family Formation." *Social Casework* 60 (May 1979): 296–305.

Festinger, Trudy. *Necessary Risk.* New York: CWLA, 1986.

Fisher, Florence. *The Search for Anna Fisher.* New York: Arthur Fields, 1973.

Foster, Henry H., and D. Jonas Freed. "Children and the Law." *Family Law Quarterly* 2 (March 1968): 41–49.

Fraser, F. Murray, and H. D. Kirk. "Cui Bono? Some Questions Concerning the 'Best Interests of the Child' Principle in Canadian Adoption Laws and Practices." Unpublished ms., 1983.

Gediman, Judith S., and L. P. Brown. *Birth Bond: Reunions Between Birth-parents and Adoptees.* Far Hills, N.J.: New Horizon, 1989.

Giddens, Anthony. *Sociology: A Brief But Critical Introduction.* New York: Harcourt Brace Jovanovich, 1987.

Gill, Dereck. *Illegitimacy, Sexuality and the Status of Women.* Oxford: Basil Blackwell, 1977.

Gill, Margaret M., and C. M. Amadio. "Social Work and Law in a Foster Care/Adoption Program." *Child Welfare* 62 (1983): 455–467.

Ginsburg, Faye. *Contested Lives.* Berkeley: University of California Press, 1989.

———. "Procreation Stories: Reproduction, Nurturance, and Procreation in Life Narratives of Abortion Activists." *American Ethnologist* 14 (November 1987): 623–636.

Goffman, Erving. *Stigma.* New York: Penguin, 1968.

Goldstein, Joseph, A. Freud, and A. J. Solnit. *Before the Best Interests of the Child.* New York: Free Press, 1979a.

———. *Beyond the Best Interests of the Child.* New York: Free Press, 1979b.

Goldstein, Joseph, A. Freud, A. J. Solnit, and S. Goldstein. *In the Best Interests of the Child.* New York: Free Press, 1986.

Goodrich, Frederick W., Jr. *Infant Care: The United States Government Guide.* Supplemented and annotated by F. W. Goodrich. Englewood Cliffs, N.J.: Prentice-Hall, 1968.

Goody, Esther. *Contexts of Kinship: An Essay in the Family Sociology of the Gonja of Northern Ghana.* New York: Cambridge University Press, 1973.

———. *Parenthood and Social Reproduction.* New York: Cambridge University Press, 1982.

Goody, Jack. "Adoption in Cross-Cultural Perspective." *Comparative Studies in Society and History* 2 (1969): 55–78.

———, ed. *The Character of Kinship.* New York: Cambridge University Press, 1973.

———, ed. *Production and Reproduction.* New York: Cambridge University Press, 1976.

Goody, Jack, J. Thirsk, and E. P. Thompson, eds. *Family and Inheritance.* New York: Cambridge University Press, 1976.

Gordon, Linda. *Heroes of Their Own Lives.* New York: Viking, 1988.

Grieff, Geoffrey L., and M. S. Pabst. *Mothers Without Custody.* Lexington, Mass.: D. C. Heath, 1988.

Grossberg, Michael. *Governing the Hearth.* Chapel Hill: University of North Carolina Press, 1985.

Gusfield, Joseph. *The Culture of Public Problems: Drinking, Driving and the Symbolic Order.* Chicago and London: University of Chicago Press, 1981.

Haimes, Erica, and N. Timms. *Adoption, Identity and Social Policy: The Search for Distant Relatives.* Brookfield, Vt.: Gower, 1985.

Hallinan, Helen. "Who Are the Children Available for Adoption?" In *Adoption Principles and Services (Collected Papers),* pp. 21–27. New York: Family Service Association of America, 1952.

Hanssen, Gail. *Before You Search.* Dover, N.H.: CUB Headquarters, n.d.

———. *Coping with Rejection.* Dover, N.H.: CUB Headquarters, n.d.

Harrington, Joseph D. "The Courts Contend with Sealed Adoption Records." *Public Welfare* 38 (1980): 30–43.

———. "Legislative Reform Moves Slowly." *Public Welfare* 37 (1979): 49–57.

Hartman, Ann. *Finding Families.* Human Services Guide #7. Beverly Hills, Calif.: Sage, 1979.

———. *Working with Adoptive Families Beyond Placement.* New York: CWLA, 1984.

Hemphill, Sandra, S. McDaniel, and H. D. Kirk. "Adoption in Canada: A Neglected Area of Data Collection for Research." *Journal of Comparative Family Studies* 12 (Autumn 1981): 509–515.

Herbenick, Raymond M. "Remarks on Abortion, Abandonment, and Adoption Opportunities." In *Having Children,* edited by O. O'Neill and W. Ruddick. New York: Oxford University Press, 1979.

Hermann, Kenneth. "There Is Insight When the Tables Turn." *Ours* (September/October 1983): 22–23.

Heyden, Eric. "Seal of Sorrow." *Human Rights* 9 (1981): 28–31, 53–54.

Holman, Robert. *Trading in Children: A Study of Private Fostering.* Boston: Routledge and Kegan Paul, 1973.

Hoopes, Janet L. "Adoption and Identity Formation." In *The Psychology of Adoption,* edited by D. M. Brodzinsky and M. D. Schechter, pp. 144–166. New York: Oxford University Press, 1990.

———. *Prediction in Child Development.* New York: CWLA, 1982.

Horejsi, Charles R. "Increasing Bio-Parent Involvement in Foster Care." *Foster Care Journal* 4 (October 1987): 74–80.

Houlgate, Laurence D. *The Child and the State.* Baltimore: Johns Hopkins University Press, 1980.

Howe, Ruth Arlene. "Adoption Practice, Issues and Laws, 1958–1983." *Family Law Quarterly* 17 (1983): 173–197.

Huard, Leo Albert. "The Law of Adoption: Ancient and Modern." *Vanderbilt Law Review* 9 (1956): 743–763.

Hubbell, Ruth. "Foster Care and Families." In *Changing Families,* edited by Irving E. Sigel and L. M. Laosa, pp. 247–266. New York and London: Plenum, 1983.

Humphrey, Michael. *The Hostage Seekers: A Study of Childless and Adopting Couples.* New York: Humanities Press, 1969.

Humphrey, Michael, and H. Humphrey. *Families with a Difference.* New York: Routledge, 1988.

Inglis, Kate. *Living Mistakes: Mothers Who Consented to Adoption.* Boston: George Allen and Unwin, 1984.

Jaffe, Benson. "Adoption Outcome: A Two-Generation View." *Child Welfare* 53 (1974): 211–224.

Jaffe, Benson, and D. Fanshel. *How They Fared in Adoption: A Follow-Up Study.* New York: Columbia University Press, 1970.

James, P. D. *Innocent Blood.* New York: Warner, 1980.

Jewett, Claudia L. *A Parent's Guide to Adopting an Older Child.* Ms. prepared for the Northeast Adoption Council, n.d.

Joe, Barbara. *Public Policies Toward Adoption*. Washington, D.C.: The Urban Institute, 1979.

Jonassohn, Kurt. "On the Use and Construction of Adoption Rates." *Journal of Marriage and the Family* 27 (1965): 514–521.

Kadushin, Alfred. "Child Welfare." In *Encyclopedia of Social Work*, vol. 1, pp. 265–274. Silver Springs, Md.: National Association of Social Workers, 1987.

———, ed. *Child Welfare Services: A Sourcebook*. New York: Macmillan, 1970.

Kagan, Jerome. "The Child in the Family." In *The Family*, edited by A. Rossi, J. Kagan, and T. Hareven, pp. 35–56. New York: W. W. Norton, 1978.

Katz, Sanford N. "Judicial and Statutory Trends in the Laws of Adoption." *Georgetown Law Journal* 51 (1962): 64–95.

———. "Rewriting the Adoption Story." *Family Advocate* 5 (1982): n.p.

———. *When Parents Fail*. New York: Beacon, 1971.

Kawashima, Yasuhide. "Adoption in Early America." *Journal of Family Law* 20 (1981–1982): 677–696.

Kirk, H. David. *Adoptive Kinship*. Toronto: Butterworths, 1981.

———. "A Dilemma of Adoptive Parenthood: Incongruous Role Obligations." *Marriage and Family Living* 21 (1959): 316–328.

———. *Exploring Adoptive Family Life: The Collected Adoption Papers of H. David Kirk*, edited by B. J. Tansey. Port Angeles, Wash.: Ben-Simon, 1988.

———. "Forward." In *Chosen Children*, by W. Feigelman and A. R. Silverman, pp. ix–xviii. New York: Praeger, 1983.

———. *Shared Fate: A Theory of Adoption and Mental Health*. [1964] Port Angeles, Wash.: Ben-Simon, 1984.

Kittay, Eva Feder. *Metaphor: Its Cognitive Force and Linguistic Structure*. Oxford: Clarendon, 1987.

Kittson, Ruthena Hill. *See* Paton, Jean.

Krementz, Jill. *How It Feels to be Adopted*. New York: Alfred A. Knopf, 1982.

Krugman, Dorothy C. "Reality in Adoption." *Child Welfare* 43 (1964): 349–358.

Kuhlmann, Frieda, and H. P. Robinson. "Rorschach Tests as a Diagnostic Tool in Adoption Studies." In *Adoption Principles and Services (Collected Papers)*, pp. 7–14. New York: Family Service Association of America, 1952.

Lakoff, George, and M. Johnson. *Metaphors We Live By*. Chicago: University of Chicago Press, 1980.

Landes, Elizabeth, and R. Posner. "The Economics of the Baby Shortage." *Journal of Legal Studies* 7 (June 1978): 323–348.

Lawder, Elizabeth, K. D. Lower, R. G. Andrews, E. A. Sherman, and J. G. Hill. *A Follow-up Study of Adoptions: Post-Placement Functioning of Adoptive Families*. Vol. 1. New York: CWLA, 1969a.

———. *A Follow-up Study of Adoptions: Post-Placement Functioning of Adopted Children*. Vol. 2. New York: CWLA, 1969b.

Leavy, Morton L., and R. D. Weinberg. *Law of Adoption*. Dobbs Ferry, N.Y.: Oceana, 1979.

Leichter, Hope J., and W. E. Mitchell. *Kinship and Casework*. New York: Russell Sage Foundation, 1967.

Lewin, Kurt. "Bringing up the Jewish Child" [1940]. In *Resolving Social Conflicts*, edited by G. Weiss Lewin, pp. 169–185. New York: Harper and Row, 1948.

Lewontin, R. C., S. Rose, and L. J. Kamin. *Not in Our Genes: Biology, Ideology and Human Nature*. New York: Pantheon, 1984.

Lifton, Betty Jean. *I'm Still Me*. New York: Bantam, 1982.

———. *Lost and Found: The Adoption Experience*. New York: Dial, 1979.

———. *Twice Born: Memoirs of an Adopted Daughter* [1975]. New York: Penguin, 1977.

Lindsay, Jeanne W. *Open Adoption: A Caring Option*. Buena Park, Calif.: Morning Glory Press, 1987.

Lockridge, Frances, with S. Van Senden Theis. *Adopting a Child*. New York: Greenberg, 1947.

Lomas, Peter, ed. *The Predicament of the Family: A Psychoanalytical Symposium*. New York: International Universities Press, 1967.

Luker, Kristin. *Abortion and the Politics of Motherhood*. Berkeley: University of California Press, 1984.

Maas, Henry S., and R. E. Engler, Jr. *Children in Need of Parents*. New York: Columbia University Press, 1959.

Maine, H. S. *Ancient Law*. London: J. Murray, 1861.

Malinowski, Bronislaw. "Parenthood—The Basis of Social Structure." In *The New Generation*, edited by F. Calverton and S. Schmalhausen, pp. 136–166. New York: Macaulay, 1930.

Mandell, Betty Reid. *Where Are the Children? A Class Analysis of Foster Care and Adoption*. Lexington, Mass.: D. C. Heath, 1973.

Martin, Emily. *The Woman in the Body: A Cultural Analysis of Reproduction*. Boston: Beacon, 1987.

Maxtone-Graham, Katrina. *An Adopted Woman*. New York: Remi, 1983.

Maza, Penelope. *Adoption Trends: 1944–1975*. Child Welfare Research Notes #9. Washington, D.C.: Children's Bureau, 1984.

———. "What We Do—and Don't—Know About Adoption Statistics." *Permanent Families for Children* 3 (1985): 5.

McCauliff, C. M. A. "The First English Adoption Law and Its American Precursors." *Seton Hall Law Review* 16 (1986): 656–677.

McRoy, Ruth, H. D. Grotevant, and K. L. White. *Openness in Adoption: New Practices, New Issues*. New York: Praeger, 1988.

McWhinnie, Alexina Mary. *Adopted Children: How They Grow Up; A Study of Their Adjustment as Adults*. New York: Humanities Press, 1967.

Meezan, William, S. Katz, and E. M. Russo. *Adoptions Without Agencies: A Study of Independent Adoptions*. New York: CWLA, 1978.

Meezan, William, and J. F. Shireman. *Care and Commitment: Foster Parent Adoption Decisions*. Albany: State University of New York Press, 1985.

Melina, Lois Ruskai. *Raising Adopted Children*. New York: Harper and Row, 1986.

Miall, Charlene E. "The Stigma of Adoptive Parent Status." *Family Relations* 36 (1987): 34–39.

Miller, Daniel, and G. Swanson. *The Changing American Parent: A Study in the Detroit Area*. New York: Wiley, 1958.

Miller, Warren B., and L. F. Newman, eds. *The First Child and Family Formation*. Chapel Hill: University of North Carolina Press, 1978.

Mishler, Elliot G. "The Analysis of Interview Narratives." In *Narrative Psychology: The Storied Nature of Human Conduct*, edited by T. R. Sarbin. New York: Praeger, 1986.

Mnookin, Robert H. *Child, Family and State: Problems and Materials on Children and the Law*. Boston: Little, Brown, 1978.

————. "Foster Care: In Whose Best Interest?" In *Parents of Children in Placement*, edited by P. Sinanoglu and A. W. Maluccio, pp. 191–233. New York: CWLA, 1981.

————. *In the Interest of Children: Advocacy, Law Reform, and Public Policy*. New York: W. H. Freeman, 1985.

Mnookin, Robert H., and Lewis Kornhauser. "Bargaining in the Shadow of the Law: The Case of Divorce." *Yale Law Journal* 88 (1979): 950–997.

Modell, Judith. "'How do you introduce yourself as a childless mother?'" In *Storied Lives*, edited by G. Rosenwald and R. Ochberg, pp. 76–94. New Haven: Yale University Press, 1992.

————. "Last Chance Babies." *Medical Anthropology Quarterly* 3 (1989): 124–138.

Momjian, Albert, and N. Perlberger. *Pennsylvania Family Law*. Philadelphia: George Bisel, 1978.

Moorman, Jeanne E., and D. J. Hernandez. "Married-Couple Families with Step, Adopted, and Biological Children." *Demography* 26 (1989): 267–277.

Morning Sentinel (Waterville, Maine). 1982–1984.

Musser, Sandra Kay. *I Would Have Searched Forever*. Plainfield, N.J.: Haven Books, 1979.

National Center for Health Statistics. *Questionnaires: National Survey of Family Growth*. Hyattsville, Md.: National Center for Health Statistics, 1973, 1976, 1987.

National Committee for Adoption. *Adoption Factbook: U.S. Data, Issues, Regulations and Resources*. Washington, D.C.: NCFA, 1985.

"Natural Versus Adoptive Parents: Divided Children and the Wisdom of Solomon." *Iowa Law Review* 57 (1971): 171–198.

Nickman, Steven L. "Losses in Adoption." In *The Psychoanalytic Study of the Child*, edited by Albert J. Solnit et al., vol. 40, pp. 365–398. New Haven: Yale University Press, 1986.

Olds, Charles B. "Early Legal Adoption." *Child Welfare* 64 (1975): 392–394.

O'Neill, Onora, and W. Ruddick, eds. *Having Children: Philosophical and Legal Reflections on Parenthood*. New York: Oxford University Press, 1979.

Pascall, G. "Adoption: Perspectives in Policy." In *Adoption: Essays in Social Policy, Law, and Sociology*, edited by Philip Bean, pp. 9–23. New York: Tavistock, 1984.

Paton, Jean (Ruthena Hill Kittson). *Orphan Voyage*. New York: Vantage, 1968.

Peck, Ellen, and W. Granzig. *The Parent Test: How to Measure and Develop Your Talent for Parenthood.* New York: Putnam, 1978.

Philipp, Elliott. *Overcoming Childlessness.* New York: Taplinger, 1975.

Phillips, Maxine. *Adopting a Child.* Public Affairs Pamphlet #585. New York: Public Affairs Committee, 1980.

Powledge, Fred. *The New Adoption Maze—And How to Get Through It.* St. Louis: Mosby Multi-Media, 1985.

Presser, Stephen B. "The Historical Background of the American Law of Adoption." *Journal of Family Law* 11 (1971–1972): 443–516.

Priel, Beatrice. "On Mirror-Image Anxiety." In *The Psychoanalytic Study of the Child,* edited by Albert J. Solnit et al., vol. 40, pp. 183–193. New Haven: Yale University Press, 1986.

Quarles, Louis. "The Law of Adoption—A Legal Anomaly." *Marquette Law Review* 32 (1949): 237–243.

Rein, Mark, T. E. Nutt, and H. Weiss. "Foster Family Care: Myth and Reality." In *Children and Decent People,* edited by A. Schorr, pp. 24–52. New York: Basic Books, 1974.

Rillera, Mary Jo, ed. *The Reunion Book.* Vol. 1. Westminster, Calif.: Triadoption Library, 1991.

———. *Searching for Minors.* Huntington Beach, Calif.: Triadoption Library, 1982.

Roberts, Robert W., ed. *The Unwed Mother.* Westport, Conn.: Greenwood, 1966.

Romanofsky, Peter. "The Early History of Adoption Practices." Ph.D. diss., University of Missouri, 1969.

Rondell, Florence, and R. Michaels. *The Adopted Family: You and Your Child; A Guide for Adoptive Parents* [1951]. New York: Crown, 1965.

Rossi, Alice. "A Biosocial Perspective on Parenting." In *The Family,* edited by A. Rossi, J. Kagan, and T. Hareven, pp. 1–32. New York: W. W. Norton, 1978.

Rothman, Barbara K. *Recreating Motherhood: Ideology and Technology in a Patriarchal Society.* New York: W. W. Norton, 1989.

Rowe, Jane. *Yours By Choice: A Guide for Adoptive Parents.* London: Routledge and Kegan Paul, 1959.

Sarbin, Theodore R., ed. *Narrative Psychology: The Storied Nature of Human Conduct.* New York: Praeger, 1986.

Schaap, Trish, and Dick Schaap. "Thank You For This Baby." In *Parade Magazine* (Pittsburgh Press), March 3, 1985, 4–7.

Schapiro, Michael. *A Study of Adoption Practice: Adoption Agencies and the Children They Serve.* Vol. 1. New York: CWLA, 1956.

Schechter, Marshall D. "About Adoptive Parents." In *Parenthood: Its Psychology and Psychopathology,* edited by E. J. Anthony and T. Benedek, pp. 355–371. Boston: Little, Brown, 1970.

Schechter, Marshall D., and D. Bertocci. "The Meaning of the Search." In *The Psychology of Adoption,* edited by D. Brodzinsky and M. Schechter, pp. 62–90. New York: Oxford University Press, 1990.

Schechter, Marshall D., P. V. Carlson, J. Q. Simmons, and H. H. Work.

"Emotional Problems in the Adoptee." *Archives of General Psychiatry* 10 (1964): 37–46.

Schneider, David. *American Kinship: A Cultural Account.* 2d ed. Chicago: University of Chicago Press, 1980.

————. *A Critique of the Study of Kinship.* Ann Arbor: University of Michigan Press, 1984.

————. "Kinship and Biology." In *Aspects of the Analysis of Family Structure,* edited by M. Levy, pp. 83–101. Princeton: Princeton University Press, 1965.

————. "What Is Kinship All About?" In *Kinship Studies in the Morgan Centennial Year,* edited by P. Reining, pp. 32–63. Washington, D.C.: Anthropological Society of Washington, 1972.

Schneider, David, and R. T. Smith. *Class Differences and Sex Roles in American Kinship and Family Structure.* Englewood Cliffs, N.J.: Prentice-Hall, 1973.

Schwartz, Edward M. "The Family Romance Fantasy in Children Adopted in Infancy." *Child Welfare* 49 (1970): 386–391.

Schwartz, Lita Linzer. "Adoption Custody and Family Therapy." *American Journal of Family Therapy* 2 (1984): 51–58.

Scott, Russell. *The Body as Property.* New York: Viking, 1981.

Seglow, J., M. K. Pringle, and P. Wedge. *Growing Up Adopted.* Windsor, Berks.: National Foundation for Educational Research in England and Wales, 1972.

Sennett, Richard, and J. Cobb. *The Hidden Injuries of Class.* New York: Vintage, 1972.

Shaw, Martin. "Growing up Adopted." In *Adoption: Essays in Social Policy, Law and Sociology,* edited by P. Bean, pp. 119–127. New York: Tavistock, 1984.

Shell, Marc. *The End of Kinship. "Measure for Measure," Incest, and the Ideal of Universal Siblinghood.* Stanford: Stanford University Press, 1988.

Silber, Kathleen, and Phylis Speedlin. *Dear Birthmother.* San Antonio, Tex.: Adoption Awareness Press, 1982.

Simon, Rita J., and H. Altstein. *Transracial Adoption.* New York: John Wiley, 1977.

Simpson, Mark, H. Timm, and H. I. McCubbin. "Adoptees in Search of Their Past: Policy Induced Strain on Adoptive Families and Birth Parents." *Family Relations* 30 (July 1981): 427–434.

Smith, Carol L. "The New Families Project." In *New Developments in Foster Care and Adoption,* by John Triseliotis, pp. 201–214. London: Routledge and Kegan Paul, 1980.

Smith, Dorothy W., and L. Nels Sherwen. *Mothers and Their Adopted Children—The Bonding Process.* New York: Tiersias, 1983.

Smith, I. Evelyn, ed. *Readings in Adoption.* New York: Philosophical Library, 1963.

Smith, Jerome, and F. I. Miroff. *You're Our Child: The Adoption Experience.* New York: Madison Books, 1987.

Sobol, Michael P., and Jeanette Cardiff. "A Sociopsychological Investigation of Adult Adoptees' Search for Birth Parents." *Family Relations* 32 (1983): 477–483.

Sonne, John C. "A Family System Perspective on Custody and Adoption." *International Journal of Family Therapy* 2 (1980): 176–192.

Sorosky, Arthur, A. Baran, and R. Pannor. *The Adoption Triangle*. New York: Doubleday, 1979.

Spock, Benjamin. *Baby and Child Care*. 4th ed. New York: Hawthorne/Dutton, 1985.

Stacey, Judith. *Brave New Families*. New York: Basic Books, 1991.

Stack, Carol. *All Our Kin*. New York: Harper and Row, 1974.

State of Pennsylvania. *Laws of the General Assembly*. Act 456. Harrisburg, Pa., 1855.

———. *Laws of the General Assembly*. Act 66. Harrisburg, Pa., 1887.

———. *Laws of Pennsylvania*. Act 1980-163. Harrisburg, Pa., 1980.

Stein, Leslie M., and J. L. Hoopes. *Identity Formation in the Adopted Adolescent*. New York: CWLA, 1985.

Steiner, Gilbert Y. *The Futility of Family Policy*. Washington, D.C.: The Brookings Institute, 1981.

Strathern, Marilyn. *Kinship at the Core*. New York: Cambridge University Press, 1981.

Thayer, Stuart W. "Moppets on the Market." In *Readings in Adoption*, edited by I. E. Smith, pp. 503–536. New York: Philosophical Library, 1963.

Thompson, Jean. *House of Tomorrow*. New York: Harper and Row, 1967.

Tiffin, Susan. *In Whose Best Interest?* Westport, Conn.: Greenwood, 1982.

Timms, Noel, ed. *The Receiving End: Consumer Accounts of Social Help for Children*. Boston: Routledge and Kegan Paul, 1973.

Titmuss, Richard M. *The Gift Relationship: From Human Blood to Social Policy*. New York: Pantheon, 1971.

Tizard, Barbara. *Adoption: A Second Chance*. New York: Free Press, 1977.

Today Show (NBC). *Interview with Birthfathers*, by Bryant Gumble and Pat Mitchell, April 1986. Audiotape.

Triseliotis, John. *In Search of Origins*. London: Routledge and Kegan Paul, 1973.

———. *New Developments in Foster Care and Adoption*. London: Routledge and Kegan Paul, 1980.

———. "Obtaining Birth Certificates." In *Adoption: Essays in Social Policy, Law and Sociology*, edited by P. Bean, pp. 38–53. New York: Tavistock, 1984.

Triseliotis, John, and M. Hill. "Contrasting Adoption, Foster Care, and Residential Rearing." In *The Psychology of Adoption*, edited by D. M. Brodzinsky and M. D. Schechter, pp. 107–120. New York: Oxford University Press, 1990.

Turner, Mark. *Death Is the Mother of Beauty*. Chicago: University of Chicago Press, 1987.

Unger, Christopher, G. Dworshuis, and E. Johnson. *Chaos, Madness, and Unpredictability: Placing the Child with Ears Like Uncle Harry's*. Chelsea, Mich.: Spaulding for Children, 1977.

United States Congress. *Adoption Assistance and Child Welfare Funding Act (Public Law 96-272)*. Washington, D.C.: Government Printing Office, 1980a.

———. *Hearings before the Subcommittee to Investigate Juvenile Delinquency of the Committee on the Judiciary*. Washington, D.C.: Government Printing Office, 1955.

———. *Oversight on Adoption Reform Act (Public Law 95-266): Hearing before the Subcommittee on Child and Human Development of the Committee on Labor and Human Resources*. Washington, D.C.: Government Printing Office, 1980b.

Vincent, Clark E. *Unmarried Mothers*. Glencoe, N.Y.: Free Press, 1961.

Viorst, Judith. *Necessary Losses*. New York: Fawcett, 1986.

Waltner, Ann. *Getting an Heir: Adoption and the Construction of Kinship in Late Imperial China*. Honolulu: University of Hawaii Press, 1990.

Ward, Margaret. "The Relationship Between Parents and Caseworker in Adoption." *Social Casework* 60 (1979): 96–103.

Watson, Kenneth, and J. Strom. *Report of the Child Welfare League of America Task Force*. New York: CWLA, 1987.

Weinstein, Eugene A. *The Self-Image of the Foster Child*. New York: Russell Sage Foundation, 1960.

Williamson, Nancy E. *Sons or Daughters: A Cross-Cultural Survey of Parental Preferences*. Beverly Hills, Calif.: Sage, 1976.

Winkler, Robin, and M. van Keppel. *Relinquishing Mothers in Adoption*. Monograph #3. Melbourne, Australia: Institute of Family Studies, 1984.

Winnicott, D. W. "Mirror Role of Mother and Family in Child Development." In *The Predicament of the Family*, edited by P. Lomas, pp. 26–33. London: Hogarth, 1967.

Witmer, Helen L., E. Herzog, E. Weinstein, and M. Sullivan. *Independent Adoptions. A Follow-Up Study*. New York: Russell Sage Foundation, 1963.

Yanigisako, Sylvia, and J. Collier. "For a Unified Analysis of Gender and Kinship." In *Gender and Kinship*, edited by J. Collier and S. Yanigisako, pp. 14–50. Stanford: Stanford University Press, 1987.

Zainaldin, Jamil. "The Emergence of a Modern American Family Law: Child Custody, Adoption, and the Courts, 1796–1851." *Northwestern University Law Review* 73 (1979): 1038–1089.

Zelizer, Viviana. *Pricing the Priceless Child*. New York: Basic Books, 1985.

Index

Abortion, 9–10, 233, 247n.5

Adoptees, 115–139; on agencies, 132; on being told/finding out, 116, 117–122, 129–135; on burden of being special/chosen, 114, 115–116, 129, 131–132; compare adoptive parents to birthparents, 123–128, 227–228; contact birthparents, 1–3, 138, 144, 159–166, 181–185, 187–188; curiosity of, 144, 145; fantasies of, 125, 126–127, 128; feel different, 118–120, 121, 122, 133–135; feeling of belonging of, 132–135; feel placed or rescued, not chosen, 132; feel purchased, 133; on having two sets of parents, 165–166, 168; identity/background, looking for, 134, 135–139, 143; inheritance rights of, 25–26; on motherhood, 189; numbers of, 11–12; for open records, 230; right to know of, 145, 156–157; search by (*see* Search, by adoptee); support groups for, 6, 7, 8, 15, 120, 144, 145, 146–147, 154–155, 156, 178; treated differently, 130–131, 210

Adoptee Search Group (ASG), 120, 128, 145–147, 154–156

Adoptees' Liberty Movement Association (ALMA), 8, 120, 144, 145, 156

Adoption, 19–35; activism (*see* Support groups); as-if-begotten as basis of, 2, 4, 5, 11, 14, 21, 22, 24, 225; of biracial child, 93; cancelled/disrupted, 113, 233–234, 251n.17; as child exchange, 4, 9, 21; in child's best interest, 19–20, 21, 26, 29–32, 34–35, 39, 40, 51, 80–81; defined, 2, 19; as fate/predestined, 206; as fictive or contrived kinship, 2, 3, 14, 20, 37, 62, 123, 125, 138–139, 225–226, 238; foster care blended with (*see* "Fost-adopt"); by foster parents, 37, 45, 47–49; gray market, 54, 247n.30; honeymoon aspect of, 205, 206; illegitimacy and, 24; independent (non-agency), 37, 52–55, 93, 104–108, 112, 237; in-family, 22, 69, 239n.3 (*see also* Adoption, open); inheritance rights in, 22, 23, 24–26; motives for, 21, 22, 71, 93, 94–95, 98, 99–100, 122–125; of older child, 43; parenthood concepts in (*see* Adoptive parents; Birthparents); permanence of, 2, 28, 92, 113–114, 138–139, 205, 206, 232; reforms/openness in, 8, 9–10, 16, 62–63, 146, 225–238 (*see also* Adoption, open); resemblance in (*see* Matching; Resemblances); rights of parents in, 32–33, 38–39; as self-conscious/unnatural, 4, 7–8; significance of, 24, 43–44, 133–135, 136–137, 161–163, 185, 186, 214–215;